Know Thyself

Know Thyself

An Essay in Social Personalism

Thomas O. Buford

LEXINGTON BOOKS
Lanham • Boulder • New York • Toronto • Plymouth, UK

Published by Lexington Books
A wholly owned subsidiary of The Rowman & Littlefield Publishing Group, Inc.
4501 Forbes Boulevard, Suite 200, Lanham, Maryland 20706
www.lexingtonbooks.com

Estover Road, Plymouth PL6 7PY, United Kingdom

Copyright © 2011 by Lexington Books

All rights reserved. No part of this book may be reproduced in any form or by any electronic or mechanical means, including information storage and retrieval systems, without written permission from the publisher, except by a reviewer who may quote passages in a review.

British Library Cataloguing in Publication Information Available

Library of Congress Cataloging-in-Publication Data

Buford, Thomas O., 1932–
  Know thyself : an essay in social personalism / Thomas O. Buford.
    p. cm.
  Includes bibliographical references and index.
  ISBN 978-0-7391-4618-7 (cloth : alk. paper)—ISBN 978-0-7391-4620-0 (electronic)
  1. Self-knowledge, Theory of. 2. Knowledge, Sociology of. 3. Personalism.
I. Title.
  BD438.5.B84 2011
  141'.5—dc23
                                                        2011030760

∞™ The paper used in this publication meets the minimum requirements of American National Standard for Information Sciences—Permanence of Paper for Printed Library Materials, ANSI/NISO Z39.48-1992.

Printed in the United States of America

Contents

Preface		vii
Acknowledgments		xxi
Chapter 1	Self-knowledge and the Problem of Suspicion	1
Chapter 2	Our Haunting Hopes	35
Chapter 3	A New Master Narrative	73
Chapter 4	Persons and Nature	107
Chapter 5	Society and Culture	127
Chapter 6	The Personal	151
Chapter 7	Dancing	171
Chapter 8	Broken Dances	189
Selected Bibliography		197
Index		209

Preface

The thesis of this book is that social Personalism can best provide for self-knowledge. In the West self-knowledge has been sought within the framework of two dominant intellectual traditions, order and the emerging self. On the one hand, ancient and medieval philosophers, living in an orderly hierarchical society governed by honor and shame bolstered by the metaphysics of being and rationalism, believed persons gain self-knowledge through uniting with the ground of their being. Once united, they would understand what they are, what they are to be, and what they are to do. On the other hand, Renaissance and modern thinkers such as Pico della Mirandola, Copernicus, Descartes, Locke, and Kant shattered the great achievement of the High Middle Ages and bequeathed to posterity an emerging self in a splintered world. Continuing their search for self-knowledge, the moderns found themselves faced with the dualism of the emerging self of the Renaissance and the natural world as understood by modern scientists. New problems spun out of the new dualism including the mind-body problem; the other minds problem; free will and determinism; the nature and possibility of social relationships; values, moral norms and their relationship to the natural and social worlds; and science, religion, and their relationships. Finding self-knowledge among these splinters without a guiding orientation has proven difficult. Even though luminaries such as Spinoza, Berkeley, and Hegel attempted to bring order to the sundered elements, their attempts proved unsatisfactory. We contend that neither order nor the emerging self can adequately provide for self-knowledge. Since those culturally embodied "master narratives," lead us to an impasse, we turn to social Personalism. Defending our thesis turns on the meaning of key terms and phrases: "self-knowledge," "social Personalism," and "can best provide." Having clarified them and the thesis, we outline the argument supporting the thesis.

SELF-KNOWLEDGE

First, what is self-knowledge? Self-knowledge can be used in many senses. They include knowing psychic phenomena at the root of emotional disorder, the characteristics of one's interpersonal relationships, ones place in biological evolution, ones chemical makeup, ones DNA, and the image of God forming us as persons. As a starting point, consider the admonition at the Oracle of Delphi, *gnothi seauton*. The definition of the words and grammatical structure of the phrase help convey its meaning. Grammatically, *gnothi* is an ingressive aorist imperative of the verb *gnosko*; as imperative it is a command, as aorist it is an action that has not started, and as ingressive the action must start now. *Seauton*, a reflexive pronoun, second person, expresses the action of a subject upon itself. Thus *gnothi seauton* means, "Start gaining a proper discernment of what you are, what you are to be, and what you are to do." What will "proper discernment" show us about ourselves?

It shows us our place in relation to each other, a natural habitat, a society, a culture, and an ultimate authoritative environment legitimating what we are, what are to be, and what we are to do. Specifically, it shows our lives are temporal; we have a past (a background), a present, and a future (a foreground). Next, life lived properly over a period of time is stable and unified. Cultural shaping prepares us to act in circumstances without conscious deliberation and choice. We act out of habit, what we shall call our second nature. For example, seeing a traffic light turn red, we apply the brakes, and stop the car. We do that most of time, fortunately. As long as traffic rules and driving patterns remain constant over time, our habituation is reliable, stable. We understand ourselves as persons who obey traffic laws; we have a unity over time. In addition, proper discernment reveals patterns connecting our background and foreground. If we continue to connect background and foreground in a particular way, we create patterns that become habitual, second nature to us. Finally, patterns are legitimated by an authority. In the case of traffic laws, they are legitimated by local, state, federal governments enacted and enforced under and within the authority of the framework of the U.S. Constitution. What is revealed in our social, cultural contexts is also the case for all others. We are commanded to gain a proper discernment of ourselves in all our contexts.

In sum, *gnothi seauton* is a command to properly discern who we are, what we are do, and what we are to be. In interpersonal relationships regarding a cause, we recognize we are not minds and bodies but whole persons who live in environments ranging from social, cultural, habitat, and natural expanse to the ultimate environment. Furthermore, contexts as lived are temporal, composed of connections between our background and foreground, patterned, stable, and unified. Both who we are and our proper way of life are legitimized by the authority of an ultimate context.

Next, what is social Personalism?

SOCIAL PERSONALISM

Consider the word "Personalism." Ralph Tyler Flewelling defined it as "a modern term applied to any philosophy that considers personality the supreme value and the key to the measuring of reality."[1] "Social" Personalism has several possible meanings. For example, in the first half of the twentieth century, most personalists believed persons are social, whether absolutists such Mary Whiton Calkins or Personalistic idealists such as Edgar Sheffield Brightman. Absolutists believed persons have no life apart from society and the metaphysical whole. Personalistic Idealists attempt to avoid absorbing individuals into the whole and to protect their freedom, autonomy, and responsibility for their individual actions. Initially, persons are independent of society and voluntarily join with each other to form communities, societies, and culture. Personalists of each type continue to investigate the nature and character of social relations within the framework of absolutism and individualism (a continuation of the Spinoza and Leibniz dispute in the eighteenth and nineteenth centuries). In contrast and working outside that formative and restrictive structure, social personalists advocate a different meaning of "social."

We shall look for "social" in the fullness of practical living, as both Borden Parker Bowne and William James advised.[2] A pattern permeates the business of ordinary living, the triadic relation, I-Thou-It, and it lies at the core of "social" Personalism. That pattern suggests a perspective for understanding the "social" and in turn, self-knowledge. The Latin root of perspective is *perspectus*, from *perspicio* (transitive verb) meaning "to look through, see clearly." Think of it as "the interrelation in which a subject or its parts are mentally viewed; the capacity to view things in their true relations or relative importance."[3] It is "seeing through" allowing one to grasp connections needed for *gnothi seauton*. The interrelation occurs from a vantage point, a *topos*, a "place," a stance from which one looks, sees, and interrelates objects. A *topos* can be limited or unlimited in scope. In contrast to perspectives of limited scope, such as political science, a master narrative is normally understood as unlimited in scope.[4] Though dangerously close to the violence of the metaphysics of Being, a master narrative is not necessarily a view of the whole, even if possible. The master narrative is a *topos* or perspective shared without judgment, a *sensus communis*, identifying and connecting persons and their environments to each other, overcoming suspicion, and allowing *gnothi seauton*. Persons live in and through a master narrative embodied in their practical living that guides the development and exercise of their personal potentials to an understanding of the relation of persons to each other and to their social, cultural, natural, and ultimate environments.

As we proceed we draw on the inspiration and insights of personalists, first articulated by Friedrich Heinrich Jacobi (1743–1819) in late eighteenth-century Germany. Personalists, as pointed out above, contend that the key to understanding reality, both social and natural, is Person. Following that insight they carefully investigate important aspects of social action, freedom, valuation, and moral responsibility. This group included, among others, such luminaries as Josiah Royce, William Ernest Hocking, John Macmurray, Emmanuel Mounier, and Karol Wojtyla, Borden Parker Bowne, Edgar Sheffield Brightman, and Peter A. Bertocci. Collectively they developed the metaphysical, epistemological, and ethical views that contribute to understanding self-knowledge. Responding to the challenges of modernity, they sought to resist both the stark autonomous radical individualism of disintegrative liberalism and the suffocating heteronomy of collectivism. Each was successful, but only up to a point. None adequately accounted for the solidarity and continuity through change present in a society that endures more than a short time. They did not help us understand the nature of trust and its place in the solidarity of a culture, and they did not explore how trust helps account for the roots of stable change. Furthermore, none of them accounted for and articulated the nature and structure of the relation of the individual to the group in such a way that the freedom of the individual is fully maintained and the unity, solidarity, and identity provided by society is fully recognized. And none gave us an adequate understanding of how Personalism provides for self-knowledge through a master narrative of the ultimate context, the Personal. Most telling, none avoided being brushed with the tar of formal impersonalism. They developed Personalism within the patterns of thought of the western philosophical tradition of Being and Rationalism. For example, Bowne contended that person is the only viable answer to the one-many and permanence-change problems. Nevertheless, shared vision and individual contributions will be included in this work. Following Jacobi, Royce, and H. Richard Niebuhr, we broaden the *topos* to include persons-in-trusting-triadic-relations.[5] Within that *topos* we can best fulfill the command to know ourselves.

THE MOST ELOQUENT STORY

Finally, what does "can best provide" mean? It means that social Personalism is the best perspective for achieving self-knowledge. Given the meaning of "perspective," what does "best" mean? We seek to tell the most complete story, to include all that should be included in the argument and omit what should be omitted. At bottom, our story must be rooted in the experience of persons, their *lebenswelt*. We offer a story whose eloquence provides compelling evidence for our thesis. That story conveys the main ways of understanding and achieving self-knowledge, the central questions they face, and the major answers given to those problems. Rather than beginning with problems and proceeding to their solution, we shall begin with a historical survey and show the central issues deeply rooted in the lives of people. That provides a historical perspective often missing in purely theoretical studies. Beginning with appealing to culture for self-knowledge from the ancient, through the Renaissance and modern periods, up to and including the contemporary, we trace the development of the problem of suspicion. To solve that problem and bolster self-knowledge through a culture, we consider theories of major philosophers in the ancient, modern, and contemporary worlds, hoping to find in them a solution to the problem of suspicion. Each seeks to bolster a cultural perspective by providing a ground for bringing into sync our background and foreground and showing that authority legitimizes that connection. Each contends it best and provides for the achievement of self-knowledge that is patterned, stable, and unified. However, problems in each major view show its internal anomalies, the strength of suspicion, and set the challenge for the remainder of the work. At bottom, each is a form of impersonalism.

What is impersonalism? Impersonalism takes two forms: substantive and formal. Substantive impersonalism includes finding eternal principles in Naturalism, Idealism, and Rationalism. Naturalism is a metaphysics that claims impersonal things in the contingent world are the basal elements of everything, including persons, their agency, subjectivity, and power to know. Idealism or "Ideism" advises us to go behind living persons and appeal "to categories of being, cause, identity, change, the absolute, and the like."[6] All are abstractions. Persons are "at best only a specification or particular case of these more general principles."[7] According to Rationalism, normal reason is expected to guide the mind to transcendent principles that are necessary, immutable, and eternal—for example, Plato's eternal forms. These three recommend themselves by their supposed objective view of our world and place within it, a helpful relief from superstition. Formal impersonalism refers to the use by personalists of the framework of substantive impersonalism to set the problems and methods of Personalism. Examples include person defined within the form and matter distinction, such as person is a soul using a body or substance with an attribute. Or, person defined within the dualism of thinking things and extended things. And, person defined as a concrete universal; logic in the hands of Hegel influenced Brightman. The universal/particular distinction influenced Bowne. Focusing on the problem of the one and the many, he argued that it can best be solved by person. These are different versions of formal impersonalism.

Furthermore, central to the Western intellectual tradition is the aspiration to find universal principles that bridge contexts, cultures, time, and place. Once found, they place us in a position to account for particular, concrete events that change over time and place. We can properly bridge changes from established cultural patterns to other emerging patterns. These universal principles include Being that allows an understanding of the whole of things. Traditionally that is the goal of metaphysics, and can be divided into a concern with a suprastructure or an infrastructure. Plato's search for the eternal forms is an example of the former, and Democritus's search for atoms moving through empty space is an example of the latter. It is also assumed that these can be achieved through reason and logic extended beyond their regular use to guide discourse to show us the way to transcendent eternal principles; Plato's divided line is a good example. This assumption is not limited to the ancients or the medievals; it is assumed throughout Western philosophy.

We grapple with the problem of suspicion by offering a *topos* generated from triadic interpersonal relations of mutual trust and show that it resolves suspicion, is moral at its core, and provides an understanding of and a way to achieve self-knowledge. The argument will show why the insight and way of seeing provided by the *topos* help us develop the most eloquent story.

In summary, faced by suspicion, we turn to an interpersonal, participatory understanding of self-knowledge and show that it is a more eloquent story than the impersonalism of rationalism and the metaphysics of being. We begin our search for self-knowledge in the midst of ordinary living. That starting point reveals an interpersonal structure, I-Thou-It, that is unified and stabilized by trust. An understanding of that structure leads to an understanding of persons and their trusting participatory relationships to each other, to nature, to society and culture, and to their ultimate environment, the Personal. In this way we answer suspicion and gain the most eloquent understanding of and our relation to the Personal; in that light we know who we are, what we are to be, and what we are to do. How shall we make good on that promise?

OUTLINE OF THE ARGUMENT

In chapter 1, we discuss self-knowledge and the problem of suspicion. We define self-knowledge as the proper discernment of what you are, what you are to be, and what you are to do. The search for self-knowledge begins in the fullness of patterned practical living. However, in everyday living with its pressing problems and requirements, persons spend little time thinking about knowing themselves. They follow the patterns their society and culture built into their habits. Their pasts or backgrounds are usually adequate guides into the ever-changing present and future or foreground. The patterned connections between Background and Foreground are accepted as legitimate, resting on Authority. Normal crises, such as those students experience during college years and those adults have in midlife, prompt us to reflect on ourselves, our goals and aspirations, on the patterns of our behavior, on self-knowledge. Usually our or society's background and Book of Knowledge guide us through a crisis to a stable and unifying pattern of life. However, changes deep and pervasive question the reliability of those patterns of living, even the possibility of any pattern being reliable. The patterns in our Background provide little help living in the present and future Foreground. The Background and Foreground are not in sync. Further, these changes penetrate to the Authority legitimating connections, questioning them, and sometimes rejecting their status and power. Self-knowledge becomes difficult, at best.

Recognizing that suspicion focuses on and subverts the temporal connections of background and foreground, we show how suspicion arises in Western culture. Viewing it from a cultural, anthropological perspective two master narratives are dominant, cultural dyadic objectivism in the ancient and medieval periods and cultural monadic subjectivism in the modern and contemporary periods. Order pervades the former, and Emerging Self the latter.

Within Order and its social structures persons learn what they are and expect to find their place and duties in the social hierarchy. Here we find ancient philosophy emerging, challenging religious contexts. When Christianity appeared in the Roman period, it blended with Greco-Roman philosophy, and eventually triumphed in a grand synthesis in the High Middle Ages, 1100–1300 CE. The hierarchy soaked medieval Christendom, limiting persons to horizontally narrow social movement but vertically unlimited religious insight.

Emerging Self finds footing in the Renaissance and loosened the bonds of hierarchical legitimacy authorized by God. Through slow social and religious leveling and accompanying conflicts, Renaissance thinkers sought a balanced tension between cultural dyadic objectivism and cultural monadic subjectivism. By the modern period the emerging self became dominant, flowering in a narcissistic individualism that is lost in its own isolation, and playing a central role in the breakdown of institutions and trust in late twentieth and early twentieth-century American culture. Under this master narrative, the self seeks knowledge of itself in itself. Under the power of modern science, industry, and technology, persons begin looking for self-knowledge outside of themselves in physics, biology, and mathematics, only to find that the self is a natural phenomenon to be studied by scientific method. A freeing monadicism ironically led to a suffocating dyadicism. The resulting crisis penetrated to the core of Western culture. We cannot know ourselves by continuing under the master narrative of the emerging self, and we cannot know ourselves by seeking to live in the ancient, medieval worlds. The crisis is genuine. Deeper than a crisis, it is also the feeling, the growing recognition that self-knowledge is not possible. Seeking our way, we cannot return to former master narratives, and it is not possible to find another one. We live in an age of suspicion.

Logically suspicion is an antinomy. Both Order and Emerging Self have evidence supporting the truth of its way of seeing and living. But they are contradictory. How can both be true, yet one be true and the other false? They are antinomies. Socially and culturally, both lodge in our Background. We can think the conflict; we live the conflict. We are a problem to ourselves. Beyond that minimal self-understanding, Self-knowledge is not possible.

Life continues. Like Dorian Gray, we live, but only peripherally. The form remains, the substance does not, not the charismatic Authority (emotional and intellectual persuasion) legitimizing connections between Background and Foreground. The traditional moorings required for self-knowledge eroded, a new is not possible. Left with exhausted master narratives that are contradictory and an antinomy that appears to be unsolvable, our rootless and shifting cultural landscape creates deep anxiety.

Yet, we continue to seek *gnothi seauton* by turning to our background, to our cultural memory, hoping to find there an authoritative root, direction, and pattern for our lives. What can we find there? From our history many can be recalled, but two underlie all of them: the metaphysics of Being and Rationalism. Can anyone of them provide an authoritative, legitimated master image required to fulfill *gnothi seauton*?

In chapter 2, we appeal to philosophy to recover and ground failed master narratives, hoping to find a way of solving the problem of suspicion. Philosophy offers the metaphysics of Being, specifically a superstructure, Idealism, and an infrastructure, Naturalism, along with a scaffolding of reflective rational insight turned toward Being, Rationalism. They attempt to ground culture and society and to show us what we are. The metaphysics of being and the rational offer only impersonalism. Though each is appealing and attempts to allay suspicion, we show that each is a haunting hope, nostalgic, nothing more. Suspicion has won, and we cannot achieve *gnothi seauton*.

Yet, we persist in seeking to know ourselves, to grasp the way things are, our place in it, what we are to be, and how we should behave in it. Finding no solution to suspicion, we boldly step outside the dominant metaphors of the western tradition. There we find a solution that breathes life into our search for self-knowledge.

In chapter 3, we turn our attention to finding and developing a new master narrative. Four questions guide the search. Where and how find the *topos*, the master narrative? Can it be accepted without question and yet established through critical thought? Can it show us both what we are and legitimate connections? Why claim success or eloquence for that master narrative? After clarifying the meaning of master narrative and authority and showing that a master narrative possesses authority, we discuss each question. The new master narrative is found through recollective imagination and creative-finding. Though submerged under layers of Western culture, triadic reciprocal trust never lost its influence; it is central to any society and culture. No society and culture can continue without Persons-in-triadic-trusting relations. Though found through reflective thought and recollective imagination, it is assumed without question. It does not implode. Further, reciprocal trust implies promising and obligating ourselves to fidelity among persons who keep promises, renounce (*kenosis*) unbridled self-interest, and seek the well-being of persons in community. What we are, though known to some extent, remains a mystery; we only glimpse the Personal of the other. Persons-in-triadic-trusting-relations is a moral relation. With an understanding of the new master narrative, we establish it as the master narrative, one to which all other *topoi* appeal for their completion and one that provides for the most complete story. Finally, we show its significance in bringing into bold relief whole persons in triadic relations of reciprocal trust, living in the environments of nature, society and culture, and the Personal, as well as the relations among those environments. Within that story suspicion is overcome and persons can gain self-knowledge.

In chapter 4, we begin discussing the environments of triads of mutual trust among whole persons. Yet, the undertow of past master narratives pulls us into the riptide of mind-body dualism. Rejecting subject-object or mind-body dualism, we distinguish but do not separate nature from practical living. Body, habitat, and the natural expanse, can be understood in at least three ways: (1) as lived, (2) as portrayed by science, and (3) understood through The Personal.

As lived, we are natural beings who are in and of nature; it is our home. We trust the natural, and the natural trusts and is trustworthy. The natural could be separated from whole persons as not persons in relation, as the negative, as the realm of the involuntary, as transcendent to yet integral to the community of trust. Social action could be understood as the integration of the positive and the negative, of personal/social agency (the voluntary) and movement (the involuntary).[8] However, through our bodies, the natural lives in and through triadic-trusting. As lived, all we are and do is natural; all trusting, all social action is natural.

As portrayed by the natural sciences, nature is a space-time continuum of law like orderliness, understood mathematically, and capable of being formulated as laws. These laws may be expressed in deterministic terms (as in Newtonian mechanics) or probabilistic terms (as in quantum mechanics, applicable at the atomic level). Portrayed by the biological sciences, nature is living and organic, developing in an evolutionary manner. Though powerful and life changing in its usefulness, the sciences objectify, control, and dominate everything to which they turn their attention. The sciences are a group of methods focusing on different aspects of the body, the habitat, natural expanse with a resultant body of knowledge. Scientists who deny *kenosis* required by lived nature and the proper practice of science may use it violently.

As distinguished within full patterned practical living and understood through the master narrative, the natural is contingent and possesses contingent freedom. Nature is integral to triads, to the fact of and development of the capabilities of triadic nexuses, and to their stability and solidarity.

In chapter 5, the discussion turns to the second of the environments highlighted by the master narrative, society and culture. Focusing on relations both within triads and among triads, four questions guide our discussion: can other persons be known (in triads, can they know each other)? Can individuals act together? What provides solidarity for society/culture? What stabilizes social solidarity? Recall that each of us begins doing philosophy in the midst of everyday living. Rejecting the impersonalism of monism and pluralism including dualism, we find ordinary living to be interpersonal and triadic in structure, I-Thou-It. The triad is the structure of social action. Triads, in contrast to systems theory and cybernetic theory, center on the mutuality of trust among persons with reference to a cause. Inherently moral, the mutuality of trust is characterized by *kenosis*, ought, transcendence, and the Other. Social action is at bottom ethical. In social action we find the basis of social solidarity, stability, crisis, and reconciliation. Social action with its triadic structure of everyday living is inherently natural and Personal. That is, without the interrelations between the natural world and the Personal, persons-in-relation would be an abstraction. Significantly, suspicion presupposes triadic trust.

In chapter 6, we turn to the third environment, the most encompassing one, the Personal. We show that an argument for the existence of the Personal is ironic. An argument can be formulated only with the backing of the triadic relation of trust, obligation, and transcendence, that is, the Personal. Finding ourselves once again in the master narrative, three questions guide our discussion. What should lead us to embrace the Personal? How best characterize the Personal? What is the relation of the Personal to triads bound and stabilized by trust, to social action, to society, culture, all governed by regnant ideals? We show how the *topos*, the master narrative, "speaks the truth," making known the Personal. We contend that the Personal is agent, relational, trustworthy, moral, authority, creator, and kenotic, yet remains the mysterious Other. The Personal participates in all triadic relations of mutual trust. Trusting triads depend on environments in which they develop and continue: nature, social action, society, culture. These acknowledge the Personal. Though beyond, the Personal is deeply involved in triadic-trusting. Further, the Personal relates to triadic-trusting and environments through *creatio ex nihilo*. The Personal creates in the sense of *ex nihilo*; unlimited by anything inherent to or beyond its personhood, as free the Personal creates triads, environments, their needs and potentials, and calls them into fruition. In our triadic relations with the Personal, we discern what we are.

In chapter 7, we focus on the relation of triads of mutual trust, environments, and the Personal to each other. Extending our understanding of the Personal through the metaphor of dancing as an art form, the Personal is the choreographer who creates the choreography guiding the dancers, who in dancing creatively-find the way of the choreography in light of their needs and potentials guided by the cause, the goal of dancing. Dancing is triadic trusting, and creative-finding. The Dance, the underlying pattern dancers follow, helps us understand primary institutions; dancers creating in dancing the Dance they find, secondary institutions. In triadic and trusting relation to each other, dancers dancing the Dance achieve the purpose of the Dance, their own well being and that of their partners. Guided and bound by promising, fidelity, *kenosis*, dancing is moral. Dancing the Dance, we are able to attain self-knowledge.

In chapter 8, we turn to broken dancing. Not only is dancing broken, but also the Dance is broken, shattering hope for self-knowledge. We have shown that suspicion may be overcome through triadic trust that points to an ultimate environment, the Personal, who as trustworthy moral Authority legitimates solidarity and stability of trusting-triads. However, questions arise again focusing on connections, this time so profoundly that trust is shattered.

Natural and social disasters, usually called evils, render us speechless. Speaking draws on our Background for a response to the Foreground. In the face of the Lisbon earthquake and Hurricane Katrina or Auschwitz and Dresden, our Background completely fails us. We stand without words, without actions. Our world is unintelligible.

Undaunted, seeking intelligibility we lay responsibility at the door step of religion, society and culture, individual persons, or natural events. If responsibility can be assigned, the responsible person could have done otherwise. Knowing that, we can investigate why it occurred and what can be done to avert future disasters. Religion says that God allowed but did not create them. Epicurus recognized the dilemma awaiting any who places responsibility on God. Societies and cultures, through their actions, build cities and carry on wars. If so, what accounts for their doing evil? If individuals through their ego centered actions create a world around them bear responsibility, how can an individual bring about such disasters? If assigned to nature, responsibility is not an issue. Lisbon and Auschwitz were natural events to be understood through the natural sciences. The question of evil does not arise. In addition to internal problems of each attempt for intelligibility, identifying the responsible party does not explain how by doing otherwise by any one of them could have prevented the evil event. Our Background stands empty in the face of Lisbon and Auschwitz. Distrust severs connections rooted in trust. Profound suspicion reigns. In the end, dancing the Dance is broken. Nothing heals and allows dancing to continue.

Ironically, we conclude that profound suspicion cannot be articulated without trust providing a basis, albeit somewhat unstable, for achieving self-knowledge. Through trust, we know and dance with each other and The Personal. Though hobbled by broken trust, we continue dancing.

Notes

1. Ralph Tyler Flewelling, "Personalism," in Dagobert D. Runes, ed. *Dictionary of Philosophy* (New York, NY: Philosophical Library, 1943), 228.

2. See Borden Parker Bowne, *Personalism* (New York, NY: Houghton Mifflin, 1908), 20, and Herbert W. Schneider, "Introductory Essay: Bowne's Radical Empiricism," in Warren E. Steinkraus (ed.), *Representative Essays of Borden Parker Bowne* (Utica, NY: Meridian Publishing Company, n.d.), xiv–xv.

3. Merriam-Webster's *Collegiate Dictionary*, 11th edition. (Springfield, MA: Merriam-Webster, Incorporated, 2005).

4. A generation ago, Lyotard used "master narrative." Yet, it continues to be useful, but with two caveats. First, its use is heavily influenced by Vico's Master Image.

See Donald Philip Verene's work on Renaissance Humanism, particularly, *Vico's Science of Imagination* (Ithaca, New York, NY: Cornell University Press, 1981); *Philosophy and the Return to Self-Knowledge* (New Haven, CT: Yale University Press, 1997); and *Speculative Philosophy* (Lanham, MD: Lexington Books, 2009). Verene continues the philosopher's search for the whole through the Imaginative Universal, the first fruit of the imagination, not the Conceptual Universal. Though this book is heavily indebted to Vico and to Verene's work and personal conversations, it is not required that the Master Image be of the whole. It must only be of that which is necessary to establish connections between Background and Foreground and allow *gnothi seauton*. Second, master narrative is an embodied story. It is not the work of Rorty's strong poet. See Richard Rorty, *Contingency, Irony, and Solidarity* (Cambridge, UK: Cambridge University Press, 1989), 26. A Master Image is embodied in Vico's sense. See chapter 2 in this book.

5. This scheme of persons-in-relation will be clarified later. Here we note that we build on the basis of the work of Giambattista Vico, *The New Science of Giambattista Vico,* trans. by Thomas G. Bergin and Max H. Fisch (Ithaca, NY: Cornell University Press, [1948] 1984), the *Autobiography,* trans. by Max H Fisch and Thomas G. Bergin (Ithaca, NY: Cornell University Press, [1944] 1983), and Stephen Pepper, *World Hypotheses* (Berkeley, CA: University of California Press, [1942] 1970). All rational thought proceeds from a way of looking at things, and that way is provided by a metaphor or image. Vico calls it the master image, Pepper the root metaphor. See Owen Barfield, *Poetic Diction, a Study in Meaning.* (Oxford, UK: Barfield Press, [1928] 2010); Donald Philip Verene, *Vico's Science of Imagination* (Ithaca, NY: Cornell University Press, 1981); and Thomas O. Buford, *In Search of a Calling* (Macon, GA: Mercer University Press, 1995), chaps 5, 6.

6. Bowne, *Personalism*, 218.

7. Bowne, *Personalism*, 218.

8. See Paul Ricoeur, *Freedom and Nature: The Voluntary and the Involuntary*, trans. with an introduction by Erazim V. Kohak (Evanston, IL: Northwestern University Press, 1966). For a book on the theory of knowledge see Frederick Will, *Induction and Justification: An Investigation of Cartesian Procedure in the Philosophy of Knowledge* (Ithaca, NY: Cornell University Press, 1974), 164–65; and Buford, *Trust*, 33.

Acknowledgments

As they think and write, philosophers work from a background. Those who influenced *Trust, Our Second Nature,* also influenced my work on this book. They include Plato, Aristotle, Augustine, Descartes, Giambattista Vico, John Dewey, Josiah Royce, the Boston Personalists, H. Richard Niebuhr, John Macmurray, and Emmanuel Levinas. At crucial points in this study the writings of Charles Taylor corrected my direction and set me on a more defensible, fruitful path. Erazim Kohak, Boston University and Charles University, in his *Embers and the Stars* continually reminded me of the power of Personalism and the failure of impersonalism. Randy Auxier, Southern Illinois University, Carbondale pressed me to study Royce that led to a fuller understanding of the triad, loyalty, and the moral life. James MacLachlin, Western Carolina University gently kept Levinas in my vision. The work of Richard Beauchamp, Christopher Newport University, on arenas of social conversation influenced my grasp of the nature and place of institutions in society. The work of Richard Prust, Saint Andrews Presbyterian College, on the phenomenology of action and the religious life pressed me to remember the wholeness of personality. My thanks to others in my immediate sphere of conversation, including Bogumil Gacka, University of Lublin, Lublin Poland; Jan Olof Bengtsson, Lund University, Lund Sweden; Charles Conti, University of Sussex, Brighton, England; and Doug Anderson, Southern Illinois University. My colleagues at Furman University provided invaluable encouragement during the preparation of the manuscript. Christopher Blackwell, classical languages, provided invaluable assistance in interpreting *gnothi seauton*; David Gandolfo, Philosophy, read and discussed portions of an early draft; and Mark Stone, Philosophy, prodded my thinking at many stages in the development of the project. John Lachs at Vanderbilt University read the completed work; his support and encouragement remain a gift for which I am grateful. Thanks to our Department Assistant, Evelyn Onofrio, for removing the tedium involved in a work of this type. Thanks especially to Dr. Jack Hansen, Associate Director of the Florida Institute for Human and Machine Cognition (2001–2007, now consultant for the CEO), for sharing his scientific expertise and gentle corrections as we talked through ideas central to this work. More than that, for his friendship.

Before we embark on our study, Valparasio University and the Lilly Program in Humanities and the Arts provided a sabbatical for study without the normal interruptions of academic life during the academic year of 1997–1998, during which time I was the Senior Fellow. The staff of the Bodelian Library, Oxford University; the Library of Congress; the Folger Institute and Library, Washington, D.C.; Duke Library, Furman University; Valparaiso University Library; and University of Notre Dame Library provided invaluable assistance researching this book. Furman University provided financial support with Mellon, Kellogg, and Dana grants. Former Academic Dean and Vice-President Tom Kazee encouraged and supported work on this essay during post retirement by providing a study, travel and book expenses, materials, and unencumbered time. Dr David Shi, former President of Furman University, continued Furman's tradition of encouragement and financial support for intellectual work. The encouragement and support of Furman's new Academic Dean and Vice-President for Academic Affairs, John Beckford and new President, Ron Smolla allowed this project to come to fruition. Leopard Forest furnished splendid Zimbabwean Peabury coffee in an atmosphere conducive to reading, thinking, and writing. Jana Wilson Hodges-Kluck, associate editor of philosophy at Lexington Books, coaxed, prodded, encouraged, and patiently worked with me through two years as this book congealed into written form. My thanks to each. My love to my family: Russ, Jack and Daniel; Anna, Scott, Emily and Sarah.

Dee, in faithful love, witnessed and discussed these ideas through over a half century of marriage, *sine qua non*.

Furman University
May 26, 2011

Chapter 1

Self-knowledge and the Problem of Suspicion

If someone asks you who you are, you can tell them. "I'm a husband, a father, a Texan who lives in South Carolina, a college professor, a Democrat, a capitalist, a regular reader of the local newspaper and the *Economist* magazine, a cellist, a flight instructor, a weight lifter, and a walker." And, if speaking to a close friend, I might add, "I believe in hard work, fair play, equal rights, commitment to ideals beyond myself, and equanimity, among others. That's the American Way." More than a description of your beliefs, connections, and your self-knowledge, they reflect accepted, assumed cultural beliefs, manifested through institutions that in turn shape habits into patterns of living. Cultural patterns shaping, stabilizing, and providing solidarity for our second nature gain their compelling power from assumed authority, from "that's just the way it is, and it's good." Such would be life in a culture with unifying, stable institutions animated by authority. But that is not our experience.

Self-knowledge, *gnothi seauton*, becomes problematic as the conditions that make it possible change into a crisis.[1] American culture and its roots are changing. Facing alternative and often competing institutional structures, we consult our cultural history for guidance as we make difficult choices presented to us in our cultural present and future. We make hard decisions, but what we gather from our history and from the alternatives in our present lack being obvious, assumed without question, believed without dissension; lacking the legitimacy of authority, we are suspicious of them. Overtly, we continue many traditional patterns of living; covertly, we do not trust their solidarity, their stability, the legitimacy of their authority.[2] Trust in any authority legitimizing personal and social patterns stabilizing us through fundamental cultural change subtlety erodes and weakens. As old institutional patterns decay and new ones slowly take their place, no cultural patterns possesses the authority and charisma to stabilize us by commanding the honor and allegiance necessary to bind, shape and hold our second nature within their boundaries. Without assumed charismatic authority, suspicion now unbridled penetrates and undermines our trust in our environmental patterns from our second nature, to institutions, to culture and nature, to the final authority itself, the Ultimate environment.[3] Without an Ultimate environment, an ultimate imperative that legitimates institutions, no culture can provide society with stability and solidarity through change, necessary for self-knowledge and living lives good to live.

More pernicious, as suspicion manifests itself in the temporal structure of our culture, the patterns of our living, it cuts the connection between unquestioned authority and the stabilizing and unifying institutional bonds reconciling our background and foreground through change. More felt than thought, suspicion penetrates into the sinews of our culture, our second nature, leaving the background and foreground dangling apart. Though fundamental cultural change has occurred before in the West, such as the transition from the Mediterranean basin to the North Atlantic rim or the transition from the medieval to the modern world, our culture and the patterns of our lives are in crisis deeper and more extensive than any preceding us. Suspicion is at the core. Beneath our confident description of who we are lies a cultural crisis fueled by suspicion that renders *gnothi seauton* highly problematic, if not impossible. Thus, we turn to three questions. What does *gnothi seauton* mean? What is suspicion, and how does it hinder fulfilling the admonition to know ourselves?[4]

As we seek answers to those questions, first keep in mind that obeying *gnothi seauton* is deeply contextual; it never occurs in a vacuum. Carrying it out is deeply influenced and supported by a natural habitat, a society, a culture, historical change, and an Ultimate environment. As we shall see, who I am, what I am to be, and what I am to do are temporal. Second, to understand suspicion, we study its nature, depth, history. Suspicion is not another form of philosophical skepticism, whether academic or pyrrhonist; both are logical without temporal dimension. Recognizing that suspicion focuses primarily on the relation within the temporal structure of our second nature and our culture, we study suspicion historically to understand it. Finally, we set self-knowledge within the context of suspicion. That allows us to focus and narrow our search through the complexities of Western culture. Focusing on the admonition, *gnothi seauton*, and appealing to our recollective memory, we move from the ancient world to the present.[5] Suspicion was rare in the ancient world. However, in the Renaissance and emerging individualism, suspicion takes root, growing to full flower in the twentieth and twenty-first centuries. In this sketch our strokes are broad but sufficient to display the core and intractability of suspicion. Now, turn to the first question, what is *gnothi seauton*?

GNOTHI SEAUTON

Meaning of *Gnothi Seauton*

Grammatically *gnothi* is an ingressive aorist imperative of the verb *gnosko*; as imperative it is a command, as aorist it is an action that has not started, and as ingressive the action must start immediately. *Seauton*, a reflexive pronoun, second person, expresses the action of a subject upon itself. Thus *gnothi seauton* means, "Start gaining a proper discernment of what you are, what you are to be, and what you are to do." Consider the imperative, *gnothi seauton*. I am commanded to learn who I am, what I am to be, what I am to do. To obey, we must discern the basis of our lives as well as the temporal relations connecting our Background and Foreground, both of our culture and second nature. Further, we must understand how our interpersonal relations stabilize and provide solidarity for that relation as well as legitimate those stabilizers and solidifiers. Discerning these, we can know what we are, and what we are to be, and what we are to do. These will be defined and clarified as we proceed.

The Fullness of Patterned Practical Living

The starting point for any serious philosophical search for *gnothi seauton* is the world of everyday living. Bowne's words focus the point, "We find such common ground in the following postulates: First, the coexistence of persons. It is a personal and social world in which we live, and with which all speculation must begin. We and the neighbors are facts which cannot be questioned. Second, there is a law of reason valid for all and binding upon all. This is the supreme condition of any mental community. Third, there is a world of common experience, actual or possible, where we meet in mutual understanding, and where the great business of life goes on."[6] Here Bowne and Jamesian pragmatists agree. James wrote in a letter to Bowne, "I think we fight in exactly the same cause, the reinstatement of the fullness of practical life, after the treatment of it by so much past philosophy as spectral. . . . [I]t is that our emphatic footsteps fall on the *same spot*. You, starting near the rationalist pole, and boxing the compass, and I traversing the diameter from the empiricist pole, reach practically very similar positions and attitudes."[7] Further, within "the fullness of practical life," we can distinguish, on the one hand, our natural shape, such as our beating heart, bones, blood coursing through our veins, and neurons firing; and on the other, our cultural shape, our second nature with its temporal span of past, present, and future nestled within a society, its culture, and what we shall later call our Ultimate environment. Only in those contexts can *gnothi seauton* be achieved. Though knowledge of what one is, learned in relation to the Personal, what one is to be and do are formed and carried out only within one's second nature, background, foreground, and culture.

Our Second Nature, Background and Foreground

Our second nature is complex. We begin by noting that it is individual, social, and temporal. Though singular individuals, we live in societies and are connected by common cultural patterns, knowledge, skills, and values we call our culture. Stable but not static, we experience change through the temporal span of our lives. Our past is our Background, and our present and future is our Foreground. In our foreground, change is usually stable and orderly, not capricious, though sometimes surprising. Our Background has two frames, the "before," the pre-conscious, pre-theoretical, pre-reflective; and the "after," the post-conscious, post-theoretical, and post-reflective. If our experiences are past, we can recollect and reflect on them. If they are "pre-," our Background is being formed through living into the future, by receiving living, by conscious choice. Its structure arises not only by the active and passive aspects of temporal living in an environment, but also by our activity potentials present to us at birth and the retentiveness of our memory. In the deepest recesses of our Background we find culturally ingrained meanings, habits, knowledge, and warrants. Our most fundamental warrants are unquestioned, obvious, held without dissension; we act within the *topos* of our culture.

What is the extent of our Background? It is all that remains with us after we undergo and act on our Foreground, including our natural and social/environments. Here we find our social place through our individual Background; we are both similar to other persons living in our society but different as we individually live out that similarity. Our Background is also historical. It can be variously structured as past, present, and future, chronologically in terms of calendars and clocks, in terms of events, such as the Reformation, or the Thirty Years War, and terms of meanings, such as the emergence of democracy. It is ordered by goals, institutions, as well as by habits, traits, attitudes, and practices. Our Background is active; its preparedness for ongoing activity and "projecting a project."[8] Finally, our Background is operative. We are aware of its presence and its absence. It is both manifest and anonymous.[9]

Our thoughts and habits present themselves, manifest themselves in the Foreground and recede into absence and anonymity in the Background, though we know the Background is ours.

Next, how are the Background and the Foreground related? Our experiences in the Foreground structured from birth by parents, guardians, and significant others, recede into the Background and having varying degrees of impact, help form its structure. Some of them deeply influence the formation of habits of a person into a distinctive pattern, sometimes referred to as character. As we grow and mature, the Background becomes richly historical and ordered. Also, the Background includes knowledge, skills, procedures, and values that are ready for action as we move into similar or new situations in the Foreground. More, the Background is operative in the Foreground. A problematic situation in the present may range from similar to past experiences to radically different, to unanticipated, to unimaginable. Our habits challenged, they fail to guide. Problems in the present range from superficial, such as a type of shoe not being available to replace the ones worn out, to more challenging, such as learning how to fly an airplane, to deeply controversial, such as gay marriage or the loss of a common system of social norms. We cannot continue our customary patterns, but we do not know how to proceed. We act, but our loss of direction deeply disturbs us. We cannot discern what we are, what we are to be, or what we are to do. The command to know one's self is a command to act in the face of confusion.

If our Foreground and our Background are in sync, we may reflectively recollect our Background, confidently seeking steady guidance for problematic presents and foreseeable futures. Or we may lose confidence in our Background, ignore it, and learn new knowledge, skills, and norms. We may challenge some aspects of the Foreground and seek reconciliation, allowing a highly valued habit in our Background to be accepted in the Foreground. In these ways one may begin the process of finding a role for one's Background as one faces the challenges in the Foreground. If we take positive steps to remedy the problematic situation, we may find a way to solidarity within and between our Background and Foreground, to an integrated personality.

Our second nature with its Background and its Foreground has many levels. Some are particular, deeply ingrained habits such as being able to fly an airplane, drive a car, or solve a problem in statistics. These may or may not be shared with other people. Others are culturally and socially shared. Their depth is so great that they define and delineate what it means to be a member of a culture. Believing in private property, individualism, and individual rights help to define one as an American. At a deeper level, humans share a belief in and a commitment to some form of social control, education, religious life, reproduction, distribution of goods and services, that is, institutions. Our interest in second nature focuses on the latter two senses. If the culture of a society is deeply disrupted, if the Background and Foreground are not in sync, the difficulty lies at the level of our deepest beliefs, those accepted without question or dissension that legitimate institutions that provide stability and solidarity through social change.

Furthermore, our second natures are interrelated simultaneously in a society. They interact and involve communication, socialization, and education. Philosophically, the other minds problem arises here. From a historical perspective we can understand that the temporal span of a second nature is more than that possessed by a numerically distinct individual. It involves the interrelation among persons in their youth, their middle years, and in their older years. For youth, their Background is formed as they acquire from their Foreground knowledge, tools, values and form habits. What they learn is sometimes individual; but it can be common to persons. From their parents, teachers, and significant elders they acquire patterns of living appropriate to homes, schools, churches, an economic system, a political system, a regulative system, and the media. As they learn they explore and nourish their individual activity potentials in steady institutional environments. By their middle years, their Backgrounds successfully formed, persons negotiate the problems they face in their Foreground and move into patterns of living available in their society. Their second nature is securely formed. At this time they assume the responsibility of helping form the Background of their children, of the next generation. Erik Erickson called this the stage of generativity.[10] Also, those in their middle years assist their parents and other older persons as health declines and they cannot care for themselves.

In their later years persons consider their second nature and assess the quality of the relation between their Background and the Foreground. If by appealing to their Background they have successfully negotiated that relation guided by their social institutions authorized by their Ultimate environment, they have a sense on integrity.[11] In stable, traditional societies, such as those in ancient Greek and Roman culture, the young emulate their seniors. The accumulated Background second nature of the old is sought and emulated by the young. In rapidly changing societies, such as in the modern west, knowledge changes rapidly. The Background of the older generation is outmoded, and for them to enter and successfully live in the institutions of society they need the latest information. The Foreground challenges the Background to update itself, rendering the old in the Background ineffective. The second nature of the older generation is a poor guide in facing the problems of the Foreground. The young do not want to emulate the older generation. The wisdom of the ages is ineffective.

Finally, the relation between Background and Foreground in an individual and their simultaneous and historical relationship help us understand where crisis is likely to occur. First, it can occur in the individual second nature during the normal process of maturing. For example, an 18 year old in college knows she cannot return home to 14 years of age. Yet she does not know what she will be when she reaches 30. She is in a crisis. Crisis in our individual second nature may be deeply emotional and require professional help. Nevertheless, a significant dimension of that crisis is the fractured relation of the Background and the Foreground. Second, the crisis can occur between groups living simultaneously. The young could reject the Backgrounds of those older than they, as between youth and their parents, teachers, or social authorities. It could occur between persons of supposedly different second natures, such as between ethnic groups, economic groups, gays and straights, or religious groups. These crises can become widespread and socially disruptive. However, crisis can become socially and culturally destructive. In this case, the Background and Foreground of a culture become so unrelated that nothing can provide stability and solidarity for a society, and it experiences deep social crisis. Suspicion appears in that crisis, undercutting the possibility of self-knowledge.

Problematic Patterns and Their Environments

The Background and Foreground of our second nature are normally in sync, stabilized and unified by cultural patterns, primarily institutions that receive their legitimacy and charisma from the authority of an Ultimate environment. Grasp the place and influence of authority legitimizing institutions and goals as they stability and solidify the temporal structure of our culture, our second nature, by considering the following scenario. After a decision in his early 20s to enter, to continue in a fuller way, or to fully commit to the legal profession, Jerry learned at mid-life that the effect of that decision extends well beyond what was imaged when the decision was made. For example, the way of life, the pattern of life of an attorney demands long hours and regular travel. Though the income is high, the impact on the family begins to show. He spends little time with the children and spouse. Little time is devoted to his children's education, and problems emerge at school. The decision is made to send them to an expensive boarding school. They can afford the best. In addition, long hours, hard work, and stress affect his eating habits and exercise; health problems appear. Though reared in the religious patterns of the Methodist Church with a strong emphasis on caring for the poor, the disenfranchised, Jerry focuses increasingly on economic power and ignores that aspect of his religious background. Increasingly he expects the government to enact laws that protect and benefit the economy, the media that support his economic interests (especially lower taxes), and the environment to be available to whatever furthers his economic welfare. His decision to enter a pattern of life connects him to other patterns and environments. Were many conscious choices made as the patterns merged into a way of living? Possibly, but more likely they simply flowed into each other. His way of life became habitual.

At the age of 38 Jerry welcomes his children home for Christmas vacation and is struck that he knows little about them, their likes, dislikes, habits, girlfriends and boyfriends, what really matters to them. Though polite, they are selfish, expecting their world to revolve around themselves. He points out the needs of the poor, the homeless, the disenfranchised; they ignore him. He remembers that he forgot them as well. He lives narcissistically, as do they. Under the impact of the dominance of the economic patterns he entered and furthered, his health fades and his business contributes to depleting the environment. Amid conflicting demands and with pangs of guilt and a sense of remorse, he ponders what if he had chosen a different life plan, possibly teaching, the ministry, government service. He would still have to feed and care for his family, educate them, help them find their way into a pattern of living, possibly a calling. How could he make enough money to pay the expenses? As he thinks through the implications of the various choices he could have made, he feels deeply the conflicts between his past way of life and his life at present.

To resolve such conflicts, we could recommend that Jerry appeal to the resources both in his Background and in the opportunities available to him in his Foreground. Searching his background through recollective memory, he could appeal to his culture's institutions, including information, skills, certified claims, sacred beliefs, and moral rightness of his Ultimate environments. Or he could seek to learn new skills, information, problem-solving techniques, certified claims, sacred beliefs and institutions from other cultures in his foreground and incorporate them into his own hoping to resolve conflicts. Though he seeks an authoritative mooring point or orientation, he finds additional problems facing him in his changing world.

He could quickly identify two examples, marriage and the economy. Regarding the institution of marriage in American life, what it means to be married changed from the 1950s to the early 2000s. In the idealized memory of some, in the 1950s men went to work while women stayed home, reared the children, and supported her husband in his work. Marriage was for a lifetime. In the early 2000s dual careers, latchkey children, high divorce rates characterize the state of marriage for many. Marriage lasts as long as love lasts, some believe. Contemplating marriage, which should one follow? The economy has changed from a national one with many trading partners to an international one with manufacturing, distribution, and sales scattered across the globe. No longer is work primarily hierarchically arranged as it was in the 1950s and 1960s; it is configured into teams of experts focusing on solving problems. The rules, procedures, and expectations of work change as institutions change.

From long habituation, institutions continue to structure our second nature even as suspicion erodes our confidence in them, and we wonder about embracing the newly forming ones. The question arises, "Which patterns are legitimate, the past ones or the future ones?" Seeking to direct one's life intelligently and morally, one could follow the authority of cultural patterns. Regarding marriage, one man and one woman; regarding economics, capitalism. Those are obviously correct, certified by the court of ultimate appeal, an Ultimate environment. However, suspicion focuses directly on the "unquestioned," the "obvious," the "taken for granted," and its relation to our temporally patterned lives. If another institutional pattern meets our needs, why accept either traditional marriage or capitalism just because they are obvious, unquestioned, or assumed? That raised, a chorus of voices call out, each claiming to be authoritative, the Ultimate environment.[12] The implication for self-knowledge is clear. To obey the command to discern who we are, what we are to be, and what we are to do in a culture in crisis leads to perplexity.

SUSPICION

Suspicion focuses on the relation between the Background and Foreground of our second nature, our culture, including an Ultimate environment and the institutional patterns that steady and unify the relation between our Background and Foreground. How did suspicion arise? To understand we turn to our cultural Background, Foreground and their relationship. Repotting the history of Western culture is both formidable and unnecessary. To limit and focus our study of the emergence of suspicion, we turn to *gnothi seauton*, know yourself, with its emphasis on the relation of persons and cultures to the Ultimate environment and to the environments it encloses.[13]

Order and Structure—Western Culture from the Greeks through the Medieval Period

Our search begins with the early formation of western culture, the Greeks, the Hebrews, and the Romans, cultures best characterized as cultural dyadic objectivist.[14] Objectivism means that persons are manifestations of the world, "chips off the old block." All knowledge and values derive from society, culture, and the order in which we live. Dyadic means that persons learn what they are through the society and culture in which they live. It was there that *gnothi seauton* rose into prominence and found its way into the mainstream of the West.

To know oneself in the ancient world what must one know? Succinctly, one must know one's station and its duties within an honor-shame culture rooted in a cosmic order. Discussion of one's individual station and duties is common in the modern world, particularly during the end of the nineteenth century among conservative thinkers such as F. H. Bradley. But such knowledge takes on a different meaning when considered within the honor-shame culture of the ancient Mediterranean basin. Central to that complex culture are limited goods, honor, shame, causality, and person. Within that order we can understand persons and how they stand to their social and cosmic order and the legitimizing Ultimate environment. Their Background and Foreground are tightly bound and apodictically authorized by an Ultimate environment.

Social Order

The Mediterranean world was composed of limited goods societies. Regarding the societies themselves,

> [T]he basic human environment into which first-century Mediterranean persons—Israelites, Romans, Greeks, or otherwise—were born was composed predominantly of agricultural or fishing villages, or both, socially tied to pre-industrial cities. The pre-industrial cities in question usually served as the administrative, religious, and market center for the villages or towns under their symbolic power. Jerusalem, Corinth, Ephesus, and even Athens and Rome were typical pre-industrial cities at this time. The only difference between Rome and the other cities of the area was that Rome served as *the* central city, the imperial hub, to which all other cities were politically tied, while each city individually had a larger or smaller number of villages or town under its sway. What resulted from this arrangement was a complex of inward-looking, closed systems that interfaced or touches upon each other: the village system, the city system, the empire system, and above all of these, the cosmic system.[15]

Only about 10 percent of the population lived in the cities; the rest lived in the villages and towns. Of that 10 percent, 2 percent were the elite, often literate, who held administrative positions in the civil and religious institutions and the wealthy absentee landowners who lived in the cities. Most important, however, the elite had responsibility for embodying and promulgating the norms and values of their society. Further, "the city itself was characterized by rigid social segregation marked by quarters or wards . . . the life of the urban elite was normally quite closed off from that of the low-status urbanite, often by a wall."[16] Below the merchants, craftsmen, day laborers stood the beggars and slaves.

Below the cities were towns and villages, where 90 percent of the population lived. Being under the control of the urban centers, these people had little control over their lives. The goods available to them were limited by powers beyond their control or influence; their existence was determined by "natural and social resources of their village, their pre-industrial city, their immediate area and world, leading to the perception that all goods available to a person are, in fact, limited."[17] Succinctly, "broad areas of behavior are patterned in such a way as to suggest . . . that in the social, economic, and natural universes—the total environment—all the desired things in life, such as land, wealth, prestige, blood, health, semen, friendship and love, manliness, honor, respect and status, power and influence, security and safety—literally all goods in life—exist in finite, limited quantity and is always in short supply."[18]

People perceived that their society's goods and services were finite in quantity, and nothing they did could change it. They believed that the gods established societies and placed families and individuals in them. The gods also distributed goods through society. Since limited goods were allotted to families and those goods were scarce, the family and individuals in them must stay in their station and perform their duties. Being born into a family with a position in society carried responsibilities that must be carried out for the well being of everyone. Any venture beyond to acquire more goods meant someone else would lose goods. Though an honorable man would not venture into the domain of someone else, he knew how to maintain his own, including defending his family and their subsistence living. Honor-shame cultures in the Mediterranean were highly stale, and one's background is a dependable guide in the foreground. It is so ordered by the gods.

What is honor, specifically regarding status and role? One's status can be defined as "the value of a person in his or her own eyes (that is one's claim to worth) *plus* that person's value in the eyes of his or her social group."[19] A person who claims worth that other people acknowledge has a justified claim to honor. Or, a person claims a position in relationship to everybody around him, and other people acknowledge that he holds that position. That is his honor. The status one holds is an intersection of *sexual role* (whether one is a man or a woman), *power* (whom does one control and by whom is one controlled), and *religion* (the "attitude and behavior one is expected to follow relative to those who control one's existence."[20]) How was honor gained? Honor comes to a person either by birth or by a gift from such notables as a king, an aristocrat, or a god. Honor can also be acquired. This is done by excelling others. In either case, each individual seeks to keep his honor, to hold on to it, and acquire what additional honor might be available.

If honor is a matter of relationship with one's equals that only they can challenge, what does dishonor mean? Dishonor is a loss of reputation. If an Augustus challenges Flavius, and Flavius does not respond appropriately, Flavius is dishonored. This meant that people would say "he cannot or does not know how to defend his honor. He thus loses his honor to the challenger, who accordingly gains in honor."[21] Clearly, this is an agonistic society of challenge and response, of winning and losing.

What is the meaning of shame, and what is its relation to honor? Shame "means sensitivity about one's reputation, sensitivity to the opinion of others."[22] It is both positive and negative. Persons with positive shame accept and "respect . . . the rules of human interaction."[23] On the other hand, persons with negative shame are shameless. They do not recognize, accept, and abide by those rules. The do not acknowledge boundaries and rules of interpersonal relationships. They are fools; fools are those who claim honor that is not recognized in the community. Their actions are called foolish. Failing to recognize, accept, and act according to the established rules of human interaction, the fool acts without understanding. Consider Greek *polis* culture. The available honor was limited by the natural world and the social resources of their polis and immediate area. What was available to a person was limited; all natural and social goods in life were finite, including honor. For the polis to function, for the needs of its citizens to be met, each person must know his place and accompanying responsibilities, stay in that place, and not venture beyond its boundaries. To do so would upset the intricately balanced social order. In *The Republic,* Plato advocates educating citizens to find their natural place, to fulfill their station and its duties, and to align their lives with the True, Good, and Beautiful. Wanting more land, a city is feverish (sick) and develops an army to take desired land and protect the citizens from attack. The bond between the True, Good, and Beautiful, the polis, and persons was strong.

Turn next to causality. At the top of the cosmic order are the gods who cause and arrange everything in its proper place, including the heavenly bodies, humans, animals, plants, and inorganic nature. The higher can affect the lower, but the lower cannot affect the higher. Causality moves from the top down. Persons higher can affect the lives of those lower, but not the other way around. One's honor can be challenged only by an equal. The gods could change human lives, but humans could not change the lives of the gods. To improve one's status required that he do so at the expense of another. If one gained, someone else lost. This, however, was a threat to the stability of the community. So, persons in honor shame societies adopt a defensive strategy and keep existing arrangements and statuses stable. To maintain harmony and stability in the community and among individuals and families, you were expected to stay in the position in which you found yourself, defend, and maintain your honor. Persons in the polis life were deeply concerned with their honor and shame. It was a matter of life and death.

Finally, consider person or personality. The word for "person" in Greek is *prosopon* and *persona* in Latin, meaning mask. An individual wears a "mask," so to speak, forming a distinction between an interior and an exterior. In an honor-shame culture the most important is the exterior. That is, individuals "internalize and make their own what others say, do, and think about them because they believe it is necessary, for being human, to live out the expectations of others. Such persons would conceivably have themselves always interrelated with other persons while occupying a distinct social position both horizontally (with others who share the same status . . .) and vertically (with others who are above and below in social rank) . . . the focus of attention (is) away from self and on the demands and expectations of others who can grant or withhold recognition."[24] The interior, on the other hand, is carefully guarded. Feelings, emotions, passions, confusions felt or thought could, if manifested, lead to foolish behavior, to overstepping the boundaries of their place and its duties. The psychological makeup of individuals is uninteresting in an honor-shame culture. Living within the order and structure of an honor-shame culture, persons in the Mediterranean world were dyadic. A person is the social dimension of his second nature.

What did *gnothi seauton* mean in the stable, cosmically ordered and authorized honor-shame culture of the Mediterranean? In one sense, to know oneself is the same as knowing one's honor and shame, one's second nature. The admonition encourages individuals to pay attention to what is most important in their lives, their place in the total scheme of things from *moira*, fate, to the gods down through the hierarchy, to the lowest forms of life below, and how they should behave.[25]

That is, know your physical, social place under the gods and behave accordingly. Avoid being a fool and shameful. The sacred texts of the poets, Homer and Hesiod in particular, teach the way of the gods, their struggles, exploits, the myths of creation, the formation of the world and institutions of order. There one can learn who you are, the place you are to occupy, and what you are to do.[26]

However, as events changed in the Mediterranean world, the understanding of the cosmic order changed for many elite from religion to philosophy. As the Mediterranean world increased trade and colonies were established in distant parts, different honor-shame cultures came into contact with each other. For example, in the Piraeus, the seaport of Athens, sailors from various parts of the Mediterranean world brought their worship of various gods. If the gods warrant a social framework, its expectations, its rules and boundary lines of human interaction, honor and shame shifted their meanings as one moved from god to god. An individual was a creature of a particular polis, a particular way of life, paid homage to the gods and all those socially above him, and exercised authority over those below. That was his second nature. But, contact with other honor-shame cultures raised questions. Which religion is correct? On what does a culture rest? Among the sophists of the fifth and fourth centuries Greek Enlightenment, the debate ensued: are societies based on custom, leaving each society to decide for it what is morally correct behavior, or are they based on divine ordained law to which one could appeal to settle such issues?

From Poets to Philosophers

To decide, some elites among the Greeks turned their search for self knowledge from narrative to Greek science, from poets to philosophers, from religion to philosophy.[27] With his claim that the unexamined life is not worth living, Socrates was the most notable. Turning from the authoritative Olympian narratives of Homer and Hesiod, for example, Socrates engaged the elite to examine rationally their own souls in search of an understanding of lives truly good to live. To gain insight into his view of *gnothi seauton*, we shall focus on his view of honor and shame and on suggestions about a cosmic order and our relation to it. To do that, consider his way of teaching.

We shall consider only one passage from the *Apology*, 28b–31c, where Socrates explains his status and role as a philosopher in the polis.[28] The passage begins with a question, one no doubt in the minds of many at the trial: "Do you feel no compunction, Socrates, at having followed a line of action which puts you in danger of the death penalty?" (*Apology* 28b) Typically, Socrates responds that life and death are not the key issues; but acting rightly or wrongly, like a good man or a bad one are. (*Apology* 28b) To illustrate, Socrates tells the jury of a scene from Troy where the *aristoi* in open field hand to hand combat took a stand on honor. A friend of Achilles, Patroclus, met death at the hands of Hector. Making "light of danger in comparison with incurring dishonor" (*Apology* 28c), he swore to avenge his friend, "being much more afraid of an ignoble life and of failing to avenge his friends." (*Apology* 28d) Calling that scene to his defense, Socrates said, "The truth of the matter is this, gentlemen. Where a man has once taken up his stand, either because it seems best to him or in obedience to his orders, there I believe he is bound to remain and face the danger, taking no account of death or anything else before dishonor." (*Apology* 28d) He recognizes that he would be guilty of a shocking inconsistency were he to leave his post. He did not do so when assigned posts at Potidaea, Amphipolis, and Delium; neither will he do so now. Indeed, "this duty I have accepted, as I said, in obedience to God's commands given in oracles and dreams and in every other way that any other divine dispensation has ever impressed a duty upon man." (*Apology* 33c)

How are we to understand this passage? In general, Socrates confirms his life. But more, he explains his status and role, his grasp of what he is up to. Though he claims not to be a teacher, he is one nevertheless. That is, he may not have a doctrine or skill to teach, as did the poets and rhetoricians; he nevertheless attempts to guide his listeners to accept their ignorance and to begin their search for self knowledge, a grasp of that which is truly good. By describing himself as one who examines himself and others, he articulates his self-concept as a teacher. However, the generality of those statements do not provide much insight into that concept. For help consider Socrates's status and role and the influence of honor on him.

First, consider his status. Socrates claims that his status in Athenian life was given him in "oracles and dreams." (Apology 33c) Given him by Apollo, his position is a matter of honor. It is a matter of a calling. Clearly, Socrates appeals to his cultural-religious heritage to account for what he is doing. Having a divinely appointed status, he understands what dishonor would mean and the accompanying shame. Analogous with Achilles, he would dishonor himself if he deserted his post. Socrates is attacked by his equals, socially at least. Meletus, Anytus, and Lycon are *aristoi*, men of the leisure class. They are free born Athenian males who are on the same social plane with Socrates. They attack him as a matter of honor, protecting the state. As the elites, there were responsible for embodying and promulgating the norms and values of their society. However, their understanding of the kind of honor Socrates claims and the kind they claim is different. Theirs is social honor; Socrates' is religious and moral honor. It's from that perspective that we should understand Socrates' comment that a good man cannot be harmed by a worse. Here we see Socrates' shift from a religiously authorized and understood *gnothi seauton* to a philosophical one. One's assigned role defines who one is, submerging the individual dimension of our second nature

Regarding the role he played with his God given status, Socrates said that God "appointed me . . . to the duty of leading the philosophical life, examining myself and others," and he will not abandon it now. Socrates asks questions to guide those to whom he is speaking in giving birth to real, essential definitions, which can reasonably be understood as the logical side to the forms. His primary way of doing this is through *elenchus*. But one can also find eristics, antilogistics, and dialectic in his discussions.[29] However, let me emphasize that Socrates appears to understand what knowledge would look like if it were forthcoming. It is gained through the structure of a craft, of *apeiron, peras*, mixture, and cause, though that way of stating it derives from one of Plato's later dialogues, the *Philebus*.[30] Nevertheless, Socrates' practice points to that, and his self understanding as one who knows that he does not know and that knowledge is of a certain sort gained through the fourfold structure just mentioned indicates it as well. As in the *Euthyphro*, Socrates believes real essential definitions articulate the stable structure of piety and point to the moral structure of reality, the eternal forms.

Through rational methods, Socrates sought to provoke his elite listeners to search for what is truly good for their souls. Through *elenchus* he encouraged them to recognize their confusion about what is best, what is truly honorable and not shameful. They must first recognize their ignorance; they do not know themselves. However, with hard thought proceeding in the right way they can come to know

His student Plato, building on Socrates insights and suggestions and armed with the insight provided by mathematics learned from the Pythagoreans, with Parmenides' arguments regarding *phusis*, with the pluralist arguments against monism on behalf of pluralism, and with Heraclitus's and the atomist such as Democritus view of *phusis*—Plato found philosophical ground for moral social interaction, stability, and solidarity. He found his identity, meaning, and intelligibility through that which is ultimately real, necessary, immutable, and eternal, the eternal forms: the Good, the True, and the Beautiful. Everything else found their reality and intelligibility through them. The eternal forms are authority, the role reserved for the gods. Though he did not escape his cultural traditions, he articulated a philosophical view of persons, social patterns, and their relationships to Reality that authorized them. What the early Greek philosophers set in motion had far reaching consequences.

By the end of the fourth century BCE two understandings of our personal and social lives, of the Ultimate environment, and their relation were clear, a Greek religious one and a philosophical one. With the rise of Christianity, philosophy found itself in conflict with yet another religion. The Christian apologists, both Eastern and Western, led the discussion between philosophy and Christianity. By the time of Emperor Constantine in the fourth century CE Christian theology had won.[31] By the High Middle Ages of the eleventh through thirteenth centuries CE philosophy had become the handmaiden of theology.[32] Both philosophy and theology accepted a tight bond between the Ultimate environment and the hierarchical structure of the social order. Authority and causality originated in God, in Reality, and spread down through the great chain of being into the farthest reaches of nature, to nothingness.

A grand synthesis

During the High Middle Ages of the twelfth into the fourteenth centuries the basic outlines of where one stands in the total scheme of things was clear. From God to the lowest form of creation stood a great chain of being peopled by angels, humans, animals, non-living beings, to the lowest forms of nature. A teleological universe governed by moral norms and powered by the will of God, this world was created out of nothing according to God's wisdom, governed by structures (social and natural) God placed in it, and directed to God's own ends. One knew oneself through an honor-shame system interpreted in terms of a Christian vision. If one chose to follow the teachings and ways of the Catholic Church one goes to heaven, and if not, to hell in eternal separation from God. One's daily life and the structures of one's society were governed by the laws God ordained for our individual, social, natural well-being. In the grand synthesis of the European High Middle Ages, constructed under the influence of Thomas Aquinas, one knew where he came from, from he is going, and what he ought to do during his life time. The honor-shame system of the ancient and medieval worlds was lodged within and legitimated by the authority of a Christian metaphysical Ultimate environment. By the fourteenth century, however, internal critiques of and external pressures on the unifying principles of a Good God; the best of all possible worlds; the hierarchy of species resting ultimately in God; an all pervasive theological, social, and natural teleology; and a Church that conveyed this synthesis and under which all earthly life found its meaning, weakened their intellectual and social adhesiveness, their authority.

Lessons from the Past

Before we move to the Renaissance, what do the ancient Greeks, Romans, Hebrews, and medievalists have that can help us with the quandary of suspicion? First, in those cultures we find a clear answer to our problem. Background and Foreground of culture and second nature are bound tightly. There we find order authorized by narratives of the way of the gods or Truth and its connection to persons in society. Persons are "masks" worn over and hiding internal feelings, thoughts, attitudes, and reactions. Our "masks," the social aspect of our second nature, are what others expect of us in light of our birth or acquired status. The patterns of our lives are given to us by social expectation, and in a limited goods society they are fixed. Men have status; women have none, other than through a male. The Ultimate environment formed and ordered nature, society, and all in them. Persons are taught their station and its duties, are expected to align their lives with the objective Ultimate environment, cosmic, social, and natural. However, fundamental social change, such as we experience in the late twentieth and early twenty-first centuries, was unknown to them. Suspicion did not arise. Their answer to social upheval is order that allows little change; the Background and Foreground of their second nature is in sync. Understanding how to behave in an unchanging society teaches us little about behaving in a changing one. The Ultimate environment authorized, legitimatized the social, cultural order and the behavior of persons who lived with Christian honor. If we adopt their worldview, especially the clear legitimacy of the gods or Truth, we learn little about reconciling conflicts we experience between our Background and Foreground.

Second, we could interpret know thyself as did the philosophically minded in the ancient world, Plato, for example. Or, we could do as the religious did, whether Olympian, Hebrew, or Christian. In each we find a hierarchically structured honor-shame culture. One might be persuaded to believe that Plato's ontology, his view of *phusis*, as developed in his theory of forms is independent of any culture, honor-shame included. Nevertheless, his moral, social, and natural cosmology bears the indelible marks of an honor-shame culture: the natural order of things is stable, hierarchical, and persons know themselves through that order, where they fit into it, and how they ought to behave. Or one could accept the religious authority of the Hebrew-Christian God, particularly the incarnation in Jesus. But it too is marked by the institutions of an honor-shame culture. Followers recite authoritative narratives of a God beyond culture, who as the creator of the heavens and the earth, orders all things in them, including the social order stabilized by the institutions of honor-shame culture.

Third, for the Greeks, Romans, Hebrews, and Christians, social space was stable and narrow; it was a matter of honor to know it, to stay there, and to perform ones duties. Social space allowed little movement up, down, or lateral. If born a peasant, one would not become a King.[33] An exception to this was open to priests in the Roman Catholic Church. Born a peasant, a man could enter the priesthood and conceivably become Pope, although Popes usually came from the social elite. Further, personal choice existed in decisions to defend or not one's honor. The narrow range of options open for consideration severely limited the possibilities of changing his life. Free will and social mobility in the modern sense was unknown.[34] Fourth, the ancients present us with two Ultimate environments: the God of the Hebrew-Christians known through narrative; and the philosophical-rational ones, such as the eternal forms of Plato, formed-matter of Aristotle, the Absolute of the

Stoics, or the One of Plotinus, known through Greek science. Conflicts ensued between Christian and philosophical ways of understanding God, nature, society, and persons. Led by Christian apologists such as Irenaeus, Origin, and Augustine, by the fifth and sixth centuries CE theology won, and by the eleventh century CE philosophy was the handmaiden of theology. However, hesitant to follow the stable, orderly, and culturally enmeshed thought of the philosophers or the Christian theologians, one recalls the hard battle for the freedom of individual persons fought in the Renaissance and modern world. Possibly there one could find a better, more acceptable interpretation of *gnothi seauton*.

The Emerging Self—Western culture from the Renaissance to the present

Returning to our more recent cultural Background, at least from the sixteenth century to the present, we find a changing understanding of *gnothi seauton*. The tight bond between God and the created order, specifically the hierarchical order of the honor-shame culture of the ancient and medieval worlds, slowly loosened in the West. As it did so, it was upstaged by a culture powered by the emerging individual self consciousness and ordered around religion, science, and the freedom of the individual. The vertical axis of the cultural dyadic objectivist order of the ancient and medieval worlds receded into the Background and a horizontal one of the cultural monadic subjectivist self surged into the Foreground of western culture.

What do we mean by cultural monadic subjectivism? In the modern period individual persons turn inward seeking to know themselves and the natural world and to create societies to meet their personal and social needs. Having rejected the ancient and medieval world of cultural dyadic objectivism, they found individual freedom and believed little external to themselves constrains their creative work, particularly the past.[35] In this realm of freedom oriented to the future, they can choose among options they imagine and can work to bring them to fruition. The freedom of each individual to develop her own psychical, spiritual, and social space seems unlimited. They find their solidarity and stability within their own lives or in a society of their own forming.[36]

Loosening the Bonds of Legitimacy

What did *gnothi seauton* mean in the western world during the Renaissance? Succinctly, it continued to focus on knowing how one stands to oneself, to other persons, to God, and to the natural world. However, during the late Middle Ages and early Renaissance, forces weakening the bonds binding

God and patterns of the social/natural orders fractured the grand medieval synthesis. The emerging self awareness of the Renaissance led to exploration beyond the doors of the Cathedral. It found and introduced diversity: "Christian and pagan, modern and classical, secular and sacred, art and science, science and religion, poetry and politics."[37] Armed with skepticism, a new scientific method and understanding of the natural world, a theory for reorganizing social life, and a reformation of theology, emerging self consciousness broke through the strictures of cultural dyadic objectivism. Persons became concrete as in the *Canterbury Tales* and Boccaccio's *De Cameron,* leaving behind the shadowy persons of the *Divine Comedy.* They epitomized a "new consciousness—expansive, rebellious, energetic, and creative, individualistic, ambitious and often unscrupulous, curious, self-confident, committed to this life and this world, open-eyed and skeptical, inspired and inspirited"— expressed in the manifesto of Renaissance humanism, Pico della Mirandola's *Oration on the Dignity of Man.*[38] Emerging persons in the Renaissance challenged authorized patterns of social stability and unity and set the stage for movements in the modern and contemporary worlds, including the Protestant emphasis on faith alone for knowledge of God; their place in and understanding of the political life of society, particularly after the Magna Carta; their loss of confidence in an all powerful and Good God after the Plague of the fourteenth century; and their new grasp of the motions of the heavenly bodies under Copernicus, Brahe, Kepler, and Galileo.

However, eroding connections between a moral order authorizing social practices and the emergence of self-consciousness and personal freedom made traditional *gnothi seauton* problematic. The tight bounds connecting the Background and Foreground loosened. To understand the erosion of that legitimating bond, turn to four central ingredients of the medieval worldview: the nature and knowledge of God, the structure of the universe, the structure of society, and the nature and structure of persons. We shall consider first, the Black Death, evil; next, science, astronomy; then, political science, society; and finally, philosophy, skepticism.

From Conflicts to Balanced Tension

The Black Death of 1348–1353 devastated Europe's population. Appeals to the Church, to a good, loving God had no effect. Many questioned the relation of God to evil in the created order, supposed to be the best of all possible worlds. Grounding the natural and social orders in the authority of God, though believed, was less secure. Depending less on theological assurances of God's relation to the world, many sought to cure disease and secure their health through observation and more refined practices. Tying medicine to chemistry, to physiology and anatomy was not far off.[39] The new science emerged.

To develop, the new science broke from the medieval dedication to Aristotle and the Bible. According to the overarching vision of the High Middle Ages, the world is the creation of God, and all things revolve around those who are made in God's image, persons. The motions of the heavenly and earthly bodies, circular and rectilinear motion respectively, are understood teleologically. The four *archai*, causes, are the principles for our world. The formal, material, efficient, and final causes collectively account for the world; it was a teleological order. In this metaphysical, hierarchical order, humans walking through this vale make life decisions either to live under God and God's governance, or under something other than God. If they choose to follow God, they go to heaven; if they choose not to do so, they go to hell. Those moral choices made in a teleologically and morally governed universe are the central concern of living. Humans know who they are, their place in the total scheme of things, and what they are to do. *Gnothi seauton* could be achieved, primarily through the Catholic Church.

However, Copernicus, Kepler, and especially Galileo with his telescope, discovered that the sun does not revolve around the earth and humans; the earth and humans revolve around the sun. Persons are decentered. No longer the center of the universe, they are grains in the cosmic sand moving in no discernible direction. Their standing in the universe is now problematic. The teleological universe, the four principles for understanding it, and ordered according to a mixture of Aristotle and Genesis 1 and 2 may be theologically and metaphysically correct, but the universe operates mechanistically. According to mechanistic causality, an adequate explanation requires only efficient causes. Determining Aristotle's formal, material, and final causes is unnecessary. To understand B, one only needs to know A, what preceded it; that to which it may be moving, a final cause, is unnecessary. Questions arose. What is the place and work of God in this new way of understanding the universe? How can God, who creates with purpose and design, legitimate a mechanistically ordered universe that has neither? What now of *gnothi seauton*, particularly the relation of our second nature to our natural, physical dimension and to a legitimate Ultimate environment?[40] Turn next to social/cultural thought, well represented by Hobbes.

In the Roman and medieval worlds the dominant philosophical view was that society was governed by laws that in turn were grounded in the laws of the universe laid in place by a Good God available to anyone through the proper exercise of reason. Bolstered by the Stoic view of law and continuing through Augustine, Aquinas carefully analyzed law, its nature and function in the universe. God governed all God created, from the eternal law, to natural moral law, to divine law, and finally to human law. However, the developing self of the Renaissance placed a premium on the will, specifically the will of persons to set their own course in life, particularly in their social relations, independent of the Church's authorizing narrative. Instead, look to science.

Hobbes argued that the state does not rest on some transcendent, metaphysical law or divine authority but on the will of the members of the society, the sovereign in particular. For Aquinas the sovereign is obligated to act according to law of God; for Hobbes law is the command of a sovereign. There are two kinds of law, natural and legal. The law as command of the sovereign is legal. Natural law rests on an understanding of the natural world and the place of humans in it. He views humans as functioning in the orderliness of nature. As natural objects move according to the laws of cause and effect, so do humans. The cause of human motion is the will to survive; good is whatever allows one to survive, and evil whatever does not. A natural law is "a precept, or general rule, found out by reason."[41] Since humans are egotistical, the first rule of nature is that persons ought to seek peace. This follows logically from natural law of human nature. The best way to survive is to live peaceably with other humans. The second states that "a man be willing, when others are so too, as far forth as for peace, and defense of himself he shall think it necessary, to lay down his right to all things; and be contented with so much liberty against other men, as he would allow other men against himself."[42] Hobbes believed that egotistical individuals would decide for themselves what is best, and anarchy would result. On the basis of the second law, however, people seeking peace would renounce their freedoms and rights and enter into a social contract, thereby creating an artificial person that he called a leviathan, the state or commonwealth. On the basis of natural law the state would be formed. On the basis of legal right the state would be governed. Legal law begins only with the command of a sovereign, whose will is the final authority. The contrast with Aquinas is obvious. As a Renaissance figure whose background lies in the Middle Ages, Hobbes is clear in his confidence in the power of reason and in interpreting the present with confidence in the new science. However, if society is best understood mechanically and not teleologically, if it rests not on God's command but on the will of its citizens, particularly that of the Sovereign, what is the relation of God to it? Is a divine legitimacy available for it? How do persons, society, and God relate? Legitimacy for socially stabilizing institutions lies in the will of persons. Turn now to persons, to Descartes.

In the early seventeenth century Descartes, seeking to resolve conflicts among God, persons, and nature, further problematized *gnothi seauton*. As a Renaissance thinker he was well schooled in medieval philosophy, especially Augustine, and metaphysics in particular; he was equally well aware both of the fissures in Christendom and the new science of Galileo. He recognized the conflicting ideas developed during the Renaissance and sought not a new synthesis, but a way of balancing opposites, a stable tension of opposites. True to the emerging self of the Renaissance, the equipoise lies in the *cogito*: I think therefore I am.

Descartes faced at least three problems, each generated in the Renaissance and its reaction to the Middle Ages: skepticism, religion, and science. Skepticism was prevalent in the Renaissance. The most persuasive form was Pyrrhonism. It argued that for each claim to truth one could find equally strong evidence against it. Since justified true beliefs are unavailable to us, we should suspend judgment. Deep fissures in the medieval synthesis, the discoveries in astronomy, the dysfunctional political life of Christendom, and the breakup of the honor system articulated by Pico della Mirandola led to deep skepticism about humans. In its traditional understanding, g*nothi seauton* was not possible. Should we stop inquiry, or should we further it? If we are to further it, the skeptic must be answered. Descartes, a son of the Church who believed its teachings and was unwilling to engage in theological matters, sought the place of religion in the lives of persons. Finally, he was aware of the work of Copernicus, Brahe, Kepler, and Galileo and believed it must find its legitimate place in our understanding of our selves and in relation to Religion. But, how suitably answer the skeptic and find a legitimate role for science and religion?

In true Renaissance fashion, he built on the emerging self-consciousness and claimed that the skeptic could be defeated. Doubt is the sword of the skeptic; cleverly used, any argument could be defeated. Descartes pointed out, however, that though all else could be doubted, one could not doubt one's own thinking as one doubts. *Cogito ergo sum.* On that firm basis, Descartes fashioned ontological and causal arguments to prove that God exists as well as the natural world. The *cogito, res cogitans*, is non-spatial, free, the arena of sense, memory, and thought. The external world, *res extensa*, is extension in motion. In *res cogitans* we find values and the basis for belief in God, non-dependent substance, who is the causal ground of both created substances. He has defeated the skeptic, made a place for religion, and a place for science. If they stay in their realms and perform their proper function, no conflict between religion and science would result. At the basis of this is the person as a thinking thing. The emergence of consciousness in the Renaissance has found its philosophical formulation and defense. Reason ascends to the final authority.

However, knowing ourselves is now even more problematic. The division of what Descartes called "secondary substances" into the dualism of *res extensa*, the external objective natural order, and *res cogitans*, the internal subjective mental order, creates major problems. What is the relation between mind and body? If in our consciousness we find free will, how is it related to the orderly movement of our bodies best understood in terms of mechanical causality of the new science? However, one now faced the free will problem.[43] And what is the relation of our sensory data to that to which they refer, such as the natural world? If we can know that to which they refer only through them, how can we justifiably claim that the world is as we perceive it to be? That is, one faces the problem of knowledge of the external world. Following on its heels is the other minds problem, and later language. Aided by Kant's Copernican revolution and the separation of the sign from the signified, all knowledge became a property of language.[44] With Descartes' placing opposites in tension, *gnothi seauton* became more elusive. The close bonds among the social/cultural world, the natural world, and authorizing Ultimate environment, understood as the Christian God, making *gnothi seauton* possible, dissolved.

As the modern world moves through the Enlightenment to the present, these problems are made more troublesome through the attempt to understand persons and the social world as possessing orderliness comparable to the natural world and legitimated by science. In the mid-nineteenth century Darwin held a view of evolution that subjected persons to the laws of biological change. Marx viewed human behavior as manifestations of economic forces. Freud understood humans in terms of biological forces, and Nietzsche in terms of the will. The emergence of problematic consciousness eclipsed the youthful exuberance of Pico della Mirandola's Renaissance and may submerge the self under the exteriority of technology.

What, then, of *gnothi seauton*? Here we find the outcome of the emergence of the self, a fully developed cultural monadic subjectivism. Recall that in the ancient world "person" meant a mask, with a public exterior and private interior. The exterior was all that mattered; the interior was subordinated to it. Our second nature defined us; we are dyadic persons. *Gnothi seauton* was possible to any self-circumspect person. However, after Descartes, deeply influenced by Augustine, a thousand years before him, the interior life of persons became increasingly important. Indeed, Descartes thought we know directly, in an unmediated manner our inner lives, and Hobbes believed what was most important for our social lives was not what was socially expected of us (a continuation of the ancient view of persons living in an honor-shame culture) but what we willed, our own survival. The duality persists in the distinction between I and me, as in I did that to myself, and as in the distinction between the person and his personality. However, for the modern, *gnothi seauton* means my private *I* knowing my private/public me or personality; where personality, though numerically mine and no one else's and to some extent private, is formed by our own choice and hand and includes our second nature, culture, institutions, an ultimate environment, and understandings of physical environments. Though we find them, what we find is our own creation. Ironically, we become again dyadic persons, contemporary but no more open than that of the ancients.

Lessons from the Emerging Self

At the outset of the Renaissance a hierarchical, stable order of honor-shame, socially defined and structured by limited goods, by Reality, and God continued, made *gnothi seauton* possible, achievable. Order, social patterns structured the temporal patterns of human living at the expense of freedom to choose patterns from among multiple options. Belief in an authoritative Ultimate environment pervaded these periods. But the grand medieval synthesis, Christendom, cracked under the internal stress of philosophical critique of Duns Scotus and William of Occam. The devastation of the plague of 1348–1353 damaged beyond repair the claim that this is the best of all possible worlds governed by God for the well-being of all persons. As personal consciousness emerged and flourished, new adventures in art, navigation, and discovery of distant lands characterized the Renaissance. In their exuberance and armed with skeptical inquiry and freedom of will, they broke tradition bound order and sought to satiate their minds with a reformed knowledge of God, nature, society, and persons. The balanced tension of Descartes initiated and became the model of modern philosophy. But in Descartes' new alignment of persons, God, patterns, and aligning one's life with God, *gnothi seauton* became difficult. Essentially, both religion and philosophy turned inward, the self became dominant, religiously with Luther, and philosophically with Descartes.[45] Now, however, how account for social patterns, the existence of God, and any alignment with God? The youthful, playful delight in freedom *from* constraints characteristic of the Renaissance, the development of modern science, and the work of Enlightenment thinkers and Kant questioned the power of Rationalism to know Ultimate Authority, such as God, and person as substance, much less understanding how Ultimate Authority and persons could be related. There is no Ultimate Authority, no person, and no relation among them.[46] Our second nature is splintered leaving an untrustworthy background unrelated to a foreground saturated with options.[47]

If *gnothi seauton* could be achieved, it most likely would occur within a culturally dominant technology, such as Net Works. The monadic self of the modern world, ironically, could become a dyadic self submerged within and defined by technical rationality. *Gnothi seauton* could be achieved through the rationalized structures of modern industrial and Net Work society. Though persons created rationalized institutions and Net Work structures for political and economic purposes, those same structures could become apodictic for persons finding their identity in them. The rational, technological structures now institutionalized would bind tightly the temporal span of our second nature. Ironically, if that occurred, cultural monadic subjectivist persons would return to the narrow, dyadic space of the ancients, but in a different form.[48]

In the meantime, we can tell someone who we are. Our personal patterns of life change, but are manageable. Institutions change, but they are stable enough for our second nature to guide us through social change. On the surface of everyday living we manage. But in the deep recesses of the Background of our second nature, we feel disquieted. We can now grasp what, though deeply submerged in our cultural and social Background, daily influences our Foreground. We call it suspicion.

We began investigating *gnothi seauton* to find, if possible, the origin of suspicion, its central characteristics, and its significance for the Background-Foreground relation. From our study we can now lay bare the problem of suspicion.

Suspicion emerges

Suspicion arises as bonds that held together the Background and Foreground of our second nature, of our culture, that were authorized by an Ultimate environment, and stabilized and unified by institutions fray and break. Our culture and its institutions, that stabilize and solidify our second nature loosen and erode. It is a long journey from dyadic selves under the authority of institutions and their authorizing Ultimate environment, to monadic selves who under their own authority both create their social/cultural worlds and submit to them, to the loss of persons, of stabilizing institutions, and of legitimating Ultimate environment, to the possible emergence of new dyadic selves defined and structured by the authority of a rationalized industrial and Net Work order. Yet, the journey reveals breaks in the temporal order of our second nature and culture, shifts in authorities, the problematic nature of persons, and the puzzling relation between authorizing Ultimate environment and the Background and Foreground relation. Elements required for *gnothi seauton* are problematic in themselves and in their relations to each other.

Consider each more carefully. What shall we make of authority? Is it authoritative narratives or objective, external Truth discovered by Greek science that we find and submit to, or is it ourselves, or is it again external to persons who created it and then submit to it? Is authority moral, accepted without discussion as in the Ancient, Roman, or Medieval worlds; or is it non-moral and accepted with dissension as in contemporary rationalized, technological world? Regarding the self, is it a substance, as in Plato, Aristotle, Augustine, Boethius, Aquinas, and Descartes? Or is it free and autonomous with no intrinsic structure, as Rousseau thought? The Renaissance humanist's emphasis on the talents and capacities of individual persons, viewed apart from God's predestining them to a place in society, has become an "individual," free and malleable but alone in the world. Though Rousseau helped usher in the modern age with his private individuals who have no center (at least the *imago dei* was cast aside) and who seek to fulfill their own interests, the identity these individuals take is the contribution of technology, industrialization, and political forces at play in industrialized Western societies, particularly in the late twentieth and early twenty first centuries. Is there no self, values, or truth other than what each person individually creates?[49] What possible relation do the various self-proclaimed final authorities have to our culture and to the Background and Foreground relation of our second nature? These issues indicate the depth, extent, and complexity of problems created by suspicion. What can we conclude regarding suspicion?

Suspicion loosens the bond between our Background and Foreground that was legitimated by an authoritative Ultimate environment stabilized and solidified through cultural and social change by institutions. That means the loss of a reliable Background enabling us to adjudicate among alternative social, cultural possibilities, including alternative *topoi* guiding our recollective memory. *Gnothi seauton* is questionable, at best.

In the meantime, we do not cease our patterns of living or break with the environments we live in simply because of these barely noticed seismic tremors. We continue them, but their Ultimate environments, their Master narratives, and Objective Truths appear to provide our institutions and culture with the legitimacy, charisma, and authority to steady our second nature, both cultural and individual, through social, cultural change. They cannot do so. Suspicion subtlety erodes any legitimization of the fullness of our temporal patterned practical living, of the possibility of genuine *gnothi seauton.*

Before we continue, note that throughout the discussion we have mentioned Ultimate environments that authorize cultures and the lives of persons living in them. We found them among the ancients. They were held apodictically by the culture. But others do not authorize and are not held without discussion, especially in the contemporary world. Look carefully at our critical study of our cultural background from the perspective of *gnothi seauton.* The study itself manifests the core of suspicion. We located and discussed key changes in western culture where resources in the cultural background became questionable aids in coping with conflicts in its foreground, leading to questioning the authority of a formerly apodictic Ultimate environment. That critical exposure shows that no authority is either "obvious," or apodictic. We can no longer simply accept without question any authorizing, legitimating Master narrative or Being; they may or may not do so. Our study opens for critical reflection the relation between the social, cultural patterns unifying, stabilizing, and solidifying our second nature, on the one hand, and the Ultimate environment that legitimates those patterns, on the other. Exposing them to questioning minds leads to critical reflective examination. Our study is an act of suspicion!

Suspicion, now exposed, leads to a loss of unquestioned acceptance of our temporal patterns of behavior and their authorizing, legitimating Ultimate environment. Once critical reflection occurs, the roots of western culture lose their "obvious," leaving us to continue living our patterns with no trustworthy authority to guide us as those patterns lose their legitimacy. Though their animating and authorizing core is lost, we continue living the patterned lives of our second nature. Nevertheless, our cultural institutions continue to provide solidarity and stability for our second nature; cultural habits do not change easily. Now, however, lacking trustworthiness, we are suspicious practitioners of them.

Suspicion Focused

Recognizing that suspicion manifests itself in the relation between the Background and Foreground in our second nature and our cultural life, we investigated our cultural/social Background from the ancient world to the present. Guided by the admonition, *gnothi seauton*, we searched the orderly stable honor-shame culture of the ancient world of the West. Agonistic societies know social change and upheaval but maintain the moral honor-shame institution. That institution, among others, authorized by their Ultimate environment, stabilized their social/cultural lives, their second nature through social change. That continued during the ascendancy of Christianity to the formation of Christendom. We then turned to the Renaissance and the emergence of the self. As the self remained religious but armed by skepticism and science freely explored the world outside the doors of the church, the old order of the Great Chain of Being slowly receded and the self expanded its freedom to explore, create, and sometimes destroy. *Gnothi seauton*, consigned to one's own self by Nietzsche and Freud, became problematic. No apodictic Ultimate environment survived, leaving institutions, individuals, and groups culturally adrift. The old order of our cultural Background was now in splinters. Our deepest cultural structures and authorities no longer stabilize and guide into our Foreground. Yet, we manage with what we have; our cultural and social well being may not need an apodictic Ultimate environment legitimating institutions providing stability for our second natures as we negotiate the relation between our Background and our Foreground. We have the technical knowledge and tools to negotiate whatever we face in the Foreground. Secure in our Background, procedures are updated as required by the problems in the Foreground. Unfortunately, that simply whitewashes the stubborn problem.

To place a fine point on suspicion, use the structure of antinomy. Consider the two dominant cultural options in our Background and Foreground, cultural dyadic objectivism or Order and cultural monadic subjectivism or the emerging self. Let "p" stand for the former and "-p" stand for latter. Formally, that would be p & -p. Logically, that is a contradiction. Cultural dyadic objectivism and cultural monadic subjectivism cannot both be true at the same time; if one is true, the other has to be false. However, it can be reasonably argued that both are true. We have examined sufficient evidence to support each conjunct. The claim is a contradiction; each statement composing it has solid supporting evidence. Thus, we have an antinomy. Our minds will not satisfactorily remain in a contradiction; we seek a resolution by showing that at least one option is false, but that is not possible. The antinomy is secure.

Now, look deeply into the antinomy, underneath its logical form into its experiential basis. Both sides of the antinomy are at the core of our cultural experience, of what makes us the persons we are, our identity, the society we live, the culture we have. In our Background and present Foreground we find elements of both cultural dyadic objectivism and cultural monadic subjectivism. That is the case for our culture and our second nature. That is our identity. We cannot help but live them, both of them. Yet they are contradictory. Our cultural identity, our second nature is an antinomy. Logically, experientially suspicion soaks our social lives.

CONCLUSION

Even while living the disquietude articulated as an antinomy, we seek to obey the command, *gnothi seauton*. Though the command is clear, obeying and achieving it is problematic. Self-knowledge rests in unifying ourselves with what is ultimately the case, and in doing so learn what we are to be and do. Such knowledge is achieved by individuals in a society with a culture, and under an authority legitimating the connections between our Background and Foreground. If that connection is lost, self-knowledge cannot be achieved. Turning to our cultural memory or to our present knowledge, we longingly hope to find a clear apodictic, authoritative Ultimate environment legitimizing a relation between our background and foreground, knowing that we will not. Yet, we recognize that we may not need that. Technical reasoning provides the skills to manage our personal and social affairs. Crisis management is sufficient without attempting to ground ourselves in being that would allow us to know what we are. Yet, the antinomy remains. Is there no way out of the antinomy of suspicion?

In our historical discussion we touched on the growth of science, on *phusis* as Being, and the power of reason. However, we did not develop the insights they offered. We ignored the infrastructure and superstructure of culture, whether the cultural dyadic objectivism of the ancients and medieval or the cultural monadic subjectivism of the Renaissance, moderns, and contemporary. What do they offer? We can best understand the infrastructure by appealing to Naturalism and the superstructure by appealing to Idealism, both guided by confidence in the power of reason (extended) to understand being, Rationalism. Is it possible that we can solve the problem of suspicion by grounding either Order or the Emerging Self either in the infrastructure of Naturalism or in the superstructure of Idealism, guided in either case by Rationalism? If so, we can confidently seek *gnothi seauton*. In the next chapter we shall examine each, hoping to find a way out of suspicion and to *gnothi seauton*. Our hopes may only haunt us.

Notes

1. The Greek words, *gnothi seauton*, mean know yourself. They appeared over the entrance to the Oracle at Delphi in Greece. In India the admonition to know yourself, *atamvidya*, appears in the Vedic (from *Veda*, "knowledge," "wisdom") texts from at least 1500 BCE. The main goal of Hindu philosophical inquiry is freedom from misery. Each system of orthodox Indian philosophy seeks to help persons to that end by giving them insight into the nature of ultimate reality and their place in it. They advocated self-knowledge; without it, the desired freedom is impossible.

2. Authority includes "ought," "good," "best." For an understanding of legitimacy see Jurgen Habermas, *Legitimation Crisis*, trans. by Thomas McCarthy (Boston: Beacon Press, (1973) 1975) and J. F. Lyotard, *The Postmodern Condition: a Report on Knowledge*, trans. by Geoff Bennington and Brian Massumi. Foreword by Frederic Jameson (Manchester, UK: Manchester University Press, 1992), 6–9.

3. Environments are like smaller boxes set inside larger ones that delimit the physical, psychical, social, and spiritual space of persons living inside them. We shall see that, though defined by those environments, through reflection and free will we can be aware of them, as well as critique and modify their influence. Deeply influential, those environments do not compel our behavior.

4. Suspicion as used here, is not an epistemological term, though it has epistemological aspects. Neither does it refer to a method of interpretation, as in Ricoeur's hermeneutics of suspicion, "a method of interpretation which assumes that the literal or surface-level meaning of a text is an effort to conceal the political interests which are served by the text. The purpose of interpretation is to strip off the concealment, unmasking those interests." (www.english.tamu.edu/pers/fac/myers/hermeneutical_lexicon.html) For the central argument of Paul Ricoeur's theory of interpretation, see his *Interpretation Theory, Discourse and the Surplus of Meaning* (Fort Worth, TX:

Texas Christian University Press, 1976). For our reasons for rejecting the subject-object distinction as formative for philosophical discussion, see Buford, *Trust, Our Second Nature*, 26–33. Furthermore, suspicion, is a metaphysical relation and not an epistemological issue; it is not a restatement of skepticism in any of its traditional forms in western philosophy, whether academic or pyrrhonist.

Rejecting the subject-object dichotomy underlying interpretation and the hermeneutics of suspicion, we submit that the origin of suspicion can be found through the recollective memory of the Background and Foreground relations that form our second nature, specifically, and culture, in general.

Finally, what we call the age of suspicion is not an attempt to group western history, or world history, into periods. Jaspers pioneered the idea of the Axial Age. Ewart Cousins and Leonard Swidler write about a second axial age that Hans Kung calls a Macro-Paradigm-Shift. Neither do we follow Oswald Spengler's "going under" of the West. In contrast, we focus on the inadequacy of western culture and its metaphysical supports to help persons gain self-knowledge, an inadequacy that congeals into the problem of suspicion. To overcome suspicion we turn to form a new Master narrative. Interestingly, this new *topos* is not limited to those living in the west; it is the master narrative for any culture and for any people seeking self-knowledge.

5. Recollective memory is an act of remembering guided by a *topos*.

6. Borden Parker, *Personalism* (New York, NY: Houghton Mifflin, 1908), 20. Though Bowne is correct that we begin doing philosophy in the midst of everyday living, his assumptions about reason and experience are questionable. In this book, see chapters 3 and 4.

7. Herbert W. Schneider, "Introductory Essay: Bowne's Radical Empiricism," in Warren E. Steinkraus, ed., *Representative Essays of Borden Parker Bowne* (Utica, NY: Meridian Publishing Company, n.d.), xiv–xv.

8. Victor Kestenbaum, *The Grace and the Severity of the Ideal, John Dewey and the Transcendent* (Chicago, IL: University of Chicago Press, 2002), 143.

9. Kestenbaum, *The Grace and Severity*, 142–430.

10. See Erik Erikson, *Childhood and society* (New York, NY: W. W. Norton and Company, [1950] 1963), 266–68.

11. Erikson, *Childhood and Society*, 268–269.

12. Kenneth J. Gergen, *The Saturated Self, Dilemmas of Identity in Contemporary Life* (New York: Basic Books, 1991), 48–80.

13. One might ask why not move directly to a logical analysis of *gnothi seauton* and forego the history of its origin and development. Simply, suspicion as understood here is at least a temporal phenomenon. It arises only within the background and its relation to the foreground, whether viewed as a cultural problem or that of our second nature. Being temporal and arising within the core of western culture, only a historical study will help us understand it.

14. See Buford, *Trust, Our Second Nature*, xii–xiii, 15–19.

15. Bruce Malina, *The New Testament World, Insights from Cultural Anthropology*, 2nd ed. (Louisville, KY: Westminster/John Knox Press, 1993), 90. For an older but helpful discussion of the cities in the ancient Mediterranean world and their religious and civil institutions, see Fustel De Coulanges, *The Ancient City, A Study on*

the Religion, Laws, and Institutions of Greece and Rome (New York, NY: Doubleday Anchor Books, 1956).

16. Malina, *The New Testament World*, 92.

17. Malina, *The New Testament World*, 94–95.

18. Malina, *The New Testament World*, 95.

19. All persons live in a culture that deeply influences their philosophical understanding. For an understanding of the culture of the ancient Mediterranean world see David D. Gilmore, ed., *Honor and Shame and the Unity of the Mediterranean* (Washington, DC: American Anthropological Association, 1987); Joseph M. Bryant, *Moral Codes and Social Structure in Ancient Greece, A Sociology of Greek Ethics from Homer to the Epicureans and Stoics* (Albany, NY: SUNY Press, 1996); and Malina, *The New Testament World*.

20. Malina, *The New Testament World*, 95.

21. Malina, *The New Testament World*, 37.

22. Malina, *The New Testament World*, 50.

23. Malina, *The New Testament World*, 51.

24. Malina, *The New Testament World*, 67.

25. See F. M. Cornford, *From Religion to Philosophy, a Study in the Origins of Western Speculation* (New York, NY: Harper and Row, Publishers, 1957), 16.

26. Jean-Pierre Vernant, *The Origins of Greek Thought* (Ithaca, NY: Cornell UP, [1962] 1982), 102.

27. Philosophy was an activity of the leisured, not of the laboring lower classes, though there were notable exceptions such as Epictetus, the Stoic.

28. See Byrant, *Moral Codes and Social Structure,* 187–188.

29. These methods are well known; no further discussion of them is needed here.

30. See *Philibus* 23 c–d.

31. It is worth noting at this point that the modern use of "person" is rooted in Christian theology, especially the thought of Augustine and the Cappadocian Fathers. In the fourth and fifth centuries CE, as the Christian church attempted to work out a satisfactory understanding of the Trinity and the individual personhood of Jesus the Christ, Greek and Hebrew-Christian understandings of person moved into focus. Central to the controversy was the understanding of the individual person. During the time of Origen (185–254 CE) under the influence of Plotinus (204/5–290 CE), *personae* lacked ontological content. Is an individual person an *attribute* of being; or is an individual person *being* who, having been created by the free and independent God and who bears God's image, is free and dependent? If the former, the Greek metaphysical word, *ousia,* expresses the Trinity, as in *una substantia* (God) and *tres personae*, where Father, Son, and the Holy Spirit is understood as three independent Gods. If the latter, person is not an attribute of *ousia*, but *upostasis*. Earlier both *ousia* and *upostasis* meant substance. Eventually, they were used separately, *ousia* referring to substance and *upostasis* referring to individual person. This means that *persona* is no longer a kind of mask worn by an ontological substrate, *ousia.* The Greek Fathers, particularly the Cappadocians, led by Gregory of Nazianus (c. 329–389 or 390 CE)

understood that individual persons are ontologically ultimate, a central thesis of Personalism. However, an understanding of the interior life of persons lay beyond their metaphysical interests.

The analysis of the interior life of persons fell to Augustine (354–430 CE) who continues the substance view by defining person as "a rational soul using a mortal and earthly body," (*substantia quaedam rationis particeps, regendo corpora accomodata*). Nevertheless, a person is one; "a soul in possession of a body does not constitute two persons but one man." His contribution to Personalism lies elsewhere. His investigation of the inner experience of persons sets a new course in philosophy that would not be developed until the modern period. In doing so he develops a key insight of Personalism, an understanding of reality as Person through an understanding of the interior life of persons. He says that knowledge of God moves "from the exterior to the interior, and from the inferior to the superior." Further, he argues that in persons, free will is superior to rationality. Yet Augustine continues the metaphysical principle that the higher can affect the lower, but the lower cannot affect the higher. Augustine is sometimes called the first modern philosopher.

32. Pierre Hadot, *Philosophy as a Way of Life. Spiritual Exercises from Socrates to Foucault*, ed. Arnold I. Davidson, trans. Michael Chase. (Oxford, UK: Blackwell Publishing Ltd. 1995), 264–276.

33. The claims made of Jesus created deep anomalies in the minds of the Jews and Romans.

34. In his *On Free Choice of the Will,* trans. Thomas Williams (Indianapolis, IN: Hackett Publishing Company, 1993) (circa 395), Augustine was the first to develop a view of free will as a psychological phenomenon and deeply influenced the Renaissance, particularly Descartes (1596–1650). Human freedom as ontological was first articulated by the Cappadocian Fathers, Nazianus in particular. See John D. Zizioulas, *Being as Communion, Studies in Personhood and the Church* (Crestwood, NY: St. Vladimir's Seminary Press, 1985).

35. See Pico della Mirandola's *Oration on the Dignity of Man* and Martin Luther's defense before the Diet at Worms, April 18, 1521.

36. See Buford, *Trust, Our Second Nature*, xii–xiii, 15–19.

37. Richard Tarnas, *The Passion of the Western Mind* (New York, NY: Ballantine Books, 1991), 229.

38. Tarnas. *The Passion of the Western Mind*, 231.

39. William C. Dampier, *A History of Science and Its Relations with Philosophy and Religion* (Cambridge, UK: Cambridge University Press, 1961), 115–123.

40. We shall consider the natural, bodily aspect of our second nature in chapters 2 and 4. The relation became an issue in the Renaissance.

41. Quoted by Samuel E. Stumpf, *Socrates to Sartre* (New York, NY: McGraw-Hill, Inc., 1993), 232.

42. Ibid.

43. This formulation contrasts with the early medieval formulation of Augustine. How can persons be free, if God created all things and has foreknowledge? See Augustine, *On Free Choice of the Will*, 74–78.

44. This is particularly true after Heidegger and issues surrounding hermeneutics. See Rudiger Bubner, *Modern German Philosophy*, trans. by Eric Matthews (Cambridge, UK: Cambridge University Press, 1981).

45. For a rich historical study of the religious dimension of the emerging self from Luther to the present, see Mark C. Taylor, *After God* (Chicago, IL: University of Chicago Press, 2007).

46. For an engaging thoughtful response to the death of the person in contemporary philosophy of mind, see Richard Moran, *Authority and Estrangement, An Essay on Self-Knowledge* (Princeton, NJ: Princeton University Press, 2001).

47. Kenneth J. Gergen, *The Saturated Self, Dilemmas of Identity in Contemporary Life* (New York, NY: Basic Books, 1991).

48. For an accessible analysis of New Work see Taylor, *After God*, 40–46. Find here the root of the modern person's arising dyadic self-knowledge. In the ancient world "person" meant a mask, with a public exterior and private interior. The exterior was all that mattered; the interior was subordinated to it. Our second nature defined us; we are dyadic persons. However, after Descartes the interior of persons became increasingly important; indeed, Descartes thought we know directly, in an unmediated manner our inner lives, and Hobbes believed in our social lives what was most important was not what was socially expected of us (a continuation of the ancient view of persons living in an honor-shame culture) but what we willed, our own survival. The duality persists in the distinction between I and me, as in I did that to myself, and as in the distinction between the person and his personality. Here the individual person is dominant and forms a second nature. We are monadic persons. However, for the modern, *gnothi seauton* means my private I knowing my private/public me or personality; where personality, though numerically mine and no one else's and to some extent private, is formed by creative findings of our own choosing and our own making, including our second nature, culture and its institutions, an ultimate environment, and understandings of physical environments. Though we find them, what we find is our own creation. Ironically, we become again dyadic persons, contemporary but no more open than that of the ancients.

49. Nietzsche thought not. He wrote, "The sole source of values and truth in the world in the autonomous individual—all rests in the rectitude of his will." Quoted by David Norton, *Personal Destinies, A Philosophy of Ethical Individualism* (Princeton, NJ: Princeton University Press, 1976), 92.

Chapter 2

Our Haunting Hopes

We yearn for self-knowledge, but deep down we despair. Nevertheless, our need to be grounded in reality, for defensible goals and right actions pull us; it can be achieved, it must be achieved! On what basis, and how? Objective Order and the Emerging Self lead to suspicion but provide no solution to it. Is it possible that grounding culture in the metaphysics of Being and rationalism would allow us to solve the problem of suspicion and provide for self-knowledge? Philosophy offers two compelling, authoritative master images, Being and Rationalism. Being, in turn, has two major interpretations that fall along a vertical axis, Naturalism, the metaphysics of the infrastructure, and Idealism, the metaphysics of the superstructure. Rationalism scaffolds our reflective reason and guides us to understand and critically support each terminus and those along the axis. Can one of them provide the support either Order or the Emerging Self needs to overcome suspicion and allow us to obey the command, *gnothi seauton*?

As we proceed, remember that suspicion arises as the background and foreground of our culture and second nature move out of sync, precipitating critical questioning and loss of stability and solidarity and an Ultimate environment legitimating the stabilizers and solidars. If Naturalism, Idealism, or Rationalism can ground either Ancient-Medieval Order or the Renaissance-Modern Emerging Self and provide for *gnothi seauton*, it must show how it can do so. We begin with Naturalism.

NATURALISM

In the age of suspicion, can Naturalism ground culture, and provide for self-knowledge? If so, we can move beyond suspicion.

The Appeal of Naturalism

Most of us do not adopt a philosophy because of the strength of the arguments used in support of it; rarely does argument alone persuade. More common, we continue living unreflectively a way of life since youth—for example, in a Christian faith community. Later, reflecting on what we were taught, anomalies begin to appear. It could be the presence of evil, or the creation of the world, or the male hierarchy permeating the Christian scriptures. Finding no meaningful way to hold to the teachings of the religious community and to the scientific understanding of the way nature works, we sometimes reject the faith and adopt the better grounded view of nature science provides. Finding in nature the ground of our social and personal lives, we also find what we are to be and what we are to do.

What is the appeal of Naturalism? It lies in the belief that the natural world is real, and the teachings of the faith community are illusions. If we define reality as that which corrects our illusions, then nature is real. Our religious imaginations conjure many wonderful possibilities; and seeking to bring them to reality, we project them onto our world, But our actions are quickly chastened by the facts of nature. Praying for God's help to play Alfredo in Verdi's *La Traviata* and sing the tenor aria "The Drinking Song," will not be realized if one has no vocal cords. Being a singer is physically not possible. Nature sobers us; its appeal is strong. All of us are occupied with physical things, whether our bodies, motion or place, work, eating, procreating, building, destroying; no one escapes. Further, no society can have a culture without involvement with nature; no society can create a viable, stable, solidar culture without being tested by the facts of nature. Persons cannot behave or think without bodies, without the surrounding natural world. There, each institution, deeply natural, finds its stability and solidarity. Institutional patterns find their charisma in their success tested by nature. Nature is real; no longer will illusory religious beliefs lead us astray. Nature is orderly, causal, predictable, and uniform. It provides solidarity with persons living around us; stability in our second nature and culture by synchronizing our Background and Foreground through stable goals, institutions, and solidars; and a real Ultimate Environment legitimating those stabilizers and solidars. Grounded in nature, we grasp what we are, and begin searching for what we are to be, and what we are to do. That is the appeal of a realistic and powerful master image. In Naturalism we find *gnothi seauton* in its inclusive sense, the whole person. As we enter Naturalism, we begin thinking it through.

Ancient-Medieval

Seeking to clarify Naturalism, we ask, "Which view of nature is implied in the master image, Ancient, Medieval, or Modern"? Succinctly, no contemporary

Naturalism builds on an ancient view of Nature. Why not? A quick historical survey reveals the answer.

Earliest known Greek philosophers, the Milesians, assumed a principle at the basis of Olympian religion, *phusis* that originally meant "the beginning, the development, and the result of the process by which a thing constitutes itself."[1] *Phusis* is becoming, birthing. Its Latin cognate is *natura*, rooted in *nascor, natus, natus sum* from which "natal" is derived. As early as the seventh century BCE, Melisian physiologists (derived from *phusis* and *logos*) developed theories to explain *phusis*. Their views and those of subsequent philosophers ranged from the power of the nature gods; fire, earth, air, and water; the *to eon*, the *what is* that is one and unchanging; ceaseless change according to fixed measure; atoms, the uncuttables, moving through space; the telic mixing of matter, the *apeiron*, the recalcitrant indefinite, and of immutable form, *peras*, the definite; to formed-matter organically moving toward a final cause. Throughout ancient Greek philosophy *phusis*, whether One or Many, is All, ultimate reality; nothing else exists, and all things find their place within it.

Consider Aristotle's view of motion. Motion is circular in the heavenly bodies and rectilinear in earthly bodies. The Unmoved Mover through its perfection, goodness, and beauty pulls all things to fulfill their essence. Matter, being inert, can be moved only by a higher cause, a First Mover. Reminiscent of the honor-shame hierarchical arrangement of cultural dyadic objectivism where the higher can affect the lower but the lower cannot affect the higher, natural beings are arranged along a hierarchy of transcendence from the necessary, immutable, and eternal at one terminus to the contingent, mutable, and temporal at the other. Later in the Middle Ages Aquinas contended that God, the Primum Mobile, set in motion all things in the created orders of heavenly and earthly bodies. Moving teleologically, natural beings, seek their natural place and rest, different for each fixed species.

Christianity's influence drastically changed the ontological view of the natural order. Anathema to Greek and Roman philosophers, God created *ex nihilo* the natural world. Only Plato in the *Timaeus* developed a view of creation, though it is creation out of preexisting materials, as an artist creates employing form, matter, and purposeful energy. In the Christian doctrine of *creatio ex nihilo*, we find a radical view of transcendence where God freely creates *ex nihilo* the natural and human worlds and stands radically other than they. However, Christian theologians, searching to show the relation of God to the created order, drew on Plato's doctrine of participation and Aristotle's view of teleological causality. In this way the connectivity of the Great Chain of Being was established and preserved, though Greek *phusis* as One and Christian *creatio ex nihilo* were inherently contradictory. In the Middle Ages, nature was the realm of change teleologically ordered by the eternal principles of God through descending created realms to nature from the highest to the lowest. Nature was understood teleologically; astrology, magic, and religion prevailed; little experimental science was practiced, even though Roger Bacon called for it.

Modern

As the Renaissance dawned, the Scholastic hierarchical teleological metaphysics (the Great Chain of Being) view of nature underwent devastating criticisms; a new form of Naturalism arose, buttressed by skepticism and a new scientific understanding of the natural world. The appeal of Nature's criterion of reality, "that which corrects our illusions," was central to the rejection of ancient and medieval views of nature and of metaphysics. For example, people living through the Plague of 1348–1350 CE pressed religion, the church, and medicine for solutions to widespread death, but what they provided did not cure the bubonic plague. Having no more credibility than magic, they were illusory. If ancient and medieval views of Nature are unacceptable, we must turn to modern scientific understanding of nature built on Roger Bacon's claim, "experimental methods alone give certainty in science."[2] Turning to those who followed Bacon's direction, what do nature and science mean in the modern world? What is science's connection to philosophical Naturalism?

To begin, consider the German word for science, *Wissenschaft*. It refers to a general type of intellectual activity that includes diverse areas from philosophy, mathematics, psychology, the natural sciences, to ethics. Modern scientists, restricting their work to the natural and socials worlds, investigate what can be empirically verifiable. Their study ranges from the inorganic, physics and chemistry, to the organic, biology and the social sciences. In each, they used an appropriate methodology for investigating them and a specialized language to express what they learned. The fields are dimensions of nature available for investigation using the "scientific method" and understood through mathematics. Consider each aspect.

First, science investigates everything in the natural continuum, including humans, dogs, cats, vines, rocks, wind, and rain, hot and cold, the firmament, genes, and quarks. That continuum is the home of humans; reflection on it runs deep in our Background. An ancient view of nature continued into the late seventeenth century CE, for example remaining the thought of Spinoza (1632–1677) as *natura naturans*, the active principle of all reality, and *natura naturata*, the effects of that principle. Earlier Descartes (1596–1650) restricted the natural world to *res extensa*, the mechanical orderliness of space and time. In addition, this continuum was assumed to be uniform. Motion and

Change in the continuum are orderly; the future will be like the past; they are related in a causal manner.[3]

Second, it is a rational method, a way of rationally investigating dimensions of the natural world available to human experience. Skeptical of the range of reason accepted in ancient and medieval worlds, many philosophers in the Renaissance and early modern period restricted reason to experience, especially in the study of nature. Puzzled by breaks in experience between two or more events, scientists sought accurate descriptions and explanations of natural events. Though some scientists, including Newton, practiced religion, magic, and alchemy, they appealed to experience and mathematics for accurate descriptions and explanations of natural events. On the basis of these, scientists looked for uniformities in nature that they expressed as natural law. Newton's three laws of motion are examples.

Third, the regularities in the natural continuum are expressed in the language of mathematics. This began early in modern scientific investigation of the inorganic. In the late 1600s CE scientists, particularly Isaac Newton, learning from the corpuscular theory of the ancient materialists, Democritus and Lucretius, that remained in the Western philosophical tradition and emerged in the thought of Gassendi, conceived the natural order as atomic. Atoms are related mathematically. The mathematization of nature's uniformity was securely in place by the early eighteenth century CE. Whether in the organic and inorganic realms, scientists continue to make discoveries and mathematics remains the common language. Scientists do not deal with absolute certainties, but only with probabilities. Kemeny reminds us first, that "statistical theories occur in many different branches of Science," and they "make heavy use of probability; second that "all measurements are subject to error," and the "theory of errors is a branch of probability theory"; and third, "when we assert a statement, we have to assign some degree of credibility to it."[4] Though the scientific use of hypothesis assumes the form of a deductive nomological explanation confirmed by appealing to past and future experienced events, inductive logic governs scientific study and discoveries.[5]

Finally, an underlying assumption of science is the uniformity of nature. This assumption is found in each period of western thought. From Heraclitus' view that all is change according to fixed measure, to the modern view that uniformity is an admirable trait and humans are able to comprehend it; nature has boundaries. Tomorrow it will obey the same laws as it does today.[6] This assumption "is needed to assure us that our past experience is a reliable guide to the future."[7] Further, order in nature is understood in terms of mechanistic causality; teleological accounts are irrelevant to a proper understanding of Nature. Teleology in the hands of religion and metaphysics led to illusions about the causal order in the natural continuum that only the rejection of teleology could correct. However, causality is not best understood in terms of hard causality, but in terms of soft causality. That is, the central traits of mechanistic causality are invariable and uniform, asymmetrical, temporal, and contiguous. Interpreting these traits in the sense of hard determinism leaves no room for probability. However, probability is central to the scientific method, and hard determinism must be rejected. We must modify the first rule, invariable and uniform, to include "unless there are intervening causes." In place of deductive nomological explanations, we would hold to hypothetical nomological explanations and to soft determinism.[8]

Persuaded by the assumption of the uniformity of nature and the power of the scientific method, we have a reliable way of "correcting our illusions." Everything from persons, their social/cultural patterns, to the natural expanse can be accounted for, at least in principle, by appealing to Naturalism supported by the scientific method and the scientific understanding of nature. Both the natural and social orders become clearer and more intelligible from this view. Finding that our humanity lies in nature, we can learn what we are to be and to do. Any religious or metaphysical philosophy leads to uncorrectable illusions; we must conclude that Nature is all there is and that the proper way to understand Nature and ourselves is to use the methods employed by scientists. Naturalism is common sense supported by a powerful method and by strong scientific evidence. If so, Naturalism must show how it can defeat suspicion and bring into sync our background and background.

Allaying Suspicion

The appeal of Naturalism lies in two claims, both crucial for self-knowledge. First, it is claimed that the natural continuum is the Real that grounds and legitimates our second nature, personal and social goals, institutions, and solidars. Second, it claims to supply the connections linking background and foreground. Both in place, we can discern what we are, what we are to be, and what we are to do.

Freud and his followers provide a classic example of the scientific theory that society and culture emerge from nature. Persons are natural beings rooted in both the inorganic world, as understood by physicists and chemists, and in the organic world, as understood by biologists and social scientists. We can trace the evolutionary path of microcosmic energy from the physical world, into biological life, into the psychic life of individuals and social groups, and finally into the macrocosmic life of persons, societies, and cultures. Walking in the paths charted by Freud, Stein points out, "psychodynamic processes are often the underpinnings (the 'core') of what we observe on the surface as the 'whole' culture (the 'crust'). . . . Culture can be understood to rest to a considerable degree upon unconscious, largely irrational, sources."[9] Persons, society, and culture are best understood in terms of the reliable and highly complex order of space-time emerging into social/cultural forms.

According to Naturalism, the temporal span of our Background and Foreground are reliably rooted through their being rooted in the uniformity of nature that emerges as the unconscious and conscious life of the individual psyche and then to society, its culture, and its institutions. That uniformity is not the work of a mysterious god or gods, of teleological forces, or free will of humans. They are patterns of Nature. Though the relation of our Background and Foreground breaks down occasioning major historical changes, and may appear to us to be precipitated by changes in master images, such as Order or the Emerging Self, cultural breakdown and conflicts are natural occurrences we now understand as conflicts among our id, ego, and superego. The orderliness of Nature resolves the conflicts between our Background and Foreground, followed by a period of cultural, personal stability and unity legitimated by the Ultimate environment, Nature. The relation between our cultural Background and Foreground is best understood as the cultural macrocosm of a more basic physical microcosm.[10] At least, that is the argument. Should we be persuaded by it?

The Haunting Hope of Naturalism

Most of us hold to or reject a metaphysical position through habit or tradition rooted deeply in our second nature and culture. For those who are critically reflective as well as committed to living the way of Naturalism, anomalies arise that create uneasiness, possibly enmeshing them in antinomies. Assuming that persons are natural beings seeking self-knowledge in the context of social living, we shall see that problems arise in the attempt to relate what we are to be in the future to what actions we are to take in the present.

Consider the following elements of personal, social living. There are four: our second nature and cultural core; stability of our Background–Foreground relation; solidarity with our society and its members, past, present, and future; and the charisma of the stabilizers and solidars legitimated by the authority of the Master Narrative. Consider these in light of the world-view of Naturalism.

Begin with our social cultural relationships. First, consider solidarity. Our second nature develops in the interrelation of two or more numerically distinct individuals. That relation is both temporal and simultaneous. As simultaneous, persons may build a bond, a solidarity, a shared experience that cannot be attributed to one isolated person. Persons do not have social solidarity with themselves; they may have personal unity, but not social solidarity. The solidarity they experience is more than the sum of individuals themselves and the structure of their relationships. It is the experience of community that has potentialities isolated individual do not possess. Such experiences include the marriage of two persons, team experience in athletics, justice under the law in court proceedings; and patriotism while celebrating a national holiday or national defense. How can we account for unity present in our social and cultural relationships?

If Naturalism means particles moving through space mechanistically related in the space-time continuum, how account for social relations and the quality of the "more"? Nothing in the individual atoms causally related can account for social relations. That is, nothing in causal relations can account for the "more" that is beyond the relation itself. Claiming emergence requires showing how the "more" of mutual trust and love can "arise" from two or more physical objects causally related. Emergence is a description, not an explanation. If Naturalism appeals to system theory, such as Weissman's or Batson's, one may account for the interrelation of individuals through the reciprocal causal relation among individuals or within the homeostasis of a cybernetic system. The relation between two lovers has a structure. What in the structural relations of a rational system accounts for the "more" experienced by two persons loving, trusting each other? There is a difference between the structure of trust and trusting each other in that structure. To say that one dimension of the relation is the "emergence" of love does not show how the structure of the relationship accounts for mutual love. The relation may be present in trusting, but love is more than the relation.

The stability of the Background–Foreground relation in individuals and society may find some help in Naturalism. The relation appears to be open to causal, evolutionary, and system analysis. However, on closer inspection, a causal relation where B follows A invariably, uniformly, temporally, and asymmetrically, cannot adequately account for the relation of the Background and Foreground. A Background is formed through interaction among persons and their present and future Foregrounds. For example, a parent, teacher, or significant other through teaching helps form the Background of their child, student, or friend. Later the student recollects the Background to guide his or her interaction with the Foreground, personal, social, and physical. The teaching and recollecting activities are not adequately understood in terms of the soft determinism of any causal theory, mechanical, biological, or system. Why not? The student is not passively receiving instruction and automatically employing it. Learning from a teacher and recollecting one's Background as one moves into her or his Foreground involves recollection, reflective choice, free will, and action. None of these can be adequately explained by appealing to any natural causal system. Nothing within a mechanistic, evolutionary, or system theory allows for two genuine options and for choosing or rejecting either or both of them. Further, recollecting from one's Background is more than a simple recall of events. Recollection is also recall of events in relation to each other where the events are related in the context of a way of seeing or grasping them, of a *topos*. Though recollection, reflection, choice are at least brain events, they are "more" than brain events and suggest the inadequacy of Naturalism.

Next, consider Ultimate Authority legitimating and providing charisma for the society's stabilizers and solidars. In a stable orderly solidar society who's institutions, goals, and fellow feeling command the honor and allegiance necessary to bind shape and hold our second nature within their boundaries, the attractiveness and legitimacy of the command derives from an Ultimate Authority believed to be morally good. What in the worldview of Naturalism provides an Ultimate Authority that is good? Any description of nature, of a space-time continuum, of causal relations, evolution, and systems within that continuum, looks in vain for moral good, moral ought, values. The is-ought problem rises here with cultural force. A culture must have moral roots for it to right itself when destabilized or threatened with dissolution. Marveling at the beauty and grandeur of nature and describing accurately its organizational and causal structure may evoke aesthetic awe and prompt a clear grasp of structure, but neither beauty or reason commands to do what is right, to act justly, and to love mercy.

Further, consider two additional aspects of the program of Naturalism: Naturalism as a participant in the search for truth and the cultural context of modern and contemporary life. As a participant in the search for the true metaphysical infrastructure, Naturalism must recognize and espouse the experience of choice among alternatives necessary for the possibility of truth-finding. To claim a conclusion to be true requires the possibility that it is false. Naturalism's appeal partly arises from the excesses, the "illusions" of less empirical worldviews. But its appeal is not dogmatic. Naturalists clarify and argue for the truth of their views. They attempt to persuade that theirs is a complete program of explanation. A person attempting to persuade another person that a proposition is true must assume that the person has genuine alternatives among which she can choose. However, the Naturalist holds to a causal theory, mechanistic, evolutionary, or system that is a soft determinism that does not allow genuine alternatives. Bowne argued that if the claim of a person that a conclusion of an argument is true is the outcome of psycho-physical or divine forces working their way through the brain, nervous system, or "soul" of that person, we cannot correctly say that the claim is based on the person's deliberating over the problem and evaluating the data presented in support of the conclusion.[11] No genuine alternative, no truth or falsity. The determinism of Naturalism renders it as neither true nor false. Though holders of Naturalism argue for their position to show it is true and not false, their assumption is inconsistent with their practice.

Last, modern Naturalism developed as internal criticism and failure to meet human need fractured and slowly dismantled medieval metaphysical Christendom and as the master image of the emerging self in the Renaissance emerged. However one views the world, it will be influenced (but not determined) by cultural perspectives, by one's Background. If that Background belongs to the individual self, one would expect scientists to give greater attention to the world as filled with individuals, and they did. Though resisted by the institutionalized Order, notably the Catholic Church in its dealing with Galileo, the skeptical, scientific activity of the individual Emerging Self won. In this context, we find the development of Newton's atomic view of nature. However, in the twentieth century and early twenty-first century CE, the excesses of individualism as well as developments in physics, evolution, and systems theory led to a rejection of atomism among some Naturalists in favor of a "social" theory of Nature. Weissman, Searle, and Batson are examples in Philosophy. However, their Naturalism ironically leads to a new scientific form of cultural dyadic objectivism. The Emerging Self and the growth of skepticism and experimental science led to independent, autonomous persons; the dominant master image of the Renaissance set in motion independence from dyadic objectivism. Industrialization, skepticism, and experimental science turned metaphysical, Naturalism, reduced the self to a natural being who possesses the same structures as any other natural being. Naturalism may save the body, the brain, but it loses the individual, the mind, the person in impersonalism. Under this new dyadic objectivism we enter the "night-view" of the world, as Fechner called it.[12]

Naturalism does not fail; it is not refuted. The strength of Naturalism, its bewitching power lies in "the completeness of its program of explanation."[13] However, anomalies within Naturalism raise questions regarding it as a complete program of explanation.

What does that imply for the claim that Naturalism is the solution to the antinomy of suspicion? Those who are self-circumspect in holding the metaphysical infrastructure of Naturalism recognize the irony. Naturalism purports to resolve the antinomy of suspicion on the basis of a world-view that is internally anomalous! With problems of its own, Naturalism is not a promising candidate to lead us beyond the antinomy of suspicion by showing an Ultimate Authority that legitimates the connection between Background and Foreground, and provides the moral charisma to hold our social, cultural behavior within boundaries, and provides for *gnothi seauton*. Turn to the superstructure, Idealism. Possibly it can bolster either order or the Emerging Self, solve suspicion, and foster self-knowledge.

IDEALISM

Seeking rich *gnothi seauton* beyond a partial, truncated sense of *gnothi seauton* garnered from Naturalism, we turn to Idealism. Ironically, Naturalism is not empirical only, though it rests its case in experience limiting reason; it is reason seeking to understand the natural context of human living and finding in that context a compelling vision of the natural world and our place in it. We do not "see" the space-time continuum, its uniformity, and causal relations within it. Neither do we see Naturalism. We think them. It is a small but important step to recognize that what we think we "see" is really thought, ideas, as Plato argued in the *Theaetetus* and Descartes in the *Meditations*. Thus, the question becomes how best to think about what we see, about the natural world. If we follow this path Naturalism leads us to Idealism, in its broadest sense.

Idealism has two senses. On the one hand, accepting without discussion that humans are *phusis*, its proponents, beginning with Parmenides and Heraclitus, claim that the real is idea or ideas. On the other, it holds that the real is mental, including ideas. Both are appealing. But, why? Can either bolster Order or the Emerging Self and provide for self-knowledge?

The Appeal of Idealism

Ancient-Medieval

Idealism's appeal lies in the power of the mind to understand and give an account of *phusis*. Look again at ancient and medieval thought, this time through the eyes of an Idealist. Western philosophical investigation began in the ancient world. It was believed that the natural world is filled with nature gods who carry the power of life and death. Though present and controlling our lives, and not always predictable, the gods are responsive to proper religious observance. A small group of elite men in Miletus, a Greek colony on the coast of Asia Minor, focused their investigations on an assumption of Olympian religion, *phusis*, that "originally meant the beginning, the development, and the result of the process by which a thing constitutes itself."[14] Believing *phusis* to be One, they attempted to understand its nature and structure, what it is and how the many differences arise from it. For example,

Thales (b. 624) believed *phusis* was water and all things came from it through transformation. Subsequent physiologists believed it to be fire or air. The Pythagoreans, also puzzled, believed *phusis* to be numbers and their relation constituting the harmony, order, and uniformity in the world. Natural things are copies of the order of numbers. Two philosophers focusing on the problem of change, Heraclitus and Parmenides introduced an understanding of *phusis* deeply influencing all subsequent philosophers. Heraclitus believed *phusis* is change according to fixed measure, the logos. Change is universal fire. The human soul is part of that fire and nourished by it. Parmenides, accepting the law of non-contradiction, claimed that change is inconceivable. What is, *phusis*, is One, internally consistent, and unchanging. For anything to change, it must become what it is not. We cannot think what is not. Change as inconceivable, *Phusis* is the *to eon,* the eternal, necessary, immovable, and internally immutable.

Remember that thought and being are identical; the rational is real, and the real is rational. The force of arguments pre-Socratic philosophers formulated derives from their cultural assumption that the mind derives its existence and characteristics from Being. Rejecting any creation, such as *creatio ex nihilo*, they assumed transcendence in the sense of a hierarchical scale, where the higher transcends the lower. The pre-Socratics, especially Parmenides, planted the seeds of Idealism.

The Ionian and Eleatic philosophers were monists, quantitative and qualitative. However, differences between the views of Heraclitus and Parmenides regarding *phusis* urged some philosophers to account for both permanence and change. These were the pluralists. They argued that *phusis, what is*, is many, each a miniature *to eon.* On the one hand, they agreed with Parmenides' powerful argument. Though *phusis* cannot change internally or absolutely, as many each *to eon* can change place. On the other hand, they agreed with Heraclitus, *phusis* changes. Various views of pluralism developed under the careful reflection of Empedocles, Anaxagoras, and Democritus; they were quantitative pluralists and either qualitative monists or qualitative pluralists.

The stage was set for the first major Idealist, Plato. As Athens entered a democratic period in the fifth century BCE, Socrates shifted the discussion from the nature and structure of the natural world to the human concern of *gnothi seauton*. Called by the gods to a status higher than available in Athenian honor-shame culture, Socrates sought to fulfill his new station and its duties. Understanding his duty to question every person about their soul, he moved among the Athenians, stinging them to know themselves. Though he claimed he did not know the answer to that question, he could recognize a proper answer. It will be found in thought, in ideas. Plato, drawn from writing poetry to the search for self knowledge, interpreted Socrates's search in terms, reminiscent of the Pythagoreans, of forms that are necessary, immutable, and eternal. The natural world is a mixture of forms and formless *hyle,* the principle of change itself. The constant principle providing structure through change is idea, the eternal forms. Being is innumerable Forms unified in the Good, the True, and the Beautiful; all things derive their existence through participating in the Forms; and change is the teleological movement of all things to realize to the fullest their own essence. As necessary, immutable, and eternal, Being negates the possibility of an absolute beginning and an absolute, final end, *what is* can only move in a circle, as Plato attests in the myth of Er.[15] In his later thought Plato, recognizing the importance of initiating change, argued in the *Timaeus* that the Demiurges, being good and not begrudging existence to anything that can have it, looks to the Good and initiates change by persuading the Receptacle, *hyle,* to take into itself an exhaustive replica of the possible forms.[16] The mixed world, the best of all possible worlds, results. Nothing exists outside of Being. Plato's creation is from preexisting materials, Beings.

In his early writings, Aristotle, Plato's student, followed his teacher but soon found his own voice. Instead of following Plato's hand directed to the heavens, Aristotle points his hand to the natural world. Rejecting the separation of form and matter, he argued that substance is formed-matter. Change is best understood organically, as growth in the world of plants and animals, according to four causes, *aitia* or principles of change, material, formal, efficient, and final. Every being or substance seeks to fulfill its own perfection, finally desiring Being, the Unmoved Mover. We come to know ourselves, both physically and mentally, through the lower, productive intellect aiding us in building, making; the practical intellect guiding us in *oikonomia* (household management); and ultimately through the higher, theoretical intellect guiding us to first principles. Through the intellect we achieve a correct understanding of reality and its order, particularly our place in it.

Living in a hierarchical honor-shame culture, Greek Idealist philosophers sought *gnothi seauton* through an understanding of first principles, eternal forms, gained not through experience but through reason. Most subsequent philosophers in their search for self-knowledge learned from the "Ideaism" of Idealism of the pre-Socratics, Plato, and Aristotle. At core, they sought to understand themselves through ideas of the objective, moral order of Being, to which they are subject. Persons, derived from objective Being and dyadically limited by it, find *gnothi seauton* through it. Their philosophical search for *gnothi seauton* through ideas and the moral order of the Good, of ultimate values, reflected the ground of their cultural dyadic objectivism, the water in which they swim.

With the confluence of Judeo-Christian religion and Greek-Roman life and culture, a new way to *gnothi seauton* emerged. It is achieved through a relation with a personal God who calls people to love God and others as themselves, to love mercy, do justly, and walk humbly with God. The philosophers of the day saw the Jesus followers as advocates of a philosophy. Desiring to do more than work out a theology of faith and practice, as the apostle Paul did in his letters to the early churches, some attempted to show their "philosophy" was creditable. The church fathers such as Gregory of Nazianus, Irenaeus, Origen, and Augustine presented arguments in support of their Christian "philosophy." By the time of Augustine (late fourth century CE into the early fifth century CE), Christians could declare victory (aided by the edict of Milan in 313 CE requiring tolerance for Christians); philosophy became the handmaiden of Christian theology.

For example, in Augustine's thought, God is Person and Being. The necessary, immutable, eternal Forms of Plato take residence in the memory of the Personal God. Rejecting the Greco-Roman tradition of *what is* is Being and *ex nihilo nilil fit* as well as Plato's creation out of preexisting materials, Christians asserted the sovereignty of God through *creatio ex nihilo*. Created (*creatio ex nihilo*) *phusis*, persons, and society are sustained (*creatio continua*) through God's will and the created order's participation in the eternal forms. Though the created order is good, Augustine considered it less valuable than the eternal forms in which it participated. The marriage of Form and Person continued with variations through the Middle Ages.

In the High Middle Ages Aquinas continued the Augustinian view that the eternal forms reside in the mind of God and that God created *ex nihilo* and *continua*. Influenced by Aristotle, he also thought that a second principle, matter, was required to account for the world of natural objects. Nature is a union of matter and form. Forms (structure) account for the essence, the common in created being. Matter (the potentiality to take on particular structures) accounts for diversity, the differences in the created order. Humans are formed-matter and differ from one another on the basis of the matter peculiar to each one. In its final form, the objective moral order ranges from the transcendent God as substance (pure form, that whose essence is to exist) to the lowest (*creatio ex nihilo*) matter. In reverse, the lower stages are matter for the next higher species, that is forms to them, on to the end of the series, God. Thus, the Great Chain of Being is in place. Humans created in the image of God, the *imago dei*, find their meaning and value as creatures of God. In this philosophical theology, one achieves *gnothi seauton* in its rich sense; Aquinas has a doctrine of the body as well as the mind. Yet the ambiguity of persons as created and as causally participating in the Divine Exemplars remained. As created they are fully persons; as causally participating in the forms they are shadows of God. For example, a devoted follower of Thomas, Dante pictured the souls in the *Interno* as shadowy creatures. Chaucer presented full personhood. It was this Christian metaphysics, and its inherent ambiguities that philosophers contested as they ushered in the Renaissance.

The second form of Idealism is Mind, developed during the formative period of cultural monadic subjectivism, and sought to understand God or Being and to provide an alternative ground for values, religious and moral. Reacting to Descartes' bifurcation of the created order into *res extensa* and *res cogitans* and deeply influenced by the British empiricists' view that knowledge extends only to sense experience and not to innate ideas, one of the earliest advocates, George Berkeley argued that *esse est percipici aut percipere*, that is, to be is to perceive or to be perceived. Only mind is substance and all things are expression of mind. Values, the purposive activity of mind, find their source in mental substance. Besides Berkeley, Hegel was the most profound proponent of idealism as Mind. In the nineteenth century CE in Europe and later in America this form of Idealism was slightly modified into Personalism, in Germany by Jacobi and Lotze; Thomas Hill Green in England; by Charles-Bernard Renouvier and Mounier in France; in Scotland by John MacMurray; in America by Royce and Hocking at Harvard, by Bowne, Brightman, and Bertocci at Boston University, Ralph Tyler Flewelling at University of Southern California, by George Holmes Howison at University of California at Berkeley; among others in Scandinavia, Italy, Russia, and Spain.[17] Personalists can be divided into absolutists with Royce or pluralists with Bowne and Edgar Sheffield Brightman. They developed the emerging self of the Renaissance to a full metaphysics. *Gnothi seauton* was achieved through the recognition that they are finite persons that are either manifestations of or directly dependent on God (the absolutists) or are individuals best accounted for by appealing to Creator Person as substance (pluralists). In either case reality is Mind and values are grounded in purposive Mind.

Allaying Suspicion

Can Idealism, either ancient or modern, allay suspicion and provide for rich *gnothi seauton*? If so, it must show how the experiences of personal, natural, and social living fit into the reality of Ideas or Mind, provide a context that allows self-knowledge: (1) grounding our second nature and cultural core; (2) stability of our Background–Foreground relation; (3) solidarity with our society and its members, past, present, and future; (4) authority legitimating the stabilizers and solidars; and (5) the place of each of these in nature.

Specifically, to ground any social-cultural system, Idealism must provide connections between our background and background that solve the problem of suspicion. Consider these in light of the world-view of Idealism.

Ancient-Medieval

The Background and Foreground relation in highly stabilized societies remains in sync. The Background successfully equips and guides society and the individuals in them to cope with their Foreground. Culturally the future emulates the past. More, in the ancient world before Philosophy, *phusis* was understood as dynamic and moves cyclically, as do the seasons of nature; history is circular. As dyadic, persons have their place in and are defined by the cyclical scheme of *phusis*, culture, and society. After philosophers discovered Idealism, they articulated a moral Ultimate environment providing legitimacy and charisma for social institutions that gave solidarity and stability for our second natures and social/cultural living. Though particular societies were agonistic, their underlying culture was grasped under the framework of Ideas on which ground it finally rested. Regarding the natural aspect of a culture, nature was conceived as a kind of shadow of reality, an indefinite something whose structure was derived from something other than itself. For example, Plato claimed that nature, the world of orderly change, is a mixture of *hyle*, a bastard form of being, and the Forms. In the *Timaeus*, nature results from the demiurgos' persuasion of *hyle* to take unto itself an exhaustive replica of the *possibles*, of the eternal forms. The same principle of form structuring indefinite matter is found in Aristotle and later in the Stoics. In Stoic thought, the circular movement of what Plato called Necessity is clear; after a great conflagration, all, including all things cultural and social, return to repeat over and over the cyclical, necessary, never ending development from spirit and matter to a fiery end of all individual, social, natural forms.

By the fifth and sixth centuries CE, the Christian doctrine of God's *creatio ex nihilo* subordinated being and rejected the denial of anything absolutely new coming into existence or going out of existence. Christians argued for an absolute beginning and end of the created order, including nature, society, persons, culture, as well as time and space. Being, the eternal forms lodge in the memory of God as the exemplars guiding God's creating activity. The result is a Great Chain of Being from God the *Primum Mobile*, First Cause to the created order culture, society, persons, and nature, to the last glimmer of eternal light, all structured according to divine reason, the divine exemplars, to fulfill the eternal purposes of the divine free will. The higher is cause and form of the lower, and the lower is effect and matter to the higher form. Cultures, society, and persons find their solidarity and stability in the will, eternal principles, and eternal purposes of God. The Background and Foreground relation is in sync, and institutions and purposes or causes provide stability and solidarity for culture and society.

Parmenides's argument is so deeply ingrained in the Christian mind that the divine Person-Being is necessary, immutable, and eternal. Though Augustine and Aquinas argued for God's existence, their offerings were more designed to show philosophers that Christians can also argue. Christians won, and Philosophy was subordinated to Theology. God legitimates the stabilizers and solidars that provide coherence to the Background and Foreground of society and our second nature. Under the medieval theologian/philosophers, the Christian God, in the free act of *creatio ex nihilo,* brought into existence the natural world, social existence, and heavenly bodies; further, God through *creatio continua* providentially and purposefully guides the created order to God's own transcendent ends. The necessary, immutable, eternal Substance, whose essence it is to exist, as Aquinas taught, provides stability and solidar. In the sense that all things are sacramental, social/cultural institutions have the charisma to form, guide, and hold our second nature and behavior in the way of God. The human body was believed to be transformed into a resurrected body after death; the earthly body and nature will pass away at the end of the created order.

Modern

As the Renaissance grew in influence, fissures in the Medieval worldview, were revealed, as Scotus and Occam, Magellan, Marco Polo, Copernicus, exploring beyond the gates of the Church, opened new horizons of navigation and astronomy. Elements formerly woven together in the fabric of the teleological structure of the Great Chain of Being were reinterpreted within the Master Image of the emerging self, the growing influence of skepticism, and the new science. A new form of Idealism emerged, drawing sustenance from the new Master Image of the Renaissance and in response to of the impact of materialism on the Christian way of life. Rooted in Substance and its two modes and spawned in the Cartesian subject-object framework of *res cognitans and res extensa*, two alternatives were open to a metaphysician in the seventeenth and eighteenth centuries CE. Either mind could be explained by physical nature, or physical nature could be explained by the mind. Remembering the medieval marriage of Being and Person and drawing on the Renaissance belief that mind is rational, purposive, and free, modern Idealism fought materialism. Under Descartes' influential dualism, Idealism pursued two forms, individualism and absolutism. Focusing on the problem of the physical world and the threat of materialism to Christianity, Idealists said little about central cultural changes. The seeds of suspicion were sown. Can modern Idealism, either Individual or Absolute allay suspicion's full flowering?

Can modern Idealism synchronize the Background and Foreground of persons and cultures so that institutions and social goals providing stability and solidarity for our second nature can be trusted? Does Idealism present an Ultimate environment whose authority legitimizes institutions and goals we can eagerly embrace? In the free activity of rational, purposive Mind or God, Idealists find an Ultimate environment, an authority that accounts for and legitimizes goals, stabilizers, and solidars of any culture, any society. Institutions and cultural goals that we find can be accounted for only by appealing to Mind, to God, the Ultimate environment. Furthermore, as those institutions and goals change they sometimes do so because of the personal failures of individuals and societies. They could fail to remember that persons are ends in themselves, and not means only, as Kant declared. They could be drawn into Naturalism that fails to recognize that social behavior is a form of action and not simply of movement of natural objects in social space and time. Correct social, cultural behavior is governed by values, specifically standards of right and wrong written into the fabric of existence, placed there by an objective, rational, purposeful God. Though that insight is shared by modern Idealists, Hegel carried it further and claimed that our highest ethical law is found in objective reason. Hocking summarizes, "The art of life is to discern what is universal in the laws and institutions, and to ally ourselves with that. Our highest ethical law is, *Identify thyself with objective Reason, as found in the institutions of mankind.*"[18] Recognizing that institutions change, Royce argued that since institutions were subject to decay, we should attach ourselves to causes (or goals) that rationally ought to be realized in institutions. If Reason is not adequately embodied in them, institutions will not have stability and solidarity. Though equally conscientious persons will disagree about causes, they come together in the absolute rule, *"Be loyal to loyalty wherever found."*[19] Royce points to the core problem facing *gnothi seauton*, and finds in Idealism the solution to it and to the problem of suspicion.

The Haunting Hope of Idealism

First, regarding uniting with being, which Idealist view of being is most defensible? Which one best grounds society, culture and provides for self-knowledge? Idealists of the ancient, medieval, and modern type believe they can through the eternal forms and *creatio ex nihilo* of God, account for cultural experience, nature, and authority and charisma of stabilizers and solidars. However, Greek thinkers who hold to Being as substance from which all things are derived, whether persons, society, culture, or nature severely limit the ontological (that is, freedom of the will), political, and anarchic freedom of persons. Persons are metaphysically dyadic as well as culturally dyadic. Under the influence of *creatio ex nihilo* Christians believed that God in God's ontological freedom created out of nothing, a notion anathema to the Greeks. For the Greeks, *What Is* must come from something; whatever is in the effect must preexist in the cause; *ex nihilo nihil fit*. *Creatio ex nihilo* directly contradicts that belief. Even Plato's creation was contingent on Being. God as freely (ontologically) creating with a view to the eternal forms (a carryover of Greek substance) was a contradiction: God is ontologically free, and it is not the case that God is ontologically free. Thus, if one gains *gnothi seauton* through union with God, which view of God does one hold? Greek, Jewish, Christian? What, then, is reality that grounds and allows *gnothi seauton*?

Modern Idealism, either absolutist or pluralist, fares no better. If Absolutism is true, how account for the discontinuity between the Background and Foreground of our second nature? A culture, who's stable and solidar institutions habituate under the authority, legitimacy, charisma of an Ultimate environment and calls persons to compliance, must account for continuity between Background and Foreground. If continuity is lost through severe questioning and loses its legitimacy, that loss is a loss of the Absolute. If the loss is laid at the feet of persons whose free will led them to missing the mark (*hamartia*), how can persons act freely, without compulsion of any kind, if their actions are those of the Absolute? Stability is bought at a high price, a price the Renaissance or earlier Augustine was unwilling to pay.[20] Regarding solidarity, can Absolutism account for it? Since all things are dependent on and are metaphysically of the same substance as the Absolute, unity is assured. All correct goals central to our second nature are authorized and legitimated by Absolute Mind, God. Unity is achieved by subordinating all personal and social/cultural life to the Absolute. If all is One Mind, God, the individuality of persons becomes problematic, if not impossible. The ancient problem of the One and the Many, lingering in the penumbra of personal, social, cultural life, moves to the center of focus, again causing consternation for philosophical understanding. Solidarity is purchased at the price of individual freedom; Absolutism leads us straight into social/cultural dyadic objectivism, authorized and legitimated by Objective Mind.

If Absolutism's strength is stability and solidarity, as well as its greatest weakness, pluralism's strength lies in the freedom and dignity of the individual. In seeking *gnothi seauton*, persons often fail; they miss the mark, they are guilty of *hamartia*. To account for missing the mark morally and/or religiously, philosophers and theologians attribute it to in the freedom of the will. Though Plato, Aristotle, Epicurus, and the Stoics gave a variety of interpretations, the doctrine of free will labors under the cultural weight of dyadic objectivism and philosophical weight of Being. It emerges into clarity in Augustine, continues in the medieval debate whether the intellect or will is ultimate in God, is adopted in the Renaissance as *sine qua non* of the emerging self, and becomes central to the ethics of Kant. With its emphasis on individual moral responsibility and religious sin, freedom of the will etched itself deeply into the second nature and activity potentials of persons.

Pluralism's strength creates a difficult problem. How can pluralism account for interpersonal relations, for stability and solidarity of a social world composed of a cosmic personal God and finite persons? Regarding solidarity, to call on the "will circuits" of Hocking leaves open the basis on which individual persons unite on a single project.[21] To appeal to the analogy argument to solve the other minds problem leaves intact the problem of social solidarity. Furthermore, accounting for stability requires a basis for bringing into continuity the Background and Foreground of our second nature. That basis must exist within the individual, external to the individual, or both. If external to and imposed on individual persons by some Ultimate environment, the problems of Absolutism arise, particularly of cultural dyadic objectivism. If external to the individual but freely chosen by the individual, the problem arises of knowing the Ultimate environment and certifying that the institution rests in God and is authorized and legitimated by God. In addition, the other minds problem arises, again. How can finite persons know that a cosmic person exists along with its contents? One could appeal to "faith," and raise the problem of which "faith" is correct? And insofar as "faith" is seen as a psychological act, one is drawn into a labyrinth of private emotions, feelings, thoughts from which there is no escape, no criterion on the basis of which all in society could agree. How can one decide among various "faiths"? Or, one could hold that stability and solidarity in society is the free creation of individual persons, and that the ultimate authority is the individual person. If so, what basis is there for agreement on social goals and institutions that could connect the Background and the Foreground? Faced with the problem of suspicion, pluralistic Idealism (including pluralistic, Personalistic Idealism) is inept, stymied by its internal anomalies.

Finally, how can Idealism account for the natural, physical environment of any society, culture, or person, including a person's body? *Phusis* as material or natural was pervasive in the thought of the pre-Socratics, including the atomists, Leucippus and Democritus, the hedonists, Epicurus and Lucretius, and the naturalists, Stoicism. However, Idealists, predominantly Pythagoras and Plato undergirded by the arguments of Parmenides, found stability in the eternal forms. Nature and experience are indefinite, unstable, the roots of change and discord. Stability for one's life and for society can only be found in Being, the eternal forms. If the eternal forms are *phusis*, nature must be less than Being and find its structure in something other than itself. Ontologically higher, the forms structure subordinate nature and provide the basis for whatever order is present in the mixed world.

What does that imply for the rich life of *gnothi seauton,* connections between the Background and Foreground, stability and solidarity of those connections, and the structure of action in time and place? If a manifestation of Being or eternal forms, the Idealist must agree that self-knowledge is less valuable than Being, Mind, whether Cosmic or finite and is dependent on the guidance of Being, Mind, Cosmic or finite. More, human action is not full bodied in the sense that the whole person is equally valuable and real. The hierarchical dualism between form and matter continues.

Nature, created *ex nihilo* and sustained by the Creator, is as real as anything in the created order and is of equal value. However, medievalists from Augustine through Aquinas, in holding to God as both Being and free acting Creator Person, structured the created order hierarchically from the divine exemplars in God's mind to nature. Nature is less valuable than mind. Modern Idealism cannot adequately account for nature. Mind is non-spatial. Building on Descartes' dualism, *res cogitans* and *res estensa,* modern idealists appeal to *res cogitans* to account for *res extensa*. However, *res extensa* interpreted as space-time has characteristics not found in *res cogitans*, such as nextness or contiguity. To argue that *res extensa* are ideas does not account for the spatial characteristics of extended objects.

Further, continuity between Background and Foreground rests in various environments, including personal, social/cultural, natural, and Ultimate environment. Limited to Ideas and/or Mind, Idealism cannot account for the natural environment, a necessary environment for social action, its stability, solidar, and physical continuity. Idealism runs aground on the shoals of its own internal anomalies, including its failure to give an adequate account of the natural environment underlying and supporting the continuity of social action. Succinctly, Idealism cannot provide an adequate understanding of our environments in terms of which one can achieve rich *gnothi seauton*. Naturalism can account for body without purposive mind, and Idealism can account for purposive mind without body. Neither can provide for rich *gnothi seauton*.

Neither ancient/medieval Idealism nor Modern Idealism can allay suspicion and guide us beyond it. Though Idealism was advocated by some of the most gifted minds in western thought, faced with suspicion it is only a haunting hope. Two of the three master images guiding western thought provide no help with the problem of suspicion. In our discussion we often mentioned reason. Can reason, sufficiently extended, successful allay suspicion?

RATIONALISM

The Appeal of Rationalism

Reason to Rationalism

In response to the narratives and cultic practices in Greek religious life, Rationalism took root and developed. To understand that, look again at ancient Greek thought, this time from the perspective of Rationalism.

Greek religion thrived within cultural dyadic objectivism, where priests narrated in myths the way of the gods and performed the required rituals. Homer and Hesiod organized the stories into narratives of the origin of the gods, nature, humans, their interrelationships and society. Their formulations were accepted without dissension in the Greek world. In that act, poets and priests, without being aware of it, reason. In this sense reason is part of human living, as are sensation, feeling, emotion, and desire; there is nothing special about it. Nevertheless, reason played its part as the poets and priests in their giftedness and elite role gained through insight, and revelation an understanding of the gods and their relation to humans and nature. As Greek city states changed, discussion, argument and counter argument played a role; reason in action.

In the sixth century BCE, on the coast of Asia Minor in Miletus a group of men, reflecting on the teachings of the poets and priests and exercising their reasoning skills, recognized the poets assumed a common element of the world of the gods, *phusis*. Recall that p*husis* "originally meant the beginning, the development, and the result of the process by which a thing constitutes itself."[22] The Milesian philosophers or physiologists reflectively reasoned, asked questions, and proposed answers from water, to fire, to the indefinite. As they did so they went beyond the mythopoeic narratives of priests and poets and held the views of their colleagues to critical assessment (*historia peri physeus*). If Thales is correct and *phusis* is water, how can it as one and definite, become many definites, fire, earth, and air? How can One become many and yet be One? How can the One become other than itself? Thales replied that change came as water transformed into the other elements and back to water. Anaximander, in response, claimed that *phusis* is the Indefinite, the Boundless. Eternally in motion, change occurs through separating out of the Boundless, the Indefinite, the elements; eventually they return to their original source. Without dissension or discussion The Greeks assumed harmony, balance in all things. Once reflective reason occurred, Greek science began.

Reasoning is a natural act of all humans. However, in critical reflection Greek philosophers isolated and elevated reason to the role of a special tool of insight or intelligence (*intus legere*) and focused it on *phusis*; Rationalism was born. By the sixth century BCE Greek science (*historia*) emerges, scaffolding and guiding their investigations. Seeking knowledge they assumed it is gained through two sources, reason and experience, on which two types of logic rest, deductive and inductive.

Ancient

What are the essential elements of the scaffolding Milesians and subsequent philosophers assumed as they critically reflected on *phusis*, on Being? First, they assumed the law of contradiction. Thales' answer puzzled some members of the Milesian school. If *phusis* is water, how can it also be fire, earth, and air? How can the One also be Many? Second, they employed concepts, where a concept is a relation that two or more things have in common. Sharing a common characteristic, the Many are One. Later these two structural assumptions guided Parmenides and the Eleatics as they brought into sharp clarity the nature of *phusis*. Deduction dominates their thinking. *What is, phusis*, Being, cannot be both what it is, necessary, immutable, and eternal and also change. Change involves the One becoming what it is not, many. If that could occur, something new without basis in *phusis* could come into existence. If *ex nihilo nihil fit, creatio ex nihilo* cannot occur. Building on the generally held assumption that humans are of *phusis*, Parmenides could say that the real is the rational and the rational is the real. We cannot think change; we cannot think what is not. Change cannot occur. Therefore, *phusis* or Being is One and Unchanging. It is *to eon*, What Is. If Parmenides is correct, empirically oriented philosophers, puzzled how change can be accounted for. They sought an answer.

What the pre-Socratics used in their critical reflection on the religious datum, *phusis*, Socrates employs as he obeys the call of the gods and carries out the duties accompanying the station. Prodding and cajoling his fellow Athenians, he employs Rationalism in the search for *gnothi seauton*, particularly the virtues required by it. He asks what all cases of justice share in common by virtue of which they are called justice. The question of the *Meno* can be answered by employing dialectic and its fundamental principles: the law of contradiction, excluded middle, identity, concepts; definitions; propositions;

inference; elements central to what would be called logic in the second century CE. In his search for the moral life, he practiced the major outlines of Greek science, of Rationalism.

Plato continued the dialectical practices of Socrates and the early philosophers of *phusis*. Appealing to the insights of the Pythagoreans and guided by their study of mathematical form, he sought to move closer to understanding Being. Mathematics and its necessary principles provided the scaffold for moving beyond experience to that which can be grasped by reason alone. Experience must be subordinated to reason, and mathematics shows how reason can move with certainty beyond inherently unstable experience to stable forms, to what can be grasped only by critical, reflective reason. Aristotle, reflecting on reason from its everyday practice to the Rationalistic practices of Plato and his predecessors formulated the fundamental principles of reasoning in six books on dialectic, later called Logic and the *Organon*, the instrument of science.[23] His work dominated Greek and medieval scientific investigation until challenged by the advent and flourishing of modern science. In the hands of ancient and medieval Idealists, concept was elevated to the Conceptual Universal, the *esse* of Being itself, whether in its monistic form, such as Parmenides, or pluralist form, such as Anaxagoras, Empedocles, Democritus, and Plato. The pluralists accepted Being as Parmenides argued; however, nothing in Parmenides precludes many Beings. Though Being remains One and Unchanging, each Being can change place. Change is relative, not absolute. Being, *esse*, the essential character of everything was grasped through the concept, and critical reasoning about being was properly carried out in terms of concepts, their definitions, classifications, and relations. Once the essence of something is grasped, new knowledge can be deduced. Knowledge of something's essence allowed one to predict its behavior, including natural objects and Being. Rationalism continued its reign in the Middle Ages.

Medieval

In the Middle Ages, the confluence of the way of thinking developed around the Jesus people and Greek and Roman thought, ushered in a new way of thinking, yet it was deeply influenced by the tradition of Greek, Roman, and Jewish thought. Though Christian theology gained the ascendancy over Greek and Roman philosophy, theology contained some insights gained from Plato, Aristotle, and Stoicism. Christian life and thought was deeply Hellenistic. With the breakdown of traditional understandings of the gods and the world and Alaric's sacking of Rome in 410 CE, Romans lamented leaving their local gods for the Christian God. Augustine responded with the *City of God*.

Careful scrutiny of the theological philosophy he developed reveals Augustine held fast to the central challenge to Greco-Roman thought, God created out of nothing subordinating Being on which all things depend and from which all things followed to *creatio ex nihilo*. Nevertheless, Being found its way as eternal forms, divine exemplars, into the mind of God. That marriage of Being subordinated to God as *creatio ex nihilo* indicates that Augustine continued the Platonic tradition, but he subordinated it to the creative sovereignty of the Christian God. The logical framework provided by Rationalism was the same as Plato's, mathematics from the Pythagoreans and subject-predicate logic from the pre-Socratics, Socrates, and Aristotle.

Though tradition was melted into and subordinated to Christian theological understanding, Augustine's blending created a problem for Rationalism. With Being he must hold to transcendence of an ordered and hierarchical series; with the Creator God, *ex nihilo*, he must hold to radical transcendence. He must hold to one unified Being, and he must hold to the transcendent God and the created order that is of a different order than God, one eternal and the other created *ex nihilo*, finite, temporal, contingent, and mutable. Internal consistency was problematic. Nevertheless, God thinking in an orderly manner, created laws to assist humans curb their sinful ways and to provide continuity between their Background and Foreground. Interestingly, though the metaphysics changed, rational ordering principles of culture did not. As God wills order, so the natural and social worlds are also orderly, the violation of which arises from humans attempting to create their own worlds, setting themselves up as gods and ignoring the true God. If breakdown in our second nature occurs, it does on the basis of willing that which can be taken away from you against your will. If we will that which cannot be taken away from us against our will, no discontinuity between Background and Foreground can lead us to suspicion. We can know the way to live properly; we must learn it, accept it, and act consistently within it. Good thinking guided by a will that is good solves the problem of suspicion.

Yet, the seeds of *creatio ex nihilo* sown in the early centuries of the Christian period grew into the independence of the emerging self of the Renaissance. Whereas in Being, the person is essentially the same as Being, in *creatio ex nihilo* the person is completely other than God, as the painting is other than the artist. The *imago dei* was an attempt to maintain identity, but it could do so only through the relation of the particular to the concept, a relation of participation. How participation can be interpreted proved a monumental task. How can persons both be of God and not of God at the same time? Christian Christology pivoted on the answer to that question. The Christian God's transcendence from the world and immanence in the world suffers from the same logical problem, the relation of the particular to the universal. With the systematic critique of Realism's understanding of Subject-Predicate logic principally by the nominalists, deep fissures appeared in the logical basis for holding together the Christian worldview of the High Middle Ages. The seeds of suspicion were planted, and the seeds of finite metaphysically independent persons planted by Augustine a thousand years earlier sprouted in the sunlight of the Renaissance.

Modern

The strong appeal of Rationalism in the ancient and medieval worlds remains in the contemporary period. The modern person emerged in the Renaissance aided by skepticism and modern science. The Aristotelian system undergirding the grand medieval system underwent sustained attacks form skeptics such as Montaigne and Sanchez. Peter Ramus attacked Aristotelian logic and prepared the ground for the Port Royal Logic. Logic as the form of Rationalism changed from Aristotelianism, but to what was yet unclear. Under the spirit of skepticism and the critique of traditional logic, many recalled Roger Bacon's direction that only experimental methods can produce reliable knowledge of the natural world. A new organon slowly emerged as scientists, notably Galileo, telescope in hand, challenged the Ptolemaic view of the universe and advocated a heliocentric one. Research in astronomy, physics, and chemistry followed. Along with major advances in the natural sciences, the nineteenth century CE ushered in a full bodied biology and the formation of the social sciences, the promise of the Enlightenment.

Rationalism shifted emphasis as the hierarchical system slowly moved from the Great Chain of Being to the horizontal one of the Renaissance and the Modern-Contemporary periods. On the one hand, hierarchy remained with a modified subject-predicate logic and without teleological explanation for natural events; it rested on the foundations of the self and mathematics. Descartes sought to build his system on two kinds of certitude, subjective and objective. The certitude of *cogito ergo sum* provided a subjective, factual foundation guaranteeing of the creditability of reason and experience as reliable sources of evidence. The certitude of mathematics provided an objective, logical foundation; if mathematics is the form of nature, then the certitude of nature as mathematical could be called objective. Inductive reasoning remained alive, only subordinate to deductive; deduction first, then induction. On certitude of the thinking thing and mathematics, Descartes argued for innate ideas (mind-born, not birth-born), clear and distinct ones without which we could not recognize an example of instances of a circle or a line. Important among all others is causality, a necessity of thought and actual happenings and as such an ideal field for divine and human reason. The universe is inherently rational, offering a clear separation of res *cognitans* and *res extensa*. Descartes birthed a scientifically based philosophic Rationalism. Its fruit were two grand systems, Spinoza's and Leibniz's.

On the other hand, the British Locke questioned the possibility of innate ideas. He questioned the nature, limits, and extent of knowledge. Innate ideas cannot be found either through the inner senses or the external ones. Rather, ideas arise from sensation or reflection. Knowledge rests in propositions, and propositions connect two ideas, at least, knowledge can only arise from experience. Knowledge arises through induction, through which we achieve generalities that are probable only, never necessary. Thus, knowledge arises first inductively and then deductively.

Rationalism continues both in induction and deduction. Rationalists, such as Descartes, and Empiricists, such as Locke, hold to Rationalism and differ primarily regarding the basis of general ideas. Kant mediated the debated issue of generalities. He argued that for the mind to know causality in the natural world, it must presuppose the concept, the category of causality. That is, the category of causality is the condition for the possibility of knowing causality in nature. However, Kant limited pure reason to the possibilities of experience. In experience he finds a particular with a universal character that experience cannot by itself account for. Causality, the principle of reliable relations in nature, is the presupposition of all learning and teaching. Under Kant the way of viewing the world changed; no longer does the mind revolve around the world, the world revolves around the mind. The world is the way the categories of understanding present it to be; not arbitrary, the presentation, however, is the universal structure guiding all minds seeking to understand the universe. This change added depth and credibility to the emerging self, to cultural monadic subjectivism; the monadic self is the center of knowledge of the world, natural or social.

Meanwhile, Rationalism underwent a transformation in the sciences. Under the influence of modern science, however, the formation of a *Novum Organon*, a new instrument was formed. Rationalism underwent a transformation. The dominance of deductive logic was soon challenged by inductive logic. Under the scaffold in inductive logic, science became experimental, as advocated by Roger Bacon in the thirteenth century CE and Francis Bacon in the sixteenth and seventeenth centuries CE. Though scientific method was variously understood in Descartes' *Discourse on Method*, Francis Bacon's *Novum Organum*, Galileo's *The Assayer*, and Giambattista Vico's *New Science*, it became experimental and mathematical. Under the influence of the success of mathematics in scientific discourse and the inability of subject-predicate logic, particularly the concept, to express asymmetrical and transitive relations, logic expanded to include mathematical forms. In the middle to late nineteenth century Boole invented a mathematical symbolization, and Peano and Frege independently recognized the difference between "Socrates is moral" and "All men are mortal," requiring reinterpretation of the traditional Square of the Opposition.[24] In the early twentieth century, Russell argued that Philosophy is logic. Late in the twentieth century CE, such disciplines as economics became mathematical; calculus is necessary for the study of economics. Succinctly, mathematics is the language of the sciences, both natural and social.

Thus, Rationalism plays a central role in making Idealism's case, whether ancient, medieval, or modern. Interestingly, it is also central to Naturalism (modern) when understood as scientific naturalism. The former subordinated experience to Rationalism, and the latter subordinated Rationalism to experience. Reflective critical reason needs a secure scaffold, and the appeal of Rationalism lies in its structure and methods, in Logic. As we grapple with suspicion, can Rationalism provide an answer to it? Let's see.

Allaying Suspicion

As we consider whether Rationalism can allay suspicion, remember that suspicion arises as the Background and Foreground of our second nature and culture move out of sync precipitating critical questioning and possible loss of stable goals, institutions, solidars; persons having rich knowledge of themselves; authorized and legitimated goals, institutions, stabilizers, and solidar by an Ultimate environment; and care of the body. As suspicion arises, fanged Rationalism moves into our cultural Background, possibly lost, and no rational structure remains to guide critical reflection. Can recollected Rationalism allay suspicion and provide for rich *gnothi seauton*? It must integrate the following experiences of personal, natural, and social living fit together: (1) our second nature and cultural core; (2) stability of our Background–Foreground relation; (3) solidarity with our society and its members, past, present, and future; (4) the charisma of the stabilizers and solidars supplied by and authorized by the Ultimate environment; and (5) the place of each of these in nature. Each involves relations among different aspects of persons in society living in natural, social/cultural, and Ultimate environments. Supposedly, only critical reflective reason or Rationalism can supply the required relations. We have two logics available to Rationalism, inductive and deductive, whether subject-predicate logic or mathematical logic, whether the propositional calculus, predicate calculus, or one the logics based on them, such as modal.[25] Can either one allay suspicion?

Rationalism that can claim the problem of suspicion has two central elements. First, we live in a period of fundamental cultural change. Weather changes, but that not disconcerting. We predict with reasonable probability the weather over a ten day period of time. A culture in crisis is different. That change precipitating suspicion appears to lack order. Second, change is never random; it has an order to it; orderly change. The claim that change that is suspicion is a crisis in which in which there is no order is incorrect. In any deep crisis, the problem is not the lack or possibility of order; life has a temporal structure; using ordinary reason, we can predict events based on past experience. It is reasonable to believe that even in suspicion an order is present and can be found. To find that order we must think dispassionately, critically, consistently, and make inferences on the basis of proper evidence. Suspicion carries with it a deep emotional reaction to events that seem to be unrelated. That is, the Background and the Foreground are disconnected and there seems to be no way to reconnect them. It is felt that no logic can guide us to restructure the relation. No scaffolding is available. At this point, in the darkest moments of suspicion, the way to stability is not through emotion of feeling; it is good thinking, Rationalism. If so, what can it claim?

First, a general point. Central to suspicion is the logical disconnection between the Background and the Foreground. The Background–Foreground relation forms on the basis of deductive and inductive reasoning. Backgrounds of our second nature develop under the guidance of an authority figure, a parent, guardian, brothers and sisters, minister, teacher. The culture learned, "absorbed," is unquestioned, accepted without discussion or dissension. As one engages problems, issues in the Background, one infers from the content of the Background what action should be taken. However, as circumstances change the "absorbed" beliefs do not fit all cases in the Background. One relies on imagination to come up with new ways of coping with the Background. One chooses a hypothetical solution, acts on it, and if it fits the problem, solves the problem we continue to act on it hoping to gain stability. Of course, inductive work does not occur in a vacuum; it is built on previous beliefs drawn from the culture about new ways of living into the Background. Once established, the relation between the Foreground and the Background moves in sync.

Now, can Rationalism allay suspicion? Recall that rich *gnothi seauton* includes at least five areas of living: (1) our second nature and cultural core; (2) stability of our Background–Foreground relation; (3) solidarity with our society and its members, past, present, and future; (4) the charisma of the stabilizers and solidars authorized by the Ultimate Environment; and (5) the place of each of these in nature. Common to these is relation, specifically between the Background and Foreground. Suspicion arises when the unreliability of that relation becomes pervasive, as in contemporary Western culture. Can Rationalism reestablish that relation and account for stability, solidarity, an Ultimate Environment, and the relation of these key aspects of a culture to nature? Let's turn first to the issue of reestablishing the relation between the Background and Foreground.

We have seen that the strength of Rationalism lies in logic, and Logic is the study of relations and their reliability. If relations are fractured, the problem lies in unreliable relations, and correction is achieved by finding reliable ones, not by denying the resourcefulness and power of logic, of good thinking. The Background-Foreground relation develops on authority and later inductively. Once established, we deduce, reason from the Background to how we should behave in the Foreground. If that meaningful relation is lost and suspicion arises, the root lies in violating fundamental principles of logic. Suspicion is general; to overcome it, we must reason inductively about specific issues in the Foreground and form a new Background with general principles to guide action. As new principles establish themselves, the Background is slowly reformed, and we are rehabituated. Conflicts between our former, inconsequential Background and the new one will continue; our past remains in our memory, in our habituation. Slowly the discontinuities are accepted, integrated into our lives; we learn to live in them. But the secure, authorizing, legitimating basis for continuing to rely on our Background as we face the Foreground is good thinking, is appealing to Rationalism's logical scaffold.

Good thinking restored stability and solidarity follow. The information available to us points to the importance of stable patterns of living in education, economics, government, religion, reproduction, regulation, and media. Without them and a relatively stable physical environment, we cannot develop a way of life in society. These relations require cooperation. Since humans behave in common ways, we can show by analogy what other persons need and are thinking and feeling. Furthermore, good thinking shows us we are limited and depend on an Ultimate Environment grasped through Rationalism. Our social, cultural, and natural worlds are rooted in order. Good thinking also shows us that we cannot continue to live stable, solidar lives without healthy bodies and reasonably stable physical environments. Thus, induction and deduction, if correctly practiced, can overcome the threat of suspicion. Though powerful, Rationalism has its anomalies.

The Haunting Hope of Rationalism

Anomalies arise in two basic dimensions of Rationalism's scaffolding, the concept and inference, whether inductive and deductive. Consider the concept. As used in ordinary living, it is valuable and not problematic. Logically the class-member relation helps to group things that possess a common characteristic, under a concept. If the logical relation between class and members becomes the metaphysical relation between the universal and particulars, it provides insight into Being and its relation to ordinary things and events in the world around us, the Many. Parmenides,' Plato's, Aristotle's, and Leibniz's philosophies, for example, clearly demonstrate the power of a universal to guide the mind to grasp universal Being and its relation to the many particulars. Regarding the relation between the Background and Foreground (the Many particulars), their relations can be accounted for by placing them under the concept or Conceptual Universal, whether Being (phusis), God (Person-Being), Nature (space-time continuum), or the Absolutism of Cosmic Mind. Following Rationalism guided by the Conceptual Universal has implications. Consider two.

First, the problem of individuation arises. The Background–Foreground relation focuses on an individual who makes choices renegotiating the Foreground under the guidance of the Background. Further, the Background–Foreground relation of a culture is deeply influenced by individuals choosing at least between genuine alternatives. Specifically, in the conceptual universal relation among particulars, what accounts for individual personality and freedom? Concepts assist persons in the fullness of practical living; Rationalism asks concepts to do metaphysical work, to give insight into reality and to say what it is. Reality finds its meaning within the Conceptual Universal. Rationalism as a metaphysics is totalizing. Every particular must be placed under the Universal, Being. If the Conceptual Universal approach were taken to trusting and coughing of the free person, we should expect to come to a full rational comprehension of persons, particularly of moral beings. If so, how account through the Universal for individual persons and their free moral acts? One could reply that the actions of the individual are the actions of Being. If so, and Being is believed to be Good, how account for the moral *hamartia* of individuals? If one attributes to Being immoral behavior, as one must on this account, Being would be both good and not good at the same time. Being must be internally consistent, as a class term must be internally consistent to function as a basis for organizing members. If internally inconsistent, particulars could both be placed under the concept and not under the concept. Regarding freedom of the individual, if only Being is free, the freedom of the individual rests beyond itself in Being. It finds its freedom in complete subordination to Being, ironically in determinism.

Could the problem of individuation be solved by understanding the Conceptual Universal within the symbolic language of mathematical logic rather than deductive subject-predicate logic? Let's see. Mathematical logic focuses on relations subject-predicate logic cannot adequately express. If the Conceptual Universal were expressed in the predicate calculus, in a three member universe, p, q, r, we would say (x) Mx is logically equivalent to Mp & Mq &

Mr. The Conceptual Universal, All, would be a conjunction of each member in the universe. The whole is the sum of the parts. If persons are independent of the one, how account for their relationships? They must lie in the relations among individuals. Any relation they may have would be arbitrary, depending on the purposes of the organizer. If we seek to understand their solidarity, we face the other minds problem. If we account for the relation of persons within the propositional or predicate calculus, persons would be reduced to relations, and their individual personhood would be lost, as well as their freedom.

Second, examine the problem of violence of persons, society, and culture administered by the totalizing power of the Conceptual Universal. Elements of culture and second nature include the relation of a Background and Foreground; the stability and solidarity within a society and its members; an Ultimate environment; and the relation of persons, society, and culture to nature. Each involves both the freedom of individuals to form and modify a society's culture and the independence to bring about social and cultural change. Each is dependent on the trusting and oughting relation between and among persons. To call or respond to a call as moral subjects implies their mutual transcendence. Their personhood as trusting beings who can freely break their promises is beyond the totalizing capability of reason. The triadic relation of trusting and oughting regarding a cause would be reduced to a logical relation capable of being comprehended, rationally understood. Culture or second nature would be a rational relation. Morality and Trust would be ancillary, at best. The conceptual universal, "All," does violence to persons as it gathers them under the logical wings of the concept as understood within subject-predicate or mathematical logic.

Further, consider inference. In traditional arguments, the truth of a claim (the conclusion) rests on the truth of other claims (evidence) that truth-functionally (validly) imply the claim and on the relevance of the evidence to the conclusion. But why believe the evidence is related to that claim? We do, on the basis of warrants.[26] That is, the warrant justifies the connection between the evidence and the conclusion. But then, why believe the warrant is true? We appeal to a backing to support the belief in the truth of the warrant. Clearly, this is logically an infinite regress. But, as we proceed, we seek some stopping place, some backing that rests on no further backing, but is The Backing, beyond which we cannot reasonably proceed. At that point, we are in the field of Metaphysics.

Look at this example. A person is brushing her teeth. A friend tells me that that behavior is an action. It has certain characteristics: agentive, free, temporal, triadic, norm governed, and supported by the social/physical worlds. Queried, he answers, "I have seen those characteristics before, and it is an action." If I press the discussion and ask why those characteristics are connected to action behaviors, he appeals to a reason for connecting them in just that way.

He appeals to a warrant. All actions are agentive, free, temporal, triadic, norm governed, and supported by the social/physical world in which they occur. If pressed for a justification for that generalization, he appeals to a backing. He might reasonably reply that the movement of blood in the circulatory system of the human body and brushing his teeth are different, and the difference lies in characteristics. The circulatory system does not possess them, and brushing his teeth does. The latter is voluntary, an action; the former is involuntary, a movement. And, if pressed for a justification of that belief, he could appeal to his observations of the order and nature of everyday events in his life. And, if pressed further, he would simply say, "That's just the way things are." And, if pressed further, he could simply shrug off the question by saying it is unanswerable. Or he could offer a hypothesis that would best account for "the way things are." Or he could claim that the reasoning of his argument so far implies an answer. In those two cases, he would seek backing in an Ultimate environment.

Note two anomalies, both in the relevance of premises to conclusion. One is logical, and the other is metaphysical. Consider logical relevance. In valid deductive arguments, all premises cannot be true and the conclusion false; the conclusion follows 100 percent of the time. Propositions in a valid argument are formally relevant to each other. In inductive arguments, the conclusion follows less that 100 percent of the time. On the basis of propositions rooted in the present and past, no valid inference can be inferred regarding the future. Though deductive and inductive inferences may be drawn, nothing in logical relations relates Background and Foreground. Appealing to warrants requires reference to information, to contexts in the fullness of practical living. Nothing in the formal relation itself establishes the temporal relation in our second nature. The Background–Foreground relation may be valid, but being valid does not establish the relevance of premises to conclusion. Warrants move the connection to frames of reference beyond the logical relation itself.

Pressing for a satisfactory warrant, Rationalism points to an Ultimate environment authorizing and legitimating the relevance of logical relations, whether deductive or inductive. Rationalism cannot be an Ultimate environment.

The hope of Rationalism haunts us, but it cannot solve the problem of suspicion.

THE PUZZLE BEYOND BACKINGS

In sum, neither Being, understood as Naturalism or Idealism, nor Rationalism can defeat Suspicion. The persuasiveness of each is undermined by anomalies. Naturalism presents us with a rich understanding of our bodies. But the development of the individual self, especially its freedom, meaning, and values are submerged and lost in the strict orderly causal relations within the space time continuum of Naturalism, understood in terms of the impersonalism of scientific naturalism. Idealism emphasizes the life of the mind, meaning, and values, but the body is opaque, denigrated to insignificance. And if we attempt to rescue Being, whether Naturalism or Idealism, by appealing to Rationalism, to the Conceptual Universal, we face the problems of individuation, of the relation of part and whole. Rationalism suspends freedom of choice among options and does violence to persons and their interrelationships. If we privilege inference, all interpersonal relations, specifically Background–Foreground ones (whether second nature or social-cultural) of stability, solidarity, possibly with an Ultimate environment reduce to logical only. We lose our bodies and ironically our rational minds to concepts and inference. It appears that our haunting hopes are nostalgic, nothing more.

Neither Naturalism, Idealism, nor Rationalism can reestablish the relation of the Background and Foreground and the elements of a culture resting on it. Suspicion has won, and we cannot achieve *gnothi seauton*. Yet, we persist searching for who we are, what we are to be, and what we are to do as well as their contexts that support them and arrange for their achievement. Can we find what we are looking for? The burden of the remainder of our discussion is to show that we can. We begin by searching for a new Master Narrative.[27]

Notes

1. Hadot, Pierre. *What is Ancient Philosophy?* Translated by Michael Chase (Cambridge, MA: Harvard University Press, 2002), 10.

2. William C. Dampier. A *History of Science and Its Relations with Philosophy and Religion* (Cambridge, UK: Cambridge University Press, 1961), 93.

3. Kemeny asks, "In what sense is nature to be uniform? *We are told that nature tomorrow will somehow behave just like today. We are told that the assumption is needed to assure us that our past experience is a reliable guide to the future.* In other words, somehow we are to put bounds on nature so that it is to obey the same laws tomorrow as it obeys today. Fortunately, this terminology has already been shown to be untenable. A law is no more than a description of what actually happens." (John G. Kemeny. *A Philosopher Looks at Science* (Princeton, NJ: D. Van Nostrand Company, Inc., 1959), 62–63. [italics mine]

4. Kemeny, *A Philosopher Looks at Science*, 67.

5. A deductive nomological explanation can be stated in the form of a *modus ponens* argument where the propositions are stated in the language of propositional

and predicate calculus. An example would be, "All copper expands when heated. This is a piece of copper. Therefore, it will expand when heated." Let C = copper, E = expands, H = heated. We can then say that (x)[(Cx & Hx) then Ex], Cx & Hx, therefore Ex. If we have the minor premise and the conclusion, we can confirm the predicted conclusion by adding the covering law, All copper expands when heated. That added, we know a universal characteristic of copper and can predict that in all circumstances, if heated, it expands. Remember Kemeny's point: "A law is no more than a description of what actually happens." Kemeny, *A Philosopher Looks at Science*, 63.

6. Kemeny, *A Philosopher Looks at Science*, 59.

7. See Brightman, who says, "Everything becomes chaotic unless we can believe that the events we experience can be expected to be followed by further experiences in conformity with, or continuous with, what is already experienced or known." Edgar S. Brightman, *Person and Reality, An Introduction to Metaphysics,* edited by Peter A. Bertocci, Jannette E. Newhall, and Robert S. Brightman (New York, NY: The Ronald Press, 1958), 361.

8. We must remember the history of physics as pre-Newtonian, Newtonian, and post-Newtonian. However, all three assume a natural continuum, a rational method, regularities in the natural continuum, and the uniformity of nature. We seek to lay bare some assumptions framing nature and scientific investigation that are called on to support naturalism.

9. Howard F. Stein, *Beneath the Crust of Culture, Psychoanalytic Anthropology and the Cultural Unconscious in American Life* (Amsterdam, NL: Rodopi, 2004), 121. Freud, analyzing culture, not civilization, claimed, "The events of human history ... are only the reflections of the dynamic conflicts among the ego, id, and superego which psychoanalysis studies in the individual—the same events repeated on a wider stage." From *The Future of an Illusion* quoted by Louis Menand in the Introduction to Sigmund Freud, *Civilization and Its Discontents*, introduction by Louis Menand, translated and edited by James Strachey, biographical afterward by Peter Gay (New York, NY: W. W. Norton Company, [1961] 2005), 14. An alternative account of psychology is Eliminative Materialism. See its classic statement by Paul Churchland in "Eliminative Materialism and the Propositional Attitudes," *Journal of Philosophy* 78, no. 2 (1981); reprinted in Paul Churchland, *A Neurocomputional Perspective: The Nature of Mind and the Structure of Science* (Cambridge, MA: Massachusetts Institute of Technology Press, 1989), 1–22. He states, "Eliminative Materialism is the thesis that our commonsense conception of psychological phenomena constitutes a radically false theory, a theory so fundamentally defective that both the principles and the ontology of that theory will eventually be displaced, rather than smoothly reduced, by completed neuroscience" (p.1).

10. In addition to the psychoanalytic view, other Naturalisms include Paul Churchland's *A Neurocomputational Perspective*, John Searle's speech act theory, David Weissman's system of reciprocal causal relations, and Gregory Batson's cybernetic theory of persons and society. The social sciences are not settled on this issue;

no science is. But their discoveries so far warrant Naturalism, which frees and leads us from the grip of suspicion.

11. Peter A. Bertocci, "Why Personalistic Idealism?" 10.3 *Idealistic Studies*. 10.3 (1980): 185.

12. Quoted by William Ernest Hocking in *Types of Philosophy*, with Richard B. O. Hocking, 3rd edition (New York, NY: Charles Scribner's Sons, (1929) 1959), 54.

13. Hocking, *Types of Philosophy*, 39.

14. Pierre Hadot, *What is Ancient Philosophy?* translated by Michael Chase (Cambridge, MA: Harvard University Press, 2002), 10.

15. Plato, *The Republic of Plato*, translated with notes and an interpretive essay by Allan Bloom (New York, NY: Basic Books, Inc., 1968), X 614a–621b.

16. Since *phusis* as Being is Good and the Demiurgos is a category in *phusis*, the Demiurgos can only do the good. Yet, Plato introduces self-initiated change alongside the teleological pull of the Good, in which all in the mixed world participate. See Plato, *Laws* X, 896a, translated by A. E. Taylor in Hamilton, Edith and Huntington Cairns (eds.), *The Collected Dialogues of Plato including the Letters* with Introduction and Prefatory Notes (Princeton, NJ: Princeton UP, (1961) 1994), 1225–1513.

17. Bengtsson, Jan Olof. *The Worldview of Personalism, Origins and Early Development* (Oxford, UK: Oxford University Press, 2006.)

18. Hocking, *Types of Philosophy*, 211.

19. Hocking, *Types of Philosophy*, 212.

20. Augustine, *On Free Choice of the Will*. Translated with Introduction and Notes, Thomas Williams (Indianapolis, IN: Hackett Publishing Company, 1993).

21. Thomas Buford, "Institutions and the Making of Persons: W. E. Hocking's Social Personalism," *A William Ernest Hocking Reader with Commentary*, eds. John Lacks and D. Micah Hester (Nashville, TN: Vanderbilt University Press, 2004), 290–304.

22. Hadot, *What is Ancient Philosophy*, 10. As we search each one, remember that suspicion arises as the Background and Foreground of our second nature and culture move out of sync precipitating critical questioning and possible loss of stable goals, institutions, and solidars; of persons who can know themselves; an Ultimate environment legitimating those goals, institutions, and solidar; and care of the body. If Naturalism, Idealism, or Rationalism can provide *gnothi seauton*, it must show how those cultural elements can be restored, providing solidarity for people living at the same time in history, and stability over time for our second nature and culture.

23. Not until the second century CE was the word "logic" used referring to Aristotle's work.

24. See Bertrand Russell, "Logic as the Essence of Philosophy," in Irving M. Copi and James A. Gould, eds., *Readings on Logic* (New York, NY: The Macmillan Company, 1964), 82–84.

25. Here we follow E. J. Lemmons' formulations in *Beginning Logic* (Indianapolis, IN: Hackett Publishing Company, Inc. [1965] 1978).

26. See Stephen Toulmin Richard Rieke, and Allan Janik, *An Introduction to Reasoning* (New York, NY: Macmillan Publishing Co., Inc., 1979), 23–67.

27. In his *Natural Law, Laws of Nature, Natural Rights* (New York, NY: Continuum International Publishing Group, 2005), 27–30 Francis Oakley takes a similar approach. Whitehead's distinction in the *Adventures of Ideas* (New York, NY: Free Press, 1967) between internal and external relations prods Oakley to situate his own thought between two widely separated views. Whitehead seeks a moderating position and Oakley follows. With Oakley and his predecessor, we recognize the broad gap separating Cultural Objectivism and Cultural Subjectivism and seek a moderating position. See also John Wild, "Introduction to Emmanuel Levinas," *Totality and Infinity* (Pittsburgh, PA: Duquesne University Press [1961] 1969), 15.

Chapter 3

A New Master Narrative

Our cultural shell continues; habituation is strong. Suspicion grips us, draining our cultural shell's legitimacy to provide and support self-knowledge. Vulnerable, no rescue in sight, our culture loses it efficacy to protect and guide us; death looms. Or, so it seems. Lost in a dark wood, there is a path out, beginning with a viable *topos*, perspective leading to a Master Narrative.[1]

Mining elsewhere in the western intellectual tradition turns up a fertile perspective. Submerged under and interpreted within the metaphysics of Being and Rationalism, a viable *topos* barely clings to its core of freedom, purposive social action, and community. Extricated from its suffocating bondage, it is triadic trusting, a perspective that avoids pitfalls of past master narratives, connects our Background and Foreground, and provides for *gnothi seauton*. It tells the most complete story, is eloquent; it is the Master Narrative.

To support that claim a successful search comes to grips with four problems. First, where and how find the perspective, persons-in-triadic-trusting-relations? Second, can it be the Master Narrative? If so, why? Can it possess authority without judgment, without question, and yet through critical thought be established as authoritative? Specifically, the authority of Western Master Narratives, Order and the Emerging Self, implode as the truth requirements they legitimate are turned on themselves. Can triadic trusting avoid that consequence? Third, within the *topos*, can it identify and legitimate connections required to bridge the temporal span among what I am, what I am to be, and what I am to do; to connect not only members of a triad but also triads to each other and to their social, cultural, and ultimate environments? That includes the fallout of the implosion of Master Narratives under the circularity of self-legitimation, specifically opening legitimacy to a broad range of limited narratives whose knowledge claims find legitimacy in their own practices and interactions. Yet, only specialists know the methods, procedures, and languages required to participate in the "open" narratives. Rather than openness, limited narratives create insiders and outsiders, each left to the knowledge legitimated by the limited narrative. Is it possible for any Master Narrative to bridge and legitimize truth claims common to all limited narratives? Fourth, why claim success or eloquence for Persons-in-relation to overcome suspicion and provide the basis for *gnothi seauton*? Here we shall discuss the first two questions. Questions three through four will be discussed in subsequent chapters.

SEARCHING

Before addressing those questions, three preliminaries will be considered. What does Master Narrative mean? What is meant by "authority"? And, how establish that a Master Narrative possesses authority?

Preliminary Issues

Think of Master Narrative as a perspective, accepted as Authority without discussion or dissension that connects elements necessary to self-knowledge, particularly triads of a society with a culture, nature, and ultimate environment.[2] First what is "perspective"? Its Latin root, *perspectus*, pp. of *perspicere* means "to look through, see clearly." Think of it as "the interrelation in which a subject or its parts are mentally viewed; the capacity to view things in their true relations or relative importance."[3] In a context, it is "seeing through" allowing one to grasp connections needed for *gnothi seauton*. It is the basis for cause (or purpose), solidarity, and stability. The interrelation occurs from a vantage point, a *topos*, a "place," a stance from which one sees or looks. One enters or finds oneself within a perspective that interrelates, connects objects from this "place" or viewpoint. In contrast to perspectives of limited scope, Master Narrative is normally understood as unlimited in scope.[4] Dangerously close to violence, seeking a view of the whole is not necessary, even if possible. The Master Narrative as *topos* or perspective shared without judgment, *sensus communis*, identifies and connects persons and their environments to each other, overcoming suspicion and allowing *gnothi seauton*. We live in and through Master Narratives; they encompass persons, their potentials and exercise of them, as well as their various environments, society, culture, nature, and ultimate environments.

Further clarify Master Narrative by considering what it is not. It is not a *topos*, which through critical objective reflection we identify, clarify, evaluate its strengths and weaknesses in comparison with other *topoi*, and choose as the best option to download on and provide meaning for the fullness of practical living. That view unseats Master Narrative as an all encompassing authoritative Narrative and brings it under Rationalism, reducing it to one narrative among others that embellish what is true as determined by standards of consistency, empirical coherence, or pragmatism. It assumes that truth is outside, beyond any metaphor. Appealing to truth, a knower assumes a position outside, beyond perspectives, from which she chooses among perspectives and freely adopts one and rejects the others. Truth, residing elsewhere can be found through Rationalism. From that view of narrative, self-knowledge would be a matter of knowing what Rationalism establishes though scientific methods, leaving the scientist who freely engages in scientific study a mystery unto herself. Self-knowledge ends in an unnecessary mystery. As we shall see, a Master Narrative adopted without critical, rational, objective investigation, without discussion, without dissension; that legitimates truth found through critical, rational, objective investigation, runs the risk that those legitimated under its authority may challenge the self-grounded authority of the Master Narrative; its runs the risk of imploding.

Next, what is meant by "authority"? Before addressing those questions, consider two preliminary issues: is it reasonable to search for a Master Narrative, and what is meant by Authority? On the one hand, Authority refers to a status. Consider an example from a political institution. In the United States of America the electorate chooses from among themselves members of Congress who best demonstrate their understanding of the concerns of the electorate and knowledge of possible solutions and bestows on those individuals the authority to exercise the duties of that position. On the basis of their received Authority, democratic legislative action, and in cooperation with the Judicial and Executive branches, those elected legitimize laws enacted to address the needs of the electorate and govern the actions of people. In this sense, Authority is bestowed on an individual or individuals legitimizing their actions in carrying out the duties of their station. If Authority is bestowed on a narrative, a *topos*, how does that occur, and how does the Master Narrative possessing Authority legitimize connections between Background and Foreground?

One the other hand, the Authority of a status implies power appropriate to that status and the duty to exercise that power. "Power" means to act to produce an effect, to influence, to command thought, opinion, or behavior. Power could be physical/psychological/social or moral. Physical power could be military; psychological could be emotional compulsion; social could be public opinion. Moral power could reside in ought and/or in good. For example, dignity and transcendent freedom of other persons could obligate a certain course of action. The well-being of other persons as worthwhile, such as feeding starving children, could obligate one to act to enhance it. Of course, a person occupying a status could exercise power of force granted to that status without regard to ought or good. We shall argue that such exercise of force violates the moral structure of Persons-in-Triadic-Trusting-Relations. Further, a Master Narrative's Authority of status and duties also implies the power and duty to determine and legitimize what needs to be decided and what knowledge is. As the way of seeing, *topos*, perspective, Master Narrative backs, warrants arguments supporting knowledge claims, and legitimizes knowledge. It also has the duty to exercise power to legitimize what needs to be decided.

Finally, how establish the authority of a Master Narrative? Saying a Master Narrative possesses Authority to legitimate solidars and stabilizers required for any society with a culture is a knowledge claim. During the late Renaissance and Early Modern periods, some philosophers searched by means of Rationalism, beyond Christendom, specifically outside the Master Narrative of Christian Order, for a secure foundation on which to build a culture, a foundation of rock that holds against early modern pyrrhonist skepticism's corrosive advance. Descartes' *cogito* argument and Locke's empirical argument are classic examples. They contributed to a dualism that led to insurmountable problems. Others turned to the most promising alternative, science. In the meantime some, such as Kant, turned to fideism, a foundation based on faith. Under Wittgenstein, the search for certainty underwent severe criticism. Whatever unity a foundation could bring was given up, and few continued the search. Only limited narratives survived.[5] Suspicion's grip strengthens.

Yet, Master Narratives, their possibility and Authority, continue to be deeply influential, authorizing backing and warrants. Backings and warrants drawn from the Book of Knowledge of a society and culture rest within that which neither reason nor experience can supply, a Master Narrative. Ironically, arguments deconstructing a text rest on that which arguments seek to render implausible, a Master Narrative. Arguments implode, making implausible their claims. Deepening the irony, deconstructive arguments could not be developed apart from the *topos*, Persons-in-triadic-trusting-relations. The act of deconstruction forgets what it requires, Master Narrative, specifically Persons-in-triadic-trusting-relations, as we shall see.

How can the Master Narrative, Persons-in-triadic-trusting-relations, guide us beyond suspicion and the critique of Wittgenstein, Derrida, Nietzsche as well as legitimize connections required for *gnothi seauton*? First, our search is not framed by Whole-part, whole as in Order or Emerging Self, or part as in limited narratives, as Lyotard assumes in his presentation of Postmodernism.[6] If it were, theory would be down loaded onto, dictated to experience, making it no different in form than the deductive, *sub-species aeternitatis* arguments reminiscent of metaphysics during the era of cultural dyadic objectivism. If it had, the Master Narrative as a whole would implode under the problem of self-legitimation, x is Authority and x legitimates itself. Lyotard writes approvingly of Wittgenstein, "Most people have lost its nostalgia for the lost narrative. It in no way follows that they are reduced to barbarity. What saves them from it is their knowledge that legitimation can only spring from their own linguistic practice and communicational interaction."[7] Our search, in contrast, does not begin with a conceptual universal understood as a philosophical theory, as does Searle, or a nominalist understanding as does Wittgenstein in his view of ordinary language. Rather, we begin with uneasy, weakening confidence in the solidarity and stability of our society and culture and expand to the connections within society and culture, to Nature and the Ultimate Environment and how persons within them can know themselves. The Master Narrative arises from triadic, trusting living. We move neither from practice to theory, nor theory to practice. We begin with the fullness of practical living that we find structured in triadic, trusting relations. With these preliminary clarifications, focus on the first question. Where and how find the Master Narrative, "Persons-in-Triadic-Trusting-Relation"?

Where

Where should we search for the new Master Narrative? Two options are the Background and the Foreground. Thinking historically, we could search our Background for the Master Narrative, Persons-in-relation. Its roots lie 3,000 years ago in Abram and are foundational for Jews, Christians, and Muslims. Restricted to that time and to those in that tradition, it would be a limited narrative, leaving out all others, atheists, Naturalists (scientific-metaphysical, not theological), for example. If limited to some lives, but not all, it could not be a Master Narrative. Searching our Background requires more than choosing a perspective at the root of one's own tradition. Or our search could focus on more recent past narratives uncovered through an act of cultural memory, such as the Providence of God or nineteenth century social progress through the power of science. Speaking to events in the past, they could aptly guide into them. However, exhausted and out of date, they cannot guide into the current Foreground. Further, if found and down-loaded into the present, they would be limited in scope, failing to address those who reject metanarratives. The Providence of God could not authoritatively legitimate connections for those who are atheists or scientific Naturalists. Nor could social progress through science be held without discussion by persons in the Abrahamic tradition.

Searching our Foreground fares no better. Present and future problems call for solutions; the Foreground does not present solutions or pathways to solutions, though one may be suggested. Dewey, for example, facing problems in the present and seeking future goals, appealed to the scientific method to solve problems. However, the scientific method arose within the Background of many years of scientific investigation slowly liberated from institutional authority, particularly the Catholic Church.

Where else could we look? Consider the present, the fullness of ordinary living in the present. There each of us begins doing philosophy. All philosophies must start there, and in doing so they find common ground for discussion. Consider the words of a transcendental empiricist: "We find such common ground in the following postulates: First, the coexistence of persons. It is a personal and social world in which we live, and with which all speculation must begin. We and the neighbors are facts which cannot be questioned. Secondly, there is a law of reason valid for all and binding upon all. This is the supreme condition of any mental community. Thirdly, there is a world of common experience, actual or possible, where we meet in mutual understanding, and where the great business of life goes on."[8] And "We begin with experience, which is real and valid in its way. This is the world of things and persons about us, and the general order of life. Now in serious thought there can never be any question as to the validity and truth of this experience."[9] Searching in this common ground, a new viable Master Narrative presents itself. It does so in two ways, through creative-finding and social mediation.

How

Consider persons as creative-finders. From their earliest beginnings, facing pain and death by other humans and natural forces, humans employ *techne* to transform the "world" around them. We find the beginning of human social, cultural life. In making, crafting, exploring materials with tools at hand, humans bring into existence cultures for defense and promotion of well-being, particularly *gnothi seauton*. Not *creatio ex nihilo*, they creatively-find from pre-existing materials. They imaginatively explore a medium, that includes their bodies, natural habitat, the past buried in our Background their; habituation, including present social/cultural/natural environments; and future possibilities. Creative-finding a master image roots in imaginative exploration in a broad and rich medium.

Before moving on, note the part agency plays in humans' making their world and knowing the truth about it. Humans do not simply find a social world into which they choose to move. Institutions do not have prior existence as possibilities, such as platonic forms or exemplars in the mind of

God, actualized in the mixed world through the creative imagination of God or human intellectual finding. Neither is the social world caused by natural forces nor a place where humans simply live as elements of a law-like system of natural forces. Rather social, cultural life is initiated and brought into existence by humans for their security and general well-being. Apart from self-initiating purposive agency their social-cultural world could not exist. Through creative-finding, persons transform their bodies and habitats into societies with cultures, including artifacts that do not arise unaided in the natural world, and cover, diffuse them with emotions.[10] As they do so, a perspective or *topos* guides them. To understand the place and significance of imagination in knowing, consider an opposing view: the ground of knowing lies in reason and experience, in particulars, concepts, propositions, and arguments.

Two positions have structured the search for knowledge of us and the world around. Underlying Thomistic moderate realism is the belief that mind, other persons, and the external world are deeply connected; the mind knows through abstracting forms from images conveyed *by means of* sensory experience. If so, how can minds so intertwined with the world around them fail to know? How account for error? Underlying Cartesian dualism, all knowledge rises in individual experience connecting the mind to external world *through* sensory data structured by concepts. How can minds so separated from the external world ever come to know? How account for truth? The only alternatives seem to be realism or dualism. Look again at the way the mind comes to know.

Consider how particulars and concepts arise.[11] Since Plato, this was the work of sense experience and the intellect. Sense experience, undifferentiated, without distinction, order, or structure, requires the intellect to differentiate particulars and connect them through relations, concepts. Particulars share attributes on the basis of which they can be grouped under concepts. For example, actions that share the characteristic of minding one's own business and do not have the characteristics of temperance, wisdom, and courage could be grouped under the heading or concept Justice. Justice as a general feature of our moral world is a concept. Within a culture a knower could learn from others to recognize particulars and concepts, the general features of the world. Particulars and concepts join in propositions, as in George Washington is a native of Virginia.

What are propositions and their relation to knowing? A proposition is a sentence that can be determined to true or false. The presence of a particular in one's mind does not constitute knowledge, sensing "a cup," and "white," for example. Either they are present to one or they are not. However, joining the two through the "is" copula, "The cup is white," we make a claim that can be determined true or false. If looking directly at the cup and its color, evidence is unnecessary. Knowing is occasionally direct; usually it is indirect, as in knowing that oil helps cool a Lycoming 4-cycle engine in a Cessna 172. Central to indirect knowing is argument.

What is the place of arguments in knowing? An argument requires at least two propositions, one (ground) offered in support of the other (claim). They also require warrants and backing. Consider a claim, "Socrates is mortal." What legitimates connecting Socrates and mortal? We could offer a third term, man, as in Socrates is a man, and infer, Socrates is mortal. We may be asked, why connect the two propositions, answering with another premise, a general proposition, the warrant, All men are mortal. If the two propositions constituting the premises are true, it follows necessarily that Socrates is mortal is also true.[12] However, pushing the argument, one could ask why believe All men are mortal is true. Seeking backing for the warrant, one could appeal to medical science, to principles fundamental to living organisms, to basic principles of biology and chemistry.[13] If asked for a backing for those sciences, one could appeal to the authority of science. The authority of science legitimates individual sciences. If asked for backing for science, one could appeal to metaphysics, such as Naturalism, and to Rationalism. If one asked for a backing for them, one could simply call attention to the arguments supporting Naturalism and Rationalism. Eventually, one says, "That's just the way things are." With this brief survey of the salient aspects of the place of reason and experience in knowing, its weaknesses are clear.

Are conceptual universals and undifferentiated sense experience adequate to account for this particular child, car, house? They cannot do so.[14] Regarding particulars, if sense experience lacks differences, essential to particulars, and concepts are relations, the work of the intellect, particulars cannot arise. Here find the root problem of individuation. There is no basis for differentiating undifferentiated sense experience so that different particulars arise to be connected by general concepts. If particulars could arise, and the concept could connect particulars, on what basis identify the relevance of those particulars and that concept? Reminiscent of Plato's Third Man Argument, neither nor both can do so. It is one thing to connect the ground and claim in a logical, formal manner; it is another to recognize their relevancy, the possibility of their relevancy. To recognize that possibility requires something other than concepts, generated by the intellect, and particulars arising in some mysterious fashion from undifferentiated sensation. Coming up with the possibility is the work of the imagination. The imagination forms the possibility of the connection. That possibility and manner of connection is the image. As connecting individuals the image is a type of universal; or as Vico calls it, an imaginative universal.[15] How account for particulars? They arise only on the basis of the work of the imagination.

Are propositions and arguments the basis of knowing? Concepts are neither true nor false. As frameworks for grouping, classifying, or connecting particulars, they are useful or not. Central to a concept is a characteristic, and if a particular has that characteristic, it should be grouped with all other particulars having the same characteristic. Formally, a concept is a relation based on shared characteristics. If a connection is claimed, it could be challenged, and grounds could be offered. If challenged, proceed as outlined above, to offer grounds, warrants, and backing. And if asked for a backing, simply say, "That's the way things are." As a final appeal, we move beyond logic, beyond Rationalism, beyond the conceptual universal. Yet we know. We appeal to the authority of perspective, *topos,* Master Narratives to legitimate arguments. Pushed to its limits, reasoning depends on something it cannot supply: a perspective or *topos* relating grounds, evidence, warrants, and backing. Reasoning is always from a perspective, a *topos*, and the work of the imagination in creative-finding. What, then, is creative-finding, and in what sense is it the root of thought?

Searching for the root of thought itself, "How (can) the mind . . . have something before it at all. By asking how there ever comes to be something, rather than nothing, before the mind . . . (we are) able to see knowledge as beginning directly with the image."[16] The mind rises above immediacy through the image. Images are not of something; rather they are the root of *ofness*, the basis for there being anything before the mind as individual, particular or universal (the intelligible or conceptual universal).[17] The mind forms images, the power to produce identity. Through the image the mind is able to "find again" in immediacy.[18] On the basis of this capacity the mind forms particulars and conceptual universals. Thus, the mind connects due to its capacity to form images. Forming images, as we have seen, requires *"finding again"* in immediacy and occurs through recollective imagination. What does that mean?

Thought rests in the capacity of the mind through images born of imagination to move beyond immediacy by recollection to form particulars and their relationships.[19] The power of "againness" that is present in the imagination is memory. The aspect of our cognitive life allowing for the formation of a *topos*, a Master Narratives is memory. *Memory* consists of: "(1) itself, (2) imagination . . . and (3) invention."[20] Consider each. Memory as "itself" refers to the capacity of the mind to bring before it what was once immediately before it but not before it now. We might simply call that capacity recall. This is the power of the mind for "againess" and is temporal. With this capacity, we form an image, an identity, in the midst of the flux of sensation.

Imagination is the "power to reorder what has been recalled and to shape it after the general form of the subject. . . . Through (imagination) the mind makes the object familiar; objects are not simply apprehended in themselves but are shaped as human objects."[21] I shall call this the constitutive imagination. Finally, *invention* is the power of the mind to form a topos, a perspective allowing arrangements, relationships, narratives, speeches of the elements as recalled.[22] This capacity allows us to take a name, say that of Jove (in Vico's case), realized in one instance and spread it through the whole of experience. This imaginative act coupled with technique brings forth a world not there before and not modeled on anything.[23] That is, memory is recollective imagination. Its orientation is the past; recollection is a present act collecting what is earlier remembered, ordering it under and guided by a *topos*. Through memory, as we push deep into our recollected past, a Master Narrative slowly reveals itself.[24] Under the Master Narrative, reason and experience identify and order the various elements of the world. For example, Greek science begins and understands itself through Order, Fate, and Moira that orders the gods. All three capacities of the memory function collectively to find again, to form sensation into master images. In this sense they are the primordial constitutive powers of the mind allowing the making of a Master Narrative, the *topos* that reveals itself as that within which we live, move, and have our being that in turn authorizes backings and warrants.

In contrast, Descartes, answering skepticism, finds certainty in the *cogito*, the thinking thing that abstracts sensation and imagination from their roots in bodily movements, and subordinates them to intellection. Neither sensation nor imagination provides knowledge; through mental effort, imagination provides images, metaphors illustrative of conceptions delivered by pure intellection.[25] Master Narrative is not a metaphor in the Cartesian sense. It is easy to read the preceding discussion from the perspective of Descartes and reduce the *topos* to an illustration. Illustrations lack authority to legitimate warrants and backings for arguments. Arguments could only resort to the rules governing valid arguments. Arguments and the principles on which they are based cannot provide for their own backing, as science cannot justify itself by appealing to science. Begging the question violates the principles on which logic is based. Simply, no conclusion of an argument is established by appealing to its own premises. Eschewing epistemic and metaphysical dualism, that which authorizes, legitimates warrants and backings lies in perspective, *topos*, Master Narrative. Bodily action, reaction, and sensation are initially indistinguishable. Differentiated by the powers of the mind, memory, imagination, and invention, perspective, *topos*, Master Narrative ascends to its role as Authority providing legitimacy for backings and warrants of rational arguments and meaning for the possibility of *gnothi seauton*.

Succinctly, under the dominance of Rationalism, Philosophy successfully challenging poetry for dominance separates reason and experience, arguments from their warrants and backings, sensation from its bodily roots. Sensation became under Descartes the least reliable avenue to knowledge. Locke attempted to rejoin them, but under the influence of Aristotle, Aquinas, and the Cartesian dualism of *res cogitans* and *res extensa*, sensation remained a mental event separated from bodily movements.[26] But, we contend that bodily sensation that sprouts *topos* is the act of a solitary person, but does not constitute knowledge. Mental acts of sensing and knowing are solitary, but knowledge to which those acts contribute requires environmental contexts, specifically triads, I-Thou-It. Even though rooted in bodily sensation, memory, imagination, and invention, knowledge is achieved only as we become aware by reflection within and on the fullness of ordinary practical living. There we make knowledge claims and find justification for them.

MEDIATING

Knowledge arises through exercising the powers of creative-finding resting in the potentials of individual persons to know. Knowing is an exercise of those potentials. However, the meaning of concepts, experience, and claims arising from that exercise are not formed in Cartesian isolation but are mediated by the fullness of everyday living, generally by their social/cultural environments. Those environments include institutions such as schools, churches, governments, families, economies, media, and regulations; their physical habitat, such as terrain, water, weather; and their Master Narrative limited or ultimate, exhausted or vibrant. Creative-finding always occurs within social/natural/ultimate contexts; powered by imagination, it gives rise to a perspective later specified and related internally by reasoning. To understand the place and role of mediation in knowing through creative-finding, consider two claims. (1) The underlying structure of the fullness of ordinary living is persons-in-trusting-triadic relations. (2) Central to triadic structure is trust. Analysis of these claims reveals the roots of an authorizing Master Narrative legitimating knowledge claims regarding connections required for *gnothi seauton*.

The Structure of Everyday Living

Each of us begins doing philosophy in the context of our living in the world. All philosophies must start there, and in doing so they find common ground for discussion. What do we find there?

The fullness of our practical lives is triadic, bodily, temporal, solidar, and usually stable having a past, present, and a future. Human embodiment, self-consciousness, personality, and knowing develop in the midst of events, things in the world, other persons, their communication, reflection, correction, certification, and guidance.[27] As experience becomes something for us, and not simply undergone, we become aware it is triadic in structure, composed of ourselves, other persons, and a third element, things, events, causes, norms: succinctly, I, Thou, and It.[28] Each member of the triad brings to the relation its own activity potentials.[29] However, the triad is required for each member to do what they can do. That is, the development of potentiality is always mediated. I, Thou, and It have activity potentials that develop within, on the basis of triadic interaction. All development is mediated within the triad, including potentiality of creative-finding. Also, triads are temporal; they have a past, present, and future. I and Thou as agents communicate regarding events, past, present, anticipated or sought. Thou recalls thinking through a problem in the past before speaking with I about It. Or, I and Thou could be puzzling about a possible shared goal, purpose. Should we invest our resources in a business venture later this year? Temporality includes a Background and a Foreground. The Background is recalled, and the Foreground is present and anticipated future events. Further, the triad is also to some degree stable. Facing contemporary problems in the Foreground, habituation guides us to solutions, or we recall that what we learn from others shows ways of approaching and solving the problem. "Habituation" and "ways" rely on solidar, stable relations for their formation and reliability. In the temporal, triadic structure of our lives we find both solidarity and stability.

Potentials of the members of the triad

Consider one additional aspect of the triad, the characteristics each member brings to the triad. In a straight forward sense, each I and Thou is a person we meet in everyday life, and the It is, as we have noted, the habitat and culture in which the persons live. Tom and Dee are persons having dinner in a restaurant and sharing their memories of their children. And, the four members of the quartet playing the Messiaen are persons interacting musically with musical instruments in their hands in a concert hall. Looking closer we find that each member brings to the triadic relationship a Background and a Foreground. That Background, formed from birth, influenced the Foreground of Tom and Dee as they creatively-find.[30] The potentials of I and Thou are at least what persons as persons bring to the triad. Without developing a full theory of the person, a person has at least potentials that which a person is able to do in a situation that calls for it. A list of potentials must include at least acting, sensing, reasoning, remembering, imagining, desiring, willing or initiating actions, emoting, oughting, and feeling, and aesthetic and religious appreciation.[31] Regarding persons, the agency potential to will means they can choose among genuine options. As persons, they are free. As they develop their activity potentials within a triad, their personalities develop. Yet, even though their personalities are highly influenced by the triad, their freedom and powers of reflection transcend it, allowing persons to identify, reflect on, and choose among, change or modify options.[32]

Regarding the It, we also find potentials, though they are too numerous to cite. Consider the musical instruments, especially the cello. It came to the hands of the performer from the hands of an artisan who realized that rosewood or boxwood make excellent tuning pegs, ebony for the fingerboard, maple for the neck, maple for the body of the cello, maple for the back (or willow, poplar, or sometimes beech if the "back is made from a single piece of quarter-sawn wood"[33]), spruce for the table, and ebony, pearwood, and poplar for the inlay or purfling. The cello maker recognized the aesthetic and structural potentials of these woods for an instrument that has the potentials to make aesthetically interesting sounds sought for by the discerning cellist. The beauty of the cello movement in the Messiaen is the result of these potentials realized in the hands of the artisan and musician; it arises in the interaction of I-Thou-It (including materials and causes). In the triad, "It" interacts with other members of the triad for the purpose of sustaining and promoting human life. Look further at triadic knowing.

Triadic Knowing

I shall argue that all our knowing is mediated by triadic structure of everyday living, I, Thou, It.[34] Let me explain.

In All Our Knowing there is a Believing Other People

For any solipsist to secure the claim of epistemic solipsism and overcome it to reestablish contact with the world, as Descartes attempted, contact with the social and non-social world must be assumed; we must believe other persons, our companions. As we grow up and live in the culture of our society we learn its language, its knowledge, its ways. Americans learn the English language, science, mathematics, literature, history, civics, how to balance a checkbook, and to believe in private property. As we learn these along with habits and skills, we come to know, to possess the knowledge of our culture.

Our knowledge may be either direct or indirect. Direct knowledge is unmediated; it is "the direct and immediate apprehension of truth."[35] By this we mean that a direct apprehension does not call for evidence to show that what one directly apprehends is the case. In apprehending a contradiction one does not need evidence to show that the law of non-contradiction is the case. To seek evidence for a direct knowledge claim requires that one accept it as one advances the evidence. As one looks at a piece of paper one does not need evidence to oneself that one is observing a piece of paper.[36]

Indirect knowledge is mediated. Mediation could refer to the work of concepts or first person sensory mental events through which a mind comes into contact with an object. For example, John heard the Messiaen Quartet mediated through his first person sensory mental events. The problems begin to arise as we think of knowing as the relation between a knower and a known, or more specifically, the relation between the John's first person sensory mental events and an object, such as the 1795 English cello in the hands of the cellist playing the Messiaen quartet. How show that what one is experiencing corresponds to or is identical with what is actually occurring independently of the events in one's mind? For a philosopher such as Descartes or Locke the problem is how to penetrate the veil of my sensory data and grasp directly the external world. If we can only see the external world *through* our sensory data, how can we check its accuracy? Looking at the problem more closely we find a deeper difficulty. The problem of perception is framed by the solipsism resulting from the search for new foundations. The radical skeptic led us into the thickets of first person sensory mental events without a map to guide us out. After arriving at this destination it is reasonable to ask if we have made a wrong turn.

Second, mediation could refer to the relation between knowledge and society. All knowledge is mediated through society. A mind becomes aware only within the language and physical circumstances of a society. Consider our reflecting on knowledge that leads to saying that in all knowing there is a believing other people. Take as an example the traditional definition of knowledge, "Knowledge as justified true belief." That definition cannot occur in the isolation of solipsism but only in the company of other persons living in a society in a particular locality. All believing is at least a "pro-attitude" about some object. It is easy to think of that attitude being only mine. It is mine, but it is not *only* mine. Philosophical reflections about my believing arise as questions are raised by me in company of my companions, and I formulate my answers with those companions in mind. The company of inquirers that accompanies me as I reflect on my believing includes those in the past who have thought carefully about believing, those in the present who press the issue, as well as those in the future who may learn something from my reflections. Further the form of my reflections is mediated through my society in which the form is also guiding the reflections of my companions. Reflecting within the form of Aristotelian logic or modern empirical science is a case in point. The same is the case for my reflection on justification and truth. My reflections are enmeshed in the history of investigations of knowledge, present study, as well as future expectations that occur in society.

The process and form of reflection is social, and so is the content of the reflection. Insofar as I attempt to state my reflections and to communicate them to others, I draw on words. Those I choose are those used in my society, those used by others who have engaged in similar reflections. The words carry meanings common to my companions and refer to objects all of us recognize. More occurs than my choosing words from among those used in my society to refer to common objects. I expect that they will also refer to the words in the minds of my fellows, words they use to refer to the same objects and defined in the same way.

The process, form, and content of reflection also occur in doubting as I develop a skeptical argument. My companions understand what I am saying as I express my doubts about knowledge. They are able to join me in evaluating the strength of a knowledge claim. Whether they agree with me or disagree with me, I and my company share the process of reflection as well as its form and content. We belong to the same society. A significant conflict may occur between the Background and the Foreground, but conflict can be something for us only within the company of my companions and a common language. Neurath's plank remains. It is composed of Thous with a common language, a common body of knowledge weaving through the fabric of a culture.[37]

In All Our Knowing There is a Believing Regarding an It

As I and my companions communicate within a common language, we refer to objects by directing our collective attention to them. The experience of hearing the Messiaen quartet is deeply social. As we listen we directly hear the sounds, see the movements of the players, and are aware of the staging of the quartet, the semi-darkness of the concert hall and the bright lights focused on the players. Also, we indirectly know that we are in a concert hall, the kinds of instruments being used to play the music, possibly the structure of the Messiaen quartet. We can read the printed program. The words and concepts I use to refer to objects and events: the concert hall, violin, viola, clarinet, cello, the sounds were communicated to me by the society in which I live. The words and concepts are also social. The ones I use are also used by other members of my society in situation, similar to my present one. What I hear refers to the sounds of the instruments, but their meaning refers to my society. As Niebuhr points out, "My knowledge

... seems to be through and through a social knowledge, even in its immediacy. It is not social in the sense that society is its object, but in the sense that it participates in the society's knowledge of objects."[38] Whether my comments about the quality of the performance are only my opinion, are a deeply held belief, or are a knowledge claim generated by thorough study of the Messiaen, they are mediated by society.

Furthermore, the interrelation of the I and Thou always involves a common object. The objects to which we refer include everyday cultural objects such as cellos, violins, sounds, concert halls. Our objects are also norms, standards, values, goals. We shall call these Causes.[39] Social relations are more complex than I-Thou relations alone. Both Mead and Buber corrected the Cartesianism assumed by Schutz, but they ignored the third term in the relation, an It. "Its" are also complex. They include at least causes and norms. Regarding causes, all social relations between two or more people involve that for sake of which they come together.[40] As Tom and Dee share their memories of their children they assume the reliability of their memories *about* their children. If they discussed a recent biography of George Washington, they would share a third, an object (in this case a person) to which their statements refer.[41] In addition, their conversation is governed by norms. We shall say that a norm is a principle or standard governing activities to which it applies. We can say that a person's thinking and behavior are governed by a variety of principles. The same is the case regarding the conversation between Tom and Dee. Their love for each other and for their children governs the words they use, the tone of voice, the body language, for example.

Social relations also involve norms, including rational and social ones. Look again at Tom and Dee deep in conversation over dinner at their favorite restaurant. That each understands what the other is saying indicates that their conversation is governed by principles of reason, such as the law of non-contradiction. Their speech is internally consistent. Though each speaks consistently, they are not conscious of doing so. As they speak they often do so elliptically and metaphorically. Not everything they mean is stated; drawing on their background of growing up in Texas, they speak sometimes using metaphors that only they and others with similar backgrounds would understand. Broader, social norms govern their way of dining. The contrast between their behavior and that of a typical Chinese couple makes the point. Tom and Dee have at least their own napkin, knife, fork, and spoon. Each is served an individual meal on an individual plate. And they sit across from each other, usually at a small square or rectangular table. Dining is individual. In China their counterparts have a small plate, a small bowl, a small cup, and chop sticks. They sit at a round table with a large surface rotating in the center. Food is placed on the rotating surface, and each would take from the various foods. Dining is communal. Clearly the norms governing dining in China are different than in the United States.

Further, Tom and Dee believe that each person in the marriage has equal rights. In the political process of electing governmental officials, each has the right to vote. Each can own property, such as homes, land, farms. If they lived in other societies, these rights may not be respected. From this we recognize that more is present in the conversation than the I and the Thou; norms, a third element, are also present. Emphasizing the place of norms in social relations, and particularly institutions, Parsons says, "Then in looking for the field of empirical facts with which the theory of institutions should be concerned, I should concentrate on those uniform modes of behavior and forms of relationship which are 'sanctioned,' that stand in some kind of significant relation to normative rules to a greater or lesser degree approved by the individuals subject to them. . . . It is in the particular feature of being related to norms that the institutional aspect of these uniformity's lies."[42]

In addition to norms and causes, the It can refer to the environment in which social relations occur. To grasp the complexity of the environment, distinguish among habitat, culture, and environment. By *habitat* we mean the natural setting of human existence, "the physical features of the region inhabited by a group of people; its natural resources, actually or potentially available to the inhabitants; its climate, altitude, and other geographical features to which they have adapted themselves."[43] By *culture* we refer to "that part of the total setting that includes the material objects of human manufacture, techniques, social orientations, points of view, and sanctioned ends."[44] And by *environment* we refer to "[humans] . . . in [their] . . . natural and cultural setting."[45]

From this analysis of our ordinary lives we can now see that its structure is triadic and that members of the triad bring their potentials to their relationships. The development of these potentials depends on the agency of an I in concert with the potentials of Thou and of It. As the various woods are selected and gathered by the discerning woodsman and formed by the cello artisan into a cello, the potentials of individual persons are also selected and formed by the individual and the other members of the triad. As no cello without the potentials of various woods developed by the artisan, no personality without the potentials of the person developed by herself and the other members of the triad. Furthermore, as knowing develops it does so within the triad. In all knowing there is a believing the knowledge of a society of me and my companions regarding an It.

Thus, recall James' "fullness of practical life." First, it is inherently social. This means that the starting point for all philosophical study is *within* someone's experience, broadly conceived. But how is this best understood? It is clear that Bowne believes that three elements are always present in experience, an I, a Thou, and a common object, a triad. Human self-consciousness develops only within experience, in the midst of events, of things in the world, of other persons, and their communication, reflection, correction, certification, and guidance. This means that as experience becomes something for us, and not simply undergone, we find that it is inherently triadic in structure composed of ourselves, other persons, and a third element, things, events, causes, norms: succinctly, I, Thou, and It.[46] Skepticism can be formulated only within experience. Though we find ourselves within experience, issues of knowledge and conduct arise as different aspects within experience conflict, requiring recognition, interpretation, and action. In this way this empiricism avoids Cartesian methodological skepticism, but it does not avoid skepticism altogether. As we listen to the music of Messiaen we are aware of the individual members of the quartet and the audience around us. There can be no conscious reflective experience apart from a social/cultural context.

Trust and the Triadic Structure of Experience

Most of us claim that we trust our individual experience, but we have not looked for trust in the triadic structure of everyday living.[47] To do so, consider one important aspect of the activity of persons, believing. Discussions of believing revolve around two different senses of the term. One is the *"feelings of certainty or uncertainty* that accompany our action when we hold something to be true; the other is concerned with the *activity of trusting in someone or something.*"[48] This can be further refined: the former is the "conviction of truth or reality of a thing based on grounds insufficient for positive knowledge," and the latter is the "state or habit of mind in which trust is placed in some person or thing."[49]

Consider the former meaning. To pursue an understanding of trust into the inner life of feelings of certainty and uncertainty leads us into a realm that is inherently unsteady. Feelings come and go, they are fleeting, and they strengthen and weaken without warning. If we attempt to compare one feeling of certainty with another we find no basis for distinguishing among them. To secure a claim of truth on a belief that in turn rests on feeling is to tie it to sand. Niebuhr is surely correct that "the inquiry into the nature or degrees or grounds of these feelings seems to involve us in solipsistic inquiries and in the making of arbitrary definitions that do not lead beyond themselves."[50]

Turning to the second meaning, we find a more fruitful avenue to understand of believing or trusting. Person A makes a knowledge claim to B regarding C. This claim will be either direct or indirect knowledge. Direct knowledge occurs without mediation, and indirect knowledge occurs with mediation. Direct knowledge of C occurs in the present, as in "I now directly apprehend this piece of paper" from which I read. Knowledge claims are about some persons, events, or states of affairs other than the knowledge claim itself. That is, knowledge claims are inherently contextual and are about some aspect of that context or the context itself.

We have seen that little of what we know is direct knowledge, but when direct knowledge does occur it is mediated by our cultural understanding of what counts as a piece of paper. The object I am looking at becomes known by me as a piece of paper as I learn from others a language that refers to the object. Though the senses are our avenue to the world and our cognitive powers give us capacity to interpret and organize what the senses give us, the content of the work of our sensory and rational powers, the meaning dependent on that work, lies beyond the structured and interpreted mental events and activities; it is derived from the Background and Foreground of the community of which we are a part. That all knowledge claims are mediated by language means that language is deeply social, that any knowledge claim implies a triad, I-Thou-It.

Note at this point that the recognition of our dependence on language for knowledge claims does not imply a cultural relativism or skepticism. It does mean that in all our knowing the language, definitions, and traditions of our society enter from the beginning. Human consciousness develops only within the Foreground, in the midst of other persons and events, of things in the world, communication, reflection, correction, certification, and guidance. This means that as experience becomes something for us, and not simply undergone, we find that it is inherently triadic in structure composed of ourselves, other persons, and a third element, things, events, causes, norms: I, Thou, and It.[51] Experience also includes both the Background and the Foreground.

Consider an important distinction, that between believing and trusting. Up to this point we have used trust and believing interchangeably. We shall use belief in relation to knowledge claims and trust in relation to persons. Each person remains at a distance from what she says. Let me explain. As we discuss knowledge we assume the standard definition, knowledge is justified true belief. In this sense belief is at least a pro-attitude toward the claim. It is a degree of feeling of certainty. Not wanting to leave belief and knowledge claims in the unformed morass of solipsistic feelings, we seek evidence, in principle available to everyone, that our feelings of confidence are sound. In this way we publicly secure our knowledge claims. When a knowledge claim is made, we either accept or reject it. Sometimes we discover new knowledge, but usually we learn what others have learned and pass on to us. The field of science is a case in point. A student learns the field of chemistry that in turn provides the Background for continuing research and discovery. Fortunately, the student does not have to start at the beginning and rediscover the whole body of knowledge that is chemistry. In this sense the student believes the knowledge taught to her and believes the professors who know the field. The professor is the authority for the student. Believing is inherent to knowing any field of science.

Trust can be further distinguished from belief. What students learn they accept on authority of their teacher. In all acts of believing a body of knowledge on the authority of a teacher, we find an additional attitude, trust. Trust is not placed in a teacher or authority as *knower* who is believed to be an authority. Rather, it is placed in a *person* who is a knower. This means that the relation of the teacher to the student is fundamentally moral. The student trusts the teacher, and the teacher trusts the student. In trusting an authority we implicitly acknowledge the presence of a person in whom trust is placed. In the I-Thou relation, I in trusting Thou finds itself in "the reciprocal action of I and Thou in which an I trusts a Thou and so acknowledges the latter as a person—one who has the fidelity-infidelity of moral personality."[52] All knowledge in a culture directly or indirectly occurs within the triad and rests on the reciprocal relation of trust: *fides, fiducia,* and *fidelitas* (believing, trust, loyalty). "Trust is a response to an acknowledgement of fidelity."[53] With insight, Niebuhr notes that "fides (believing) is the phenomenal element which is largely based on the fundamental interaction of *fiducia* (trust) and *fidelitas* (loyalty or fidelity)."[54] It may turn out that a person or persons are not trustworthy and Its as objects are misunderstood or ephemeral. But distrust and skepticism can be held only within the initial trust placed in persons as persons. Basic to the "conviction of truth or reality," whether or not supported by sufficient grounds, is placing trust in some person, who advances a knowledge claim, or thing regarding a person or object.

What we have said to this point could be construed as occurring only in the Foreground. If so, one could argue whether an I is justified in placing trust in a Thou. This shifts the argument away from the place of trust in the triad to the problems surrounding justification of initially placing trust in another person. Most commentators on trust, including Hollis, take the latter approach.[55] However, to do so ignores the underlying interpersonal and moral framework within which the discussion occurs. The nature and structure of that underlying interpersonal framework is central to the argument of this work.

Trust is present in what we call the Foreground. As we weigh whether to place trust in another, we find Hollis' discussion illuminating. But, we claim, the reciprocal relation of trusting in fidelity pervades the Background. The Background forms from birth, possibly earlier, and continues through change until death. Though deeply influenced by our biological inheritance, our DNA structure, that influence is not determinative for our Background, except in a boundary line sense, like shoulders on the sides of a six-lane highway. That structure is given to us as potentialities. Our potentialities both open us to possibilities but also close us to others. For example, a tone deaf person will not be able to master the cello and play the cello solo in the Messiaen. We have our limits. The potentialities of the It are developed in the context of an I-Thou relation. And, as we have seen, that relation is trusting. This means that both the initial formation and the continuance of the Background rest on the reciprocal relation of trusting in the fidelity of other persons.

In summary, insofar as a culture exists, central to which is a body of knowledge, the reciprocal relation of trusting in fidelity occurs in a triadic relation among persons in relation to objects. Insofar as we hold for true any claim, we do so mediated through the web of our relationships with other persons' Foreground and Background and our world. A belief about X, insofar as it is meaningful to me, is mediated through language and is inherently social. We learn language from persons with whom we are reciprocally related in fidelity. As we communicate, we acknowledge other persons and trust they can and will understand what we are saying. As we add "justified" to true belief, we find that trust is also present. Evidence is something for us only through language, which is also rooted in acknowledging other persons and trusting them. So we see that trust is inherent to persons communicating and knowing their world within the triadic structure of experience.

Trusting and Oughting

Furthermore, triadic trust is inherently moral. Is ought rooted in the relation of trust, and if so, in what way? Yes; let's see. Trusting is a reciprocal relation of trusting, loyalty, and trustworthiness between an I and a Thou regarding an It. That reciprocity implies promising to be loyal. As the student-teacher relation is trusting, each is obligated to live up to that trust, to be trustworthy, and loyal to the other person. There is no trust apart from fidelity; trust is the response to fidelity. The relation is reciprocal. The student's trusting the teacher and the teacher trusting the student continues as both are faithful, worthy of the other person's trust, loyal to the other. Responding to trust and acting trustworthily, implies promising; one tacitly assumes an obligation in which one is saying, "I ought to keep my promise to be trustworthy." As one enters into the reciprocal relation of mutual obligation, one chooses one course of action rather than another. Exercising freedom to promise, not to promise, or to break a promise, also exercises the potential of oughting. The decision to keep promises also implies a kind of mutual self-renunciation, a self-emptying. This means that perceived self-interest when in conflict with mutual promise keeping must be renounced. In freedom, oughting and self-emptying, one becomes a moral self, a person.[56] Trusting and loyalty are always found together. A baby born to parents has the potentiality to trust that is called forth and formed. At this pretheoretical level, trusting on the part of the child is at the deep level of sensibility, which is often thought of objectively as dependence. That dependent relation is trusted/promised to be stable. The parent/authority promises to be faithful and the child trusts them. They are its authority, and the child trusts what the authority teaches. The trusting relation is a relation of promise keeping. Consider the structure of trust in *fides, fiducia,* and *fidelitas* (believing, trust, loyalty). We have noted the place of trust in the interaction of persons in relation to a cause. We trust that the other person is loyal, faithful. In that relation the self can choose to remain faithful or to be unfaithful. If one is unfaithful, a promise is broken.

We see this especially as the personality of a person develops within the interrelation of *fides, fiducia, and fidelitas.* Succinctly, persons become moral persons in the act of freely trusting in the trustworthiness of another and in the act of promising, entering into an obligation. In trust and fidelity or trustworthiness, one is free to choose to be unfaithful, disloyal. In the relation of believing, trust, and fidelity, persons become persons only in the triadic social relation where they believe some authority and the authority is loyal.

As long as the parties freely choose to be loyal, trustworthy, and promise keeping, the solidarity of the Background and Foreground of each remains intact, as well as that of the society. However, if the fiduciary relation is violated, what one has gained through the trusting relation, now in the Background, is inconsistent with the Foreground. Disunity and instability result, both in society and in the individuals in meeting.

In the triadic relation all promises imply ought. As persons make a promise to be loyal to others, they imply that they ought to be faithful. There could be no relation of trust without the implication of ought on the part of each self. This means that ought arises and is formed only within meeting, within the triadic relation of I-Thou-It.

Compare this view with that of Levinas. Levinas's Other Disruption tends to be individualistic, person to person. Assuming the individualism of Cartesiansim, he grappled with the problem of intersubjectivity and the place of ethics in our lives. Challenging the ontology of Totality, the other as exterior confronts the ego with "you ought." Ethics is a relation; ethics is not imposed on a relation.

In contrast, we observe that ought is found only in the triad; it does not emerge only as the poor, the widowed, the fatherless address a fully formed person. In the reciprocal relation, where I and thou mutually trust each other and are faithful and trustworthy in relation to a cause, persons are formed as moral beings. Individuals bring their potentialities to the triadic relation within which the moral potentials (ought, will, and choice) are formed and grow. Thou potentials are individual; development of them is relational. The emergence of ought and its development is rooted in the triad of "I and You ought to X with regard to Y." Ought rests in the potentiality of the I and the Thou, and finds its particular formation in trust, *fides, fideliltas, fiducia* of a society and culture. We act on *fides* and seek understanding through reflection on and interpretation of our lived world (not radical reflection). In addition, solidarity is rooted in memory and in causes (such as goals) that give us hope. In memory, trust (faith), and cause we find the roots of solidarity.

Oughting and Transcending

Within the triad of I, Thou, and It, we find "believing in beings who keep faith."[57] Keeping the faith is oughting, accepting the moral obligation to be faithful to the one who is also faithful. In the reciprocal relation of trusting, the call of another to recognize a Thou and It is the beginning of the formation of the moral subject. It is the first manifestation of "oughting." Pithily, Bowne remarks that ". . . the social order is the only thing which makes individual development possible . . ."[58] Trusting calls forth the potentiality of moral ought. Actualizing the moral capacity implies freedom, memory, trust, self-renunciation for the sake of Thou, Cause, and hope (time and change being common aspects of each), all developed in a stable natural world, in the triadic relation of the potentialities of I and Thou in relation to each other and to a cause.

Deeply rooted in trust and ought, we also find transcendence. Let me explain. In any act of knowing, such as moral knowing, we believe the moral knowledge of our society through persons we trust. As we learn that other persons should be respected, we do so via persons whom we trust. In trusting, we acknowledge other persons, specifically the one teaching the moral lesson. Acknowledging another person with whom one has entered a reciprocal relation of trusting and faithfulness implies the freedom of either member of the triad to violate that trust. It also implies the obligation to tell the truth. To violate a trust is to do what one ought not to do, to tell a lie rather than the truth. Further, and here we move closer to transcendence, by which we mean that the freedom of the person to be or not to be faithful is beyond the range of concepts or any formulizing procedure. This is the Achilles heel of foundationalism. In the triadic relation of trust and ought, persons who call or who respond to a call as moral subjects are mutually transcendent. Their personhood as trusting beings who can freely break their promises is beyond the totalizing capability of reason. Since metaphysics, specifically that of Rationalism, rests on the rational capacity of the mind and seeks through a concept to gain insight into reality and to say what it is, we can say that metaphysics is totalizing. That approach means that everything, all of reality can be reduced to metaphysics, whether epistemology, ethics, aesthetics, not to speak of the "fullness of practical living." If the rational approach were taken to trusting and oughting of the free person, we should expect to come to a full rational comprehension of persons, particularly of moral beings. The triadic relation of trusting and oughting would be reduced to comprehension, understanding, knowledge. The ethical relation would then be a rational relation. Ethics would be a way of knowing.

However, if our analysis so far is correct, the act of knowing rests on a prior and more basic reciprocal relation of believing, trusting, oughting, and self-restraint or self-emptying, *kenosis*.[59] As the person responds to a call to know, she responds freely, with trust and fidelity to a Thou, bound by mutual promising. "You ought" is a call to enter into the reciprocal relation of co-knowers bound by promises to keep the reciprocal obligations of trusting as each makes or attacks knowledge claims within the book of knowledge of a society. In the I-Thou-It relation, neither member can be brought under a concept and fully grasped by it. By *kenosis*, self-restraint, members of a triad empty themselves of the desire to control any other, including through the totalizing power of Being or Rationalism, leaving an awareness of a person of infinite mysterious moral ought over against the others. Ethics in the fullness of practical living is more fundamental than any totalizing activity of reason.[60]

Before we move on, pause to note that this understanding of the relation of ethics and reason provides an interesting insight into some recent attempts to rationalize, to domesticate the infinite, the transcendent. Rationality arises in many forms, among which are classical logic, modern logic, technological reason, and modern biological science. Classical logic appealed to ideas that allow us to group together things having a common characteristic. As the pre-Socratics sought the nature of *phusis* they did so using that logic. *Phusis* is water, Thales declared. And if so, how can fire, earth, and air find their place within the concept? In what sense can water be the common element in them? Interestingly, motivated by the religious issue of the nature of *phusis*, he used his intelligence (*intus legere*) to fully comprehend it, to gain insight into it. Thales' concern with comprehension ignored the facticity of water, of water as water and its many qualities, and focused on the one characteristic that bound together everything. The One and the Many problem, we call it, is framed by the logic of the concept. In the modern period, some Europeans, enamored with Newton's success in mathematizing the universe, sought to rework logic following the ground breaking work of mathematicians. The Vienna Circle is a case in point. Hoping to find as much success in the social cultural sciences as mathematicians had in the natural sciences, they developed a powerful tool we know as mathematical logic or modern symbolic logic with its sentential and predicate calculus. The focus of that logic is on relations. What is ignored are characteristics of the x's and y's, supposedly persons and their life in society. Again, the mystery and infinity of the "fullness of practical life" is ignored as it is "comprehended," dominated through the theory of mathematical logic.

Technological thinking fares no better. In the contemporary world the moral self having been truncated, defined itself in technological terms. Gaining perspective from Descartes' *Discourse on Method, Part Two*, humans differ neither in freedom not reason. Their freedom is without bonds, as it is in God. In contrast, God's reason is infinite and human reason is finite and can act only within the narrow boundary lines of finitude. In the finitude of their reason all humans are alike; they differ in some possessing fruitful methods and some not. He then outlines his famous four step methodology. From there the story of reason is the chronicling of substantive rationality "being swept away by the onslaught of formal, practical, and theoretical rationalization processes." Reason is now dominated by "mere means-ends evaluation of self-interests" and forms the core of human identity.[61] Again, the moral self present in the "fullness of practical living" is submerged under the dominance of technological, procedural thinking. Epistemology controls, dominates ethics.

Some philosophers resisted institutionalized rationalism, though they could not completely break away. Dewey sought to restore experience but understood it in terms of concepts such as the scientific method, especially biology. The ethical was bound by the methodological, scientific, and epistemological.[62] Even the great Personalist, Borden Parker Bowne, spoke of a lower and a higher in the lives of persons. The lower includes physical nature, the instinctive, the animal, the half humanized. It is the realm of prejudice, passion, likes and dislikes, enthusiasm for worthless objects. Life lived in the lower ranges of human existence has "a strange deadness towards things revered and worthy. . . . It is the necessary outcome of our nature when uncontrolled by right reason."[63] Though Bowne's thought centers in the freedom of persons and in ethics, only right reason could guide the free will, and only through right reason can the ethical be understood.

Our conclusion that the ethical is fundamental to the rational is similar to Levinas' view. The central difference is that he assumes Cartesianism and finds morality in the call of the Other, and transcendence in the face of the Exterior. We reject Cartesianism and find not only the I-Thou relation but more fully the I-Thou-It relation. Therein, we find the call of the Other in reciprocal trust, and the transcendence in the mystery of the free Thou in relation to an equally mysterious It. Neither can be totalized by reason. The reciprocal relation is not only "about"; it is also "in." In the triad each member resisting the violence of rational Totality is mysterious, and transcendent in its otherness.

ESTABLISHING

Knowing is mediated through at least one triad. Yet, in mediation each triad is interlaced with other triads. All mediating structures are triadic. Recognizing that brings into bold relief the *topos, Persons-in-triadic-trusting-relation.* Living deep in our cultural, historical Background, in the twilight zone of forgotten-remembered, through recollective imagination, creative-finding, the *topos* is recollected. Pervading all other master narratives, the *topos* shows the limitations of each. Can it be the Master Narrative, Authoritative, *vera narratio*? If so, it must meets four requirements: (1) answers the problem of being accepted without question, discussion, dissension yet accepted through critical reflection (the problem of legitimation is a limited but penetrating form of the same issue); (2) it is the *topos* to which all other *topoi* must appeal; (3) it legitimates connections within, between, and among triads, society/culture, nature, and the Ultimate Environment; and (4) is eloquent, tells the complete story. We believe the *topos* meets these tests. Here we shall show it meets the first and second requirements, and in the remaining chapters that it meets the third and fourth requirements. Having met the four standards, it overcomes suspicion and provides for *gnothi seauton*.

First, Master narrative must be accepted without critical discussion, yet be accepted through critical discussion. But how? To understand, focus on the problem of legitimation, specifically three points: ironically, *topos* is required for any rational argument against a *topos*; a *topos* implies an ideal that may or may not be eloquent; and triadic trust is an eloquent *topos*, a Master narrative.[64] On the one hand, arguments connect premises to a conclusion. To support the connections, they appeal to warrants and to backings. To support warrants and backings, they must appeal to something beyond the content and structure of argument, whether deductive, inductive, or pragmatic, to a *topos*, a perspective. On the other hand, a perspective implies the best way to relate, though a particular *topos* may not do so. For example, if you stand here you can understand better what's happening in the basketball game. Some perspectives allow telling a more complete story than others. Some perspectives are better than others. Finally, Triadic Trust is an eloquent perspective. It implies the ideal perspective for achieving self-knowledge, who I am, what I am, and what I should do. Thus far in the discussion, we have found the perspective, the master narrative and described its fundamental characteristic. The most eloquent perspective is the ideal justifying any knowledge claim to authority, in turn to legitimacy. The problem of legitimation, where a Master narrative implodes as the trust requirements the Narrative legitimates are turned on itself, at best is exposed as a straw man. The problem does not arise.

Turn to the second requirement. Master narrative is a *topos* within which all others find their completion. Generated through creative-finding, a *topos* allows us to identify and place in their proper relationships whatever comes into view, as in "now we can see how everything fits together." And, for limited narratives, *topoi* that cannot on their own fully connect elements internal to them, the Master narrative brings them under its perspective providing a more circumspect way of seeing for those *topoi* both internally and externally.[65] Master narratives of the past, Order and Emerging persons, failing to meet those requirements, exhausted themselves and lost their status. Order, as narrated by poets such as Homer and Hesoid, is a Master narrative that provides, authorizes, legitimates, connections among Background and Foreground through gods, fate, tradition, and power. Order understood by ancient Greek and Roman philosophers, is the work of Rationalism attempting to connect the One and the many, law, persons in society, and appearance and reality through dialectic, evidence, warrants, and the backing of Being and Rationalism. However, they fail to provide fairly for the poets "seeing as," *topos*, guiding selecting and integrating elements, unless Plato's denigrating treatment of poetry in the *Republic* Bk X provides proper guidance. Neither the poet's nor the philosopher's narratives of Order account for dignity and freedom of individual persons to choose among options. Order defines persons dyadically and ignores significant potentials of individual persons. If our analysis of Order as Master narrative is correct, though it was accepted as the widest, most inclusive topos, it turns out to be a limited narrative.

Emerging persons as Master narrative fares no better.[66] Powerful in the Renaissance, it accounts for individual persons, freedom to choose among options, including types of political, economic, religious, educational, media, regulations, and familial institutions. Contributing to the development of skepticism and a scientific understanding of natural world, it helped break up Order as developed in the High Middle Ages under the Church, freeing the natural world from its metaphysical bondage of final causes. As Emerging persons did so, it allowed for the development of a limited narrative, scientific naturalism. But, it could not provide the fuller understanding of an unlimited Master narrative. Emerging Persons was a limited narrative. It could not connect *res cognitans* and *res extensa*, solve the mind-body problem it generated. Further it cannot account for relations among other persons, relation to the natural and ultimate environments, or for stable authority legitimizing these relations. Yet it assumes Persons-in-triadic-trusting-relations for its articulation and further illumination. We contend that persons-in-triadic-trusting-relations, through its wider, more inclusive *topos*, is the most elegant Master narrative.

Third, the power to connect background and foreground, required for solidarity and stability, will be discussed in the following chapter. There we turn from triadic knowing to its context, triadic action within a triad, triads in relation to each other, momentary associations and societies with cultures. The fourth, the eloquence of Persons-in-Triadic-Trusting-Relations will be shown as we discuss our other environments and their interrelationships, the natural, social/cultural, the Personal.

CONCLUSION

We have argued that suspicion challenges and subverts the legitimacy of our cultural shell imploding its underlying authority, its commanding correctness as Master narrative. The Background of our culture now guides, but only through habituating our second nature. Searching for a new Master narrative, we find it in the fullness of present practical living, persons-in-trusting-triadic-relations or triadic trust. As *topos*, perspective, the Master narrative is an image, a metaphor framing the activities of lives. It is the center piece of our Book of Knowledge, identifying and integrating our social/cultural, natural, and ultimate environments. Succinctly, the Master narrative shows us that we are persons who develop personalities mediated in triads of mutual trusting guided by regnant ideals, purposes, and causes. Also, triads live in natural environments that are integral to meeting the needs of their members, developing their potentialities, and achieving their purposes. What is the place and role of the body, habitat, and natural expanse in self-knowledge?

Notes

1. *Topos* (Greek) means place, or *locus* (Latin), carrying with it a natural or social situation. It will be used along with "perspective" to mute the tendency in contemporary usage to understand "perspective" in terms of a dualism of language and object. For example, Marcel Proust's, *Remembrance of Things Past* (New York, NY: Random House, 1981) and Jacques Derrida, *The Postcard from Socrates to Freud and Beyond*, trans. Alan Bass (Chicago, IL: University of Chicago Press, 1987) show the Background-Foreground relation can be understood from many perspectives. If they are correct, no final "story" or Master narrative is salient. Rejecting dualism and

rooting in *topos*, we shall advance a Master narrative and show that it is the most complete story.

2. Jacques Lyotard introduced "metanarrative" into French philosophical discussion in *The Postmodern Condition: a Report on Knowledge*, trans. Geoff Bennington and Brian Massumi (Manchester, UK: Manchester University Press, [1979] 1984). Concisely, a metanarrative is a globalizing narrative about limited narratives; it is a Story about stories, specifically providing legitimacy. The Emerging Self is a story about persons emerging from a dead tradition, ignorance, and unquestioned authority to individual dignity, freedom, self-creation, understanding of nature, society, skepticism, science, and faith in God. For example, in this Story, Master narrative legitimates knowledge and action in the Reformation, the birth of science, political change, and educational reform, among others. The story of the Enlightenment can be understood as the story of progress through universal human reason legitimated by the Emerging Self Story.

3. *Merriam-Webster's Collegiate Dictionary*, 11th edition, *Merriam-Webster's Collegiate Dictionary*, 11th edition, 2005.

4. Donald Philip Verene views the Imaginative Universal, the Master Image, as of the whole. See his work on Renaissance Humanism, particularly, *Vico's Science of Imagination* (Ithaca, NY: Cornell University Press, 1981); *Philosophy and the Return to Self-Knowledge* (New Haven, CT: Yale University Press, 1997); and *Speculative Philosophy* (Lanham, MD: Lexington Books, 2009). Verene continues the philosopher's search for the whole through the Imaginative Universal, the first fruit of the imagination, not the Conceptual Universal. Though this chapter is heavily indebted to his work and personal conversations, it is not required that the Master Image be of the whole. It must be only of that which is necessary for connections between Background and Foreground that allow *gnothi seauton*.

5. Lyotard hails limited narratives. He says, "We no longer have recourse to the grand narratives—we can resort neither to the dialectic of Spirit nor even to the emancipation of humanity as a validation for postmodern scientific discourse. But as we have just seen, the little narrative [*petit recit*] remains the quintessential form of imaginative invention, most particularly in science." Lyotard, *The Postmodern Condition*, 60.

6. Lyotard, *The Postmodern Condition*, 60.

7. Lyotard, *The Postmodern Condition*, 41.

8. Borden Parker Bowne, *Personalism* (New York, NY: Houghton Mifflin, 1908), 20–21.

9. Borden Parker Bowne, *Kant and Spencer, a Critical Exposition* (New York, NY: Houghton and Mifflin Company, 1912), 131; note the presumption of trust.

10. The study of emotions is beyond the confines of this study. However, articulating a framework for any adequate theory of emotions is.

11. "What is a particular" and "what is a concept" are metaphysical questions. Widely debated since Plato and Aristotle, we take no position. We assume both are present in our knowing. For good surveys of recent work, see Bruce Aune, *Metaphysics, the Elements* (Minneapolis, MN: University of Minnesota Press, 1985); Brian

102   Chapter 3

Garrett, *What is this Thing Called Metaphysics?* (London, UK: Routledge 2006); Michael J. Loux *Metaphysics, a Contemporary Introduction* (London, UK: Routledge, 1998); and Peter van Inwagen and Dean W. Zimmerman, *Metaphysics: The Big Questions*. (Oxford, UK: Blackwell, 1998).

12. This is a deductive argument. If the premises are true, the form is valid, and the premises are relevant to the claim, the claim follows 100% of the time. Inductive arguments, on the contrary, are distinguished by their conclusions, though relevant to the premises, do not follow 100% of the time; the conclusions do not follow necessarily.

13. For a fuller discussion of warrants and backing, see Stephen Toulmin, Richard Rieke, and Allan Janik, *An Introduction to Reasoning* (New York, NY: Macmillan Publishing Co., Inc., 1979).

14. The following discussion is the logical basis for not accepting Hegel. It is also the basis for Personalism not reacting to Hegel.

15. Not needing the whole, we choose not to use "universal" for the Master narrative.

16. Donald Phillip Verene. *Vico's Science of Imagination* (Ithaca, NY: Cornell University Press, 1981), 81. Also see pages 69–94 where Verene discusses the imaginative universal, which he understands "(1) as a theory of concept formation. (2) as a theory of metaphor, and (3) as a theory of the existential conditions of thought" (69). Verene, *Vico's Science of Imagination*, 97.

17. The influence of Aristotle and Aquinas is strong. However, we do not consider the image to be that by means of which form is potential for the active and passive intellect. Rather, image, the work of the imagination, allows for "againness."

18. The theory of metaphor Vico uses contrasts the theory in which metaphor is understood in terms of likeness or similarity, both of which arise from Aristotle's view of metaphor, "Metaphor is the application of the name of a thing to something else . . ." (*Poetics* 1457b 910). In addition, the metaphorical basis for finding again or "againness" is ignored by H. H. Price, *Thinking and Experience* (Cambridge, MA: Harvard UP, 1953), chapters 2 and 3 and by Peter A. Bertocci, "The Essence of a Person," *The Monist* 61.1 (1978): 28–41.

19. See this in contrast to Plato's theory of recollection. See *Meno*, 81c–86c

20. Verene, *Vico's Science of Imagination*, 97.

21. Verene, *Vico's Science of Imagination*, 104. See *In Search of a Calling* (Macon, GA: Mercer University Press, 1995), 134–135.

22. See Verene, *Vico's Science of Imagination*, 105.

23. Reminiscent of Aristotle's understanding of making discussed in the *Poetics*.

24. Vico found through recollective imagination and the study of language, the Master Image, Jove.

25. Descartes says, ". . . even bodies are not properly known by the senses nor by the faculty of imagination, but by the understanding alone; and since they are not known in so far as they are seen nor touched, but only in so far as they are understood by thinking, I see clearly that there is nothing easier for me to understand than my mind." *Meditations*, 90–91. See also *Meditations*, 126ff.

26. The relation of *topos* to bodily actions will be discussed in the next chapter.

27. Usually, persons live full, patterned, practical lives without distinguishing body, mind, soul, spirit, personality. These distinctions can be useful for therapists and psychiatrists; they become harmful under philosophical reflection that separates them for rational discussion, later attempting to reconnect them. The mind-body problem, for example. "Nature" chapter 5 focuses that issue.

28. Our experience is inherently social. Buber, Mead, and Vico recognize this, in contrast to individualists, such as Mill and Rorty, who do not. For a fuller statement of this position, see H. Richard Niebuhr, *Faith on Earth, An Inquiry into the Structure of Human Faith* (New Haven, CT: Yale University Press, 1989), 43–62

29. An activity potential is that which I, Thou, or It can do or be interpreted as when the proper occasion arises. Potential does not refer to that which can be actualized, as in Aristotelian metaphysics.

30. See Thomas O. Buford *In Search of a Calling* (Macon, GA: Mercer University Press, 1995), 134–135.

31. One reasonable candidate is the view of Peter A. Bertocci. Considering activity potentials rather than possibilities, he says that an activity potential is that which a person is able to do in a situation that calls for it. Persons have the following activity potentials: "sensing, remembering, imagining, thinking, feeling, emoting, wanting, willing, oughting, and aesthetic and religious appreciation." Peter A. Bertocci, "The Essence of a Person," *The Monist* 61 no.1(1978), 29.

32. Peter A. Bertocci, "The Person, His Personality, and Environment." *Review of Metaphysics*. no. 32,4 (June 1979), 605–20.

33. Robin Stowell (ed.), *The Cambridge Companion to the Cello* (Cambridge, UK: Cambridge University Press, 1999), 3.

34. In contrast to a direct perception of an object where nothing stands between perception and object perceived, "mediate" means to stand between, to connect, as a concept stands between, connects, and gives meaning to two individual sense experiences or two other propositions. An example of formal mediation is a standard form categorical syllogism, All S is P, All T is S, therefore All T is P; as the middle term, S stands between and connects T and P. Pragmatic mediation could refer to sensations becoming perceptions through habits of inference. Triadic mediation refers to one member of a triad standing among and connected by itself and the other two members. For example, I form an image or concept of myself, understood by me mediated by my Background and Foreground formed through language , concepts, and meanings learned from significant others whom I believe and trust. Triadic mediation is inherently social. Mediation is usually without our direct awareness of it.

35. Niebuhr, *Faith on Earth,* 32.

36. The analysis of the "fullness of practical living" reveals the triadic relation and the structures involved in it. This is not a new foundation, a new certainty, unless it is the practical certainty of our being alive in this place, time, and social circumstances.

37. Compare Josiah Royce's communities of interpretation. We have drawn on the work of H. Richard Niebuhr in developing this chapter. Niebuhr knew well Royce's

work. See Joseph Pagano, *The Origins and Development of the Triadic Structure of Faith in H. Richard Niebuhr* (Lanham, MD: University Press of America, Inc, 2005).

38. Niebuhr, *Faith on Earth*, 36.

39. Here we follow, in addition to Niebuhr, Josiah Royce. See Josiah Royce, *The Philosophy of Loyalty* (Nashville, TN: Vanderbilt University Press, [1908] 1995).

40. Niebuhr, *Faith on Earth*, 46–47.

41. We shall see later that the presence of a third participating in the relation also involves trust.

42. Talcott Parsons, "Prolegomena to a Theory of Social Institutions." *American Sociological Review* 55, no.3 (June 1990), 320.

43. Melville J. Herskovits, *Cultural Anthropology* (New York, NY: Alfred A. Knopf, 1960), 95.

44. Herskovits, *Cultural Anthropology*, 95.

45. Herskovits, *Cultural Anthropology*, 95.

46. Our experience is *inherently* social. Buber, Mead, and Vico recognize this, in contrast to individualists, such as Descartes, Mill and Rorty, who do not. Karol Wojtyla investigated the social relations of persons in community, focusing primarily on participation. But he did not discuss the triadic character of social life. See *The Acting Person*, trans. Andrzej Potocki (Dordrecht, NL: D. Reidel Publishing Company 1979), chapter seven, 261–300. For a fuller statement of this position see Niebuhr, *Faith on Earth*, chapters 3 and 4. For the historical background of Niebuhr's view, see Pagano, *The Origins and Development*.

47. In the following discussion, I am deeply indebted to Niebuhr, *Faith on Earth* For a similar view see Michael Polanyi, *Science Faith and Society* (Chicago, IL: University of Chicago Press, 1946). In contrast to Niebuhr, Polanyi does not recognize the triadic pattern of experience. Watsuji Tetsuro's discussion of Rinrigaku places trust at the core of Japanese Culture. His view differs significantly from the one presented here by its lacking a triadic structure with the accompanying freedom of the will and individual responsibility. That is, the individual gains her personal identity completely through the group. In our view the individual, though deeply formed by the group (the triad in which she lives), is nevertheless distinguishable through her capacity for transcending the group through reflection and for freedom of choice. Watsuji Tetsuro, *Rinrigaku,* trans. Yamamoto Seisaku and Robert E. Carter (Albany, NY: State University of New York Press, [1937] 1996).

48. Niebuhr, *Faith on Earth*, 31.

49. Niebuhr, *Faith on Earth*, 31.

50. Niebuhr, *Faith on Earth*, 32.

51. Our experience is inherently social. Buber, Mead, and Vico recognize this, in contrast to individualists, such as Mill and Rorty, who do not. For a fuller statement of this position see Niebuhr, *Faith on Earth,* 43–62.

52. Niebuhr, *Faith on Earth*, 47.

53. Niebuhr, *Faith on Earth*, 47.

54. Niebuhr, *Faith on Earth*, 48.

55. See for example, Martin Hollis, *Trust Within Reason* (Cambridge: Cambridge University Press, 1998). For a more circumspect view, and closer to the view developed here see Trudy Govier, *Social Trust and Human Communities* (Montreal, ON: McGill-Queen's University Press, 1997).

56. The place of promising in communication within the triadic relation is noted by Derrida. He says, "Each time I open my mouth, I am promising something. When I speak to you, I am telling you that I promise to tell you something, to tell you the truth. Even if I lie, the condition of my lie is that I promise to tell you the truth. So the promise is not just one speech act among others; every speech act is fundamentally a promise." J. D. Caputo, *Deconstruction in a Nutshell: A Conversation with Jacques Derrida* (New York, NY: Fordham University Press, 1977), 22–3.

57. Niebuhr, *Faith on Earth*, 41.

58. Borden Parker Bowne, *Principles of Ethics* (New York, NY: American Book Company, 1892), 139.

59. *Kenosis* is central to triadic trust. It is found in the triadic structure of human living. It is not only a theological event, though Yoder, Murphy and Ellis find *kenosis* the essential aspect of their theologies. See Nancey Murphy and George F. R. Ellis, *On the Moral Nature of the Universe, Theology, Cosmology, and Ethics* (Minneapolis, MN: Fortress Press, 1996), and John Howard Yoder, *The Politics of Jesus*, 2nd enlarged ed. (Grand Rapids, MI: Eerdmans, 1994).

60. In this both Kant and Levinas agree, though from different perspectives. See Emmanuel Levinas, "Is Ontology Fundamental?" chap 1 in *Entre Nous, Thinking-of-the-Other*. Trans. Michael B. Smith and Barbara Harshav (New York, NY: Columbia University Press, 1998), 1–11.

61. Stephen Kalberg, "Max Weber's Types of Rationality: Cornerstones for the Analysis of Rationalization Processes in History," *American Journal of Sociology* 85, no.5 (1980): 1176. See Buford, *In Search of a Calling*, 48–55.

62. John Dewey, *Reconstruction in Philosophy* (Boston, MA: Beacon Press, (1920) 1957).

63. Borden Parker Bowne, *Principles of Ethics.* (New York, NY: American Book Company, 1892), 126–127.

64. Lyotard hails limited narratives. He says, "We no longer have recourse to the grand narratives—we can resort neither to the dialectic of Spirit nor even to the emancipation of humanity as a validation for postmodern scientific discourse. But as we have just seen, the little narrative [*petit recit*] remains the quintessential form of imaginative invention, most particularly in science." Lyotard, *The Postmodern Condition,* 60. Ideal as used here does not imply the assumption of an ordered series with a terminus, such as does Plato, Aristotle, and later in the Great Chain of Being.

65. Lyotard points out that "the little narrative [*petit recit*] remains the quintessential form of imaginative invention, most particularly in science." *The Postmodern Condition,* p. 60.

66. The Master narrative of the Renaissance flowered into Personalism in reaction to the Spinoza-Leibniz debate in Europe during the eighteenth and nineteenth centuries, beginning with Jacobi (1743–1819), reaching maturity in the mid-nineteenth century with Hermann Lotze, and moving to America and Boston through Royce at Harvard, and Bowne, Brightman, and Bertocci at Boston University. Its two central forms are individualistic or monistic. In each, person is elevated from cultural emerging persons to metaphysical Person.

Chapter 4

Persons and Nature

Self-knowledge is an achievement of persons within and mediated by triads of persons mutually trusting each other regarding a cause. Self-knowledge is also an achievement of the body. Let me explain. Early in the search for self-knowledge, it became clear that our Background must be a reliable basis and guide into our Foreground. Suspicion blocked every attempt to provide reliable, legitimate connections. Seeking a way to allay suspicion, we turned to the fullness of practical living and found in it a structure, I-Thou-It bound stabilized by trust. Prompted by that insight, we sought and found an authoritative, moral Master Narrative, persons-in-triadic-trusting-relations. As the discussion continued, the natural world seemed pushed into the wings; I-Thou-It, trusting-triads, took center stage. However, the body intriadic-trusting must not be ignored. No body, no trusting-triad; trusting-triads are laced with the body.

However, if we were to embrace contemporary Western philosophical culture that habituates us to the faltering influence of Cartesian dualism, self-knowledge would be on the mind, and its relation to the body would be problematic, at best. Speaking of "my" body would be puzzling. Accepting our lives as mind and body, and the issue would be the relation between mind and body, action and movement. Pursuing that issue leads into philosophical *cul-de-sacs*. Within the *topos* of persons-in-trusting-triadic-relations, however, the question is not the relation of mind and body. The question is the best understanding of persons, their bodies, habitats, and natural expanse as viewed from the perspective of the Master Narrative. With that understanding, we can then speak of the whole person seeking to know what she is, what she is to be, and what she is to do.

We shall focus three topics. First, we begin with the appeal of dualism within our practical living. Next, we discuss philosophical dualisms, including those developed within *phusis*, the relation of God-Being to creation, and the mind-body relation. Each is a cul-de-sac. Finally, choosing not to follow roads leading nowhere, and entering into the Master Narrative, persons-in-trusting-triadic-relations, we address the question of how best understand the natural and its place and role in triads of trust. We shall show that the natural is as integral to the triad as are causes and persons. Turn first to the appeal of dualism.

APPEAL OF DUALISM

Everyday Dualism

Dualism originates in breaks in everyday living, from awareness of them to contrasts. Recalling living since morning, we could generalize and say that we got out of bed, dressed, ate breakfast, and went to work. Detail could be added. We ate four fried eggs, eight slices of bacon, three buttered cat-head biscuits, churned butter, blackberry jam, and four cups of hot coffee. Our normal living continues until we become aware of potential difficulties. For example, after a physical exam, my doctor tells me that being one hundred pounds overweight places my heart and blood pressure under stress that can lead to diabetes, high blood pressure, and heart failure. Making me aware of being overweight as a problem, he encourages me to change my diet and eating patterns. Becoming aware of the effects of eating patterns on weight and general health, we attempt to change those patterns. But, it is difficult.

We recognize that we control or influence some things, and some we do not. We recognize the relationship between food and body weight; by eating 8,000 calories a day, the human body will increase in weight. That we cannot control. However, the relationship between our awareness of a problematic eating habit and our doing otherwise is under our control. Eating habits lie deep in our Background. Changing them is under our control. Other examples present themselves. We can influence our health, the directions our lives take, our relations with other people and the natural world, and our relations to institutions. However, resisting our efforts includes adding four inches to the height of a full grown person, defying gravity, a deaf person hearing the voice of a child, flying without assistance, acting without a context, thinking while brain dead, and stopping a hurricane. Thus, everyday living guided by habit and thoughtful choice disturbed by difficulties leads to awareness and contrast of mental and physical events. Beyond awareness and contrast, philosophical reflection since the ancient Greeks led to interpreting contrasts as differences between mind and body and to exploring their relation, possibly their unity. We live as whole persons in triadic trusting relations; but awareness prompted by breaks in living structured by cultural monadic subjectivism, Emergence of Persons, the metaphysics of Being, and Rationalism, led to recognizing and interpreting them as mind-body philosophical dualisms. Historically, Western culture is characterized by two basic dualisms, construed along the lines of cultural dyadic objectivism and cultural monadic subjectivism. The former is a rift in the objective Order between higher mind and lower nature, the latter in the Emerging Self between minds and bodies.

Recognizing how mind-body dualisms develop in our living, their appeal is clear. We live as whole persons, yet our culture and its philosophical roots guide us to distinguish between mind and body in such terms as the voluntary and the involuntary, what we intend to do and what resists those intentions. Study of those differences led many philosophers to the dualism of mind and body. Our lived experience also pushes philosophers to account for wholeness. We contend that dualisms lead to philosophical cul-de-sacs.

Philosophical Dualisms

Philosophical dualisms arise as philosophers, whether ancient, medieval, or modern, construe mind-body differences within two assumed frameworks: the metaphysics of being and rationalism. Then, puzzled by problems dualism spawns, philosophers attempted to unify the differences without examining the structures they assumed. We shall discuss four topics: (1) *phusis*, the root of philosophical dualism, (2) philosophical dualism, (3) God-Being and the created order, and (4) modern mind-body relation. The first three are drawn from Order and its hierarchy in ancient and medieval cultures and the last from Emerging Self in the Renaissance and modern periods. Begin with nature birthing cosmic dualism among the Greeks.

Nature, the Root of Dualism

Religious beliefs prodded the ancient Greeks to interpret natural events occurring on farms, vineyards, births, eagles flying overhead at midday as acts of nature gods, the God Bacchus and vineyards, for example. Growing food expresses the power of the gods. The flight of the eagle expresses the will of a god. Dependence on food means dependence on the gods. Further, through the power of divination, priests read the particular flight of an eagle as a sign of the will of the gods. Or, divining the way of the gods in charge of food and communicating that way through stories helps to understand them. By aligning their lives with the way of the gods, crops grow, and life continues. Narrative wisdom recorded by such poets as Homer and Hesiod ranged from the origin of all things, the birth of the gods and men, their order, their way, to Fate, Moira, the order of all things and their proper place. Knowledge of the gods and the order of all things are needed for living, for food, births, marriage, organization of society, for every dimension of life. Ancient Greek religion assumed a unity in Nature, *phusis*, birthing or growing, common to gods and humans. Differences between the way of humans and of the gods encouraged religious dualism. All is *phusis*; nothing is apart from it, yet it accommodates multiple interpretations ranging from water, to air, to the unlimited (*to apeiron*), to forms.

No longer believing the wisdom of the poets, though deeply influenced by a culture energized and structured by religious belief, some lovers of wisdom reflected on an assumption deep in their religious beliefs, *phusis* or nature. Concerned with the origin and structure of all things, they asked what is *phusis*, or birthing, growing. It admitted many answers, yet everything is *phusis*; everything is like everything else; *phusis* is unity with diversity. *Phusis* manifests itself through differences in living; the differences in life lie in *phusis*. These pre-Socratic lovers of wisdom recognized the differences in living; to understand them they concentrated their critical intellect on *phusis*, and found the task puzzling. Heraclitus wrote, "Nature loves to hide," *phusis kruptesthai plilie*.[1] Whatever *phusis* might be, it is, it is One; nothing lies outside *phusis*, it always existed, never created; *ex nihilo nihil fit*.

Lived differences in the One became philosophical problems under the rational gaze of the Pre-Socratic physiologists. They assumed critical reflection had sufficient power to penetrate *phusis* and understand how all things could arise from and return to one source, as well as how the one is related to the many. The appearances of the many reveal the unity of "hiding" Nature, *phusis*. Answers ranged from quantitative monism and pluralism to qualitative monism and pluralism. Heraclitus thought *phusis* is one and changing according to fixed measure; Parmenides thought *phusis* is one and unchanging, necessary, permanent, and eternal. Formidable arguments persuaded subsequent philosophers to find a way to account for both One and Many, permanence and change. Soon another difference arose. Anaxagoras and Heraclitus believed mind of some sort pervaded *phusis*. Plato developed the first full-bodied philosophical dualism of mind and body.

Philosophical Dualism

Plato, in the *Phaedo*, said that Socrates' remaining in prison was not the movement of muscles in the body but the soul doing what is right and just.

Recognizing that difference, Plato viewed *phusis* broadly as soul moving and guiding the natural world. What is, is two, rational soul and body. The human intelligent soul and elemental body are microcosms of the macrocosm of intelligent soul guiding the organismic body. In *Timaeus* 29d-47e, Plato outlines his cosmic dualism of rational soul (the Demiurgos and the eternal forms as possibilities) and elemental body (*hyle*). The eternal forms are the possibilities of existence, and potentialities in the mixed world are grounded in the possibilities of existence, all achieved through the power of the demiurge looking to the Good, the eternal forms and persuading the Receptacle (*hyle*) to take into itself a likeness of the forms. The mixed world of permanence and change is created, and a dualism between rational soul and organic body is formulated. Plato follows the principle that the higher can affect the lower; but the lower cannot affect the higher. Form provides stable structure for the Receptacle, the changing and unstructured. Form is higher, and *hyle* is lower. Aristotle looking to the organic world rejected Plato's cosmic rational soul and body dualism and argued *phusis* is formed-matter. Asserting pluralism, each substance moves toward the fulfillment of its potentiality. Yet, Plato's cosmic dualism reappears in Aristotle as individual substances are moved or drawn by the beauty and goodness of the Unmoved Mover. The higher-lower principle underlying social structures appears as a metaphysical principle, particularly in Plato and Aristotle.

Plato set in place a cosmic dualism of rational soul and body. He did so by interpreting differences through the lenses of Being and Rationalism. Being, or the Good and each eternal form, is a Parmenidean *to eon*, one, necessary, immutable, and eternal. Sifted through the structure of the concept, each kind is a characteristic its instances share in common; in metaphysical language, a universal and particulars. Following the laws of thought supporting Rationalism, each essence is what it is, it cannot be anything other than itself, and it cannot both be itself and not itself. Further, the Receptacle, *hyle*, a bastard form of Being; having no structure of its own, takes on order and definiteness through mixture with Being. P*husis* is dual, Being and Receptacle.

Though, dualism understood as Beings through subject-predicate logic employed by Rationalism cannot be One, Plato sought their unity through participation. Logically, particulars can be brought under a concept on the basis of shared characteristics. Metaphysically, sharing characteristics under a concept means particulars participating in a universal. The particular would not be a particular without the universal. With Being and Rationalism, Greek philosophers effectively eliminated the possibility of relating Being and particulars, the One and the Many.

God-Being and the Created Order

Cosmic mind-body dualism becomes more complex as the Abram traditions merge with Greco-Roman philosophical culture. In that merger God and the created order form a new dualism. God is not *phusis*; God is the creator of *phusis*, of nature. God's creating action is free, not limited by potentialities grounded in eternal patterns (possibilities). The created order remains through God's power and love. This is a religious dualism. However, defending their views in conversation with Roman and Greek philosophers, Christian apologists such as Irenaeus, Origin, and Augustine found philosophical ideas helpful, particularly Stoic, Platonic as understood through Plotinus, and Aristotle's logic. To show the Christian God is stable and dependable, some apologists argued Plato's eternal forms are the patterns of God's thought. Greek philosophical dualism seemed to be consistent with Christian religious dualism. However, that proved to be problematic.

Greek metaphysical dualism developed in the philosophical exploration of a Greek religious datum, *phusis*, the source of everything outside of which nothing is. What occurs does so within *phusis*. It is eternal, whole, One; no creation out of nothing can occur. Creation can occur only with pre-existing materials. Whether eternal forms, soul, or organic body, it is *phusis*. Thus, philosophical conundrums arise. How can *phusis* be one and many, how can they be united, and what is the relation between the one and the many and lived life? Christian dualism lies in the contrast between God and the created order. God freely creates with no pre-existing materials.

The marriage between Greek thought and Christian theology proved to be turbulent. Amid its differences, Greek thought focused on *phusis*, birthing, of which Being and becoming are aspects. Christian thought focused on the sovereign God who freely creates an independent order, one that is dependent on the will and purposes of God. Specifically, Christians believe God, without compulsion or controlling goals, freely creates. God as free is person-like, is personal. Humans as creatures of God, share the characteristic of personal freedom of action. Acting freely, human persons are solely responsible for missing the mark (*hamartia*), for acting righteously. In contrast, Greek philosophers believed humans, defined and guided by reason; choose among options given to them, determining their options. Humans have no choice but to fulfill their essence, their best, though ignorance of that essence may keep them from doing so. Aquinas interpreted Christianity aided by the philosophical structure of Aristotle as Augustine did neo-Platonism.[2] In doing so, both Augustine and Aquinas faced the same problem. How can God be both Person and Being, free Creator and Being?

Abramic dualists offered a defense using philosophical Being and Rationalism. Augustine and Aquinas bequeathed two competing dualisms, one arising from *phusis* hiding and the other God freely creating. Both rest on philosophical understandings of religious data. These master apologists also bequeathed two views of free action, one radical and other limited. Later, in Descartes we see Christian dualism and Augustinian freedom, both contributing to the Emerging Self of the Renaissance and modern periods. They also contributed to modern dualism.

Pathway to Modern Dualism

Under the master narrative of Order, dualism appears early in Greek thought as the complexity of *phusis* is thought of as soul, as physical, one stuff with two manifestations. That distinction was developed by Plato into a microcosm, the soul and body of the individual are derived from the macrocosm, the universe, the whole, *phusis*, body and soul. Soul as rational can grasp the Good, and the body as becoming receives it structure from the Good. The rational soul acts freely within *phusis*, but only as it submits to the direction of the intellect. Knowledge is required for freedom. Rejection through ignorance, a fever, leads to the soul's death.

The body-mind distinction carried over into the Middle Ages but transformed by *creatio ex nihilo*. P*husis,* no longer bare soul and mind, is created, gifted Nature, gifted soul. Let me explain. Heraclitus' hiding nature allowed multiple interpretations. The gods guaranteed its order and justice. Nothing about *phusis* is moral; nothing about the earth giving birth to olives is moral. It simply does so. *Phusis* simply is birthing, growing. Under *creatio ex nihilo* Nature is a gift of God as is life in humans. The gift of life or soul created in the image of God is free, and according to Plato can challenge reason and the power of knowledge.[3] The soul made in God's image is free as God is free and superior in power to rational knowledge and whose essence is independent of created Nature or *phusis*. Two substances depend on God, soul and body, with God as creator of each, other than either, and that on whom both depend for their existence. Further, these created reals move teleologically toward the eternal exemplars in the mind of God. That view, articulated by Augustine, influenced Descartes, and introduced modernity one thousand years ahead.

The pathway to God is through the inner life, the life of the soul. Many Christians in the Middle Ages following Augustine's (fourth century CE) and Bonaventure's (thirteenth century CE) lead took the inward path to God, rejecting the outward path of the senses and the natural world. Many philosophers in the seventeenth century followed Descartes' path to defeat skepticism and achieve certainty through the inward path of *cogito ergo sum*. All other knowledge is problematic, including knowledge of the natural world. The Emerging Self as thinking thing, now isolated, seeks to know what is beyond itself. Descartes couples his epistemic dualism to the Medieval Christian view that God created two substances, *res cogitans* and *res extensa*, mental things and extended things. Modern dualism was born.[4]

Modern Mind-Body

A new kind of dualism emerged with the shift from ancient/medieval to modern culture, from hierarchy of cultural dyadic objectivism to individualism of cultural monadic subjectivism. Old individualism emerged within dyadicism.[5] New individualism, the Emerging Self of the Renaissance, marked the beginning of cultural monadic subjectivism. Though many contributed, Descartes' argument with skepticism and the search for certainty and understanding nature conducted by modern science set the framework for modern dualism.

Early modern scientists contributed to dualism by rejecting all but one of Aristotle's four causes, keeping only efficient cause. Rejecting final causes meant rejecting a purposive mind controlling natural events. Removing God's mind and purposes from nature's orderly processes opened the understanding of nature as bare fact to experimentation by scientists using new instruments, telescopes and microscopes, and employing mathematics. Old issues remained and new ones arose. Daily life continued to be problematic; memory of the Black Death continued to sting. Ocean voyages circumnavigating the earth led to challenge flat earth theories. Viewing the heavens through his invention, Galileo, with the telescope (early 1600's), now armed with experimental evidence, continued Copernicus' challenge of the geocentric view of the universe in favor of the heliocentric.[6] Harvey's *De Generatione Animalium* (1651) catapulted embryology from Aristotle into the modern world, and Janssen completed it with the invention of the microscope about 1590.[7] Gassendi's discussion of a corpuscular theory and the calculus proved invaluable to Newton's grasp of the physical world. The modern unveiling of nature began, its order and structure clearer, deeply impacted modern dualism.

Nature as bare fact, mindless, and inert stands over against dynamic Emerging Self. Modern dualism is formulated. As Descartes and experimental scientists charted new directions, and the medieval worldview fractured along internal metaphysical and external cultural stress lines, new philosophical problems arose. Mind-Body, perception, other minds, free-will determinism, language and reference, action and movement proved to be daunting. These gained prominence as thinkers began to accept the natural base of society and culture but also the role human intelligence plays in their formation, maintenance, and direction. Dualism became firmly entrenched in the modern mind. Unfortunately, the path of dualism leads us into various cul-de-sacs.

Dualism, Philosophical Cul-de-Sacs

Consider the first cul-de-sac. Once dualism is established, unity is elusive. Approaching specific philosophical problems, philosophers focusing on *phusis* assumed that a fuller understanding of Being and a better use of Rationalism will help solve them. Rationalism promises clear insight into Being and its relation to particulars. Plato formulated his cosmic dualism under their perspective. However, as nature or *phusis* lost its unity in dualism, neither Being nor Rationalism could help. To philosophers, *phusis* remained hidden; they continued to puzzle. In modern mind-body dualism, distinctions between mind as teleological and body as mechanistic, mind as intentional and body as non-intentional, mind as free will initiating cause and body as deterministic are articulated within the framework of Being and Rationalism. Mind and body are created substances. According to the laws of logic governing Rationalism, if x is mind, then it is mind. Either x is mind or it is not mind. X cannot be both mind and not mind. The laws of identity, excluded middle, and non-contradiction point to a logical gulf separating mind and body. We are natural beings, and we are minds. What relation bodies and minds may have is a conundrum. With no basis for crossing, the argument leads to a cul-de-sac. The unity of *phusis* remains hidden.

Look at a second cul-de-sac. *Phusis* is questionable as a basis for unifying a dualism. Pre-Socratic philosophers interested in what is true of all things, of all Nature, *phusis*, sought universality beyond the narrow range of religious poets, Homer and Hesiod. Rationalism and Being appeared to yield desired results. Yet, an assumption keeps them from it. Greek physiologists rejected claims of the poets, yet they rooted their views within the religious insights they reject. That is, the roots of philosophy lie deep in the religion of a specific culture. Its claims to universal truth beyond the limited views of the poets are blunted by their assumptions; they are limited to that culture. Assuming *phusis* or Nature and calling it Being understood through Rationalism appears to move the discussion away from limited religion and onto universal grounds. Nevertheless Being and Rationalism depend on a religious datum as a starting place. Though universalized by Rationalism as Being, phusis is at the bases of Olympian religion. Philosophers, not examining their presuppositions, rationally built their metaphysics of Being on the shifting sands of nature hiding, *phusis* of religion. *Phusis* as Nature is no more bare fact than any other unexamined religious assumption. *Phusis* as limited to a religion cannot be the basis for unifying a dualism. Dualism blindly enters a philosophical cul-de-sac.[8]

Consider a third cul-de-sac, one within nature. Philosophers and scientists continue the macrocosm/microcosm distinction; they distinguish a person's moving her arm up and down from a nerve reflex accompanying that behavior. Given that distinction among differences, what is the relation between the molecular structure of a nerve reflex and the observed up and down movement of one's arm? Could a macrocosm manifest a microcosm? What does "manifestation" mean? If the macrocosm emerges from the microcosm, what does "emerges" mean? Emerge is a description, not an explanation. A relation is claimed, but none has been established. A difference distinguished became two and nothing, apparently, could unify them.

Could a relation unite macrocosm and microcosm? If so, the evidence offered in support of a relation must be warranted. That is, the warrant must support connecting evidence and claim. There appears to be no scientific way to show a relation. If a scientist persists and appeals to a metaphysics such as Naturalism, a relevant connection can be supplied. Naturalism could support the connection by claiming that all connections among material or natural things are connected causally, where cause is "mechanistic." However, by appealing to metaphysics, a scientist, such as neuroscientist, finds support outside the bounds of science. She calls on a metaphysical relation to warrant a factual claim. Scientists who seek a warrant in metaphysics for a scientific relation commit *hubris*. They move without warrant from one language game to another, each with different rules of justification. They enter a philosophical cul-de-sac. We must avoid paths that lead to dualism.

Transition

Keep in mind that the Western philosophical tradition begins and flowers with two principles: *phusis* and critical reflection. *Phusis* as Being has two interpretations, Idealism and Naturalism; critical reflection becomes Rationalism, the belief that logic, especially its subject-predicate form, can penetrate Being, understand its essence and structure, and connect Being to the everyday world. Nature, derived from the Latin cognate of *phusis* (*nascor, natus, natus sum; natura*), is reinterpreted through cultural perspectives. *Phusis* is a datum from Greek Olympian religion and should have no meaning except for its followers. Further, Rationalism as the logical approach to a religious datum must now recognize it has no object about which to universalize. Being is vacuous apart from Greek religion. Rationalism curtailed must return to reason and reasoning in everyday living. Does this mean that neither *phusis* nor reason have legitimate meaning? No. Both refer to something that plays a part in our lives, in trusting-triads. The desire to understand the world and to achieve stable, consistent meanings amid unstable and unpredictable behavior of the gods led early Greek physiologists to interpret phusis as *on*, the what is, Being and to extend logic beyond its place in normal living, such as arguments in the agora. Doing so, they left unexamined their own presuppositions and much of Western philosophy resting on the sands of Olympian religion. With little help from unexamined Being and Rationalism, turn to the third question, what is the best understanding of the natural, its place and role as integral to the triad and to self-knowledge?[9] To answer, return to the fullness of practical living.

NATURE AND PERSONS-IN-TRIADIC-TRUSTING-RELATIONS

Fullness of Practical Living

Living normal patterns, facing regular problems, enjoying successes and aware of failures and short comings, we whole persons barely notice differences within our living.[10] Felt at first, we become aware that all is not right. It happens in many ways, most prominently as the authority of the Background, often personified as a teacher, a parent, a minister, a government official, loses legitimacy. What they claim to be true fails to fit the difficulties of the present moment. Under suspicion, habitual patterns of living provide unreliable guidance in the problems of the Foreground. Trusted government officials elected to care for the people's business, seem interested only in maintaining their positions and do not deserve trust. Awareness turns to recognition. Spread throughout the institutions of society, we recognize breaks between Background and Foreground and find no way to correct them. We are caught in suspicion. As we seek answers to suspicion, we must not walk into the problems of dualism. What path can we take? We find it by searching for the relation of triads to nature.

Society's culture, organization, artifacts, techniques, orientations, sanctioned ends reside in a natural setting, a habitat, including natural resources, climate, and altitude. More broadly, the habitat is part of the natural expanse scientists grasp as the macro of space and time of astronomy and the micro of atomic and sub-atomic particles of physics and chemistry.[11] To understand the natural dimension of triads, of society and culture, recall the structure of trusting triads.

Structure of Triads

The fullness of practical living is triadic in structure, I-Thou-It bound and stabilized by trust. Further study of the structure of the fullness of practical living, reveals Persons-in-triadic-trusting-relations, the Master Narrative authorizing and legitimating social action. Triadic relations are characterized by trusting, promising, freedom, obligation, personhood, transcendence, and *kenosis*. Seeking to know ourselves, we turn to the interrelations among trusting-triads and their environmental contexts, from society and culture, to nature, to the Personal. With a grasp of the larger environment, the Personal, we can say who we are, what we are to be, and what we are to do.

Before turning to the natural world including body, to habitat, and the natural expanse, recall that discussions of the natural begin within the fullness of practical living, within which distinctions allow us to proceed to its structure, living the natural, and environments. We begin with the characteristics of lived nature, habitat, the natural expanse.

Characteristics of the Natural

Listing characteristics of the natural could slip under the influence of mind-body dualism. Bodies would be independent of I, Thou, and It. If so, we face two independent reals whose relationships become highly problematic, leading into the cave rather than out. Resisting that pull, philosophical investigation must begin with practical living, living as whole persons. There distinctions arise among our bodies, our habitat, and the natural expanse. Distinguished, what characteristics mark them.[12]

The body participates in trust and trustworthiness. But how? Insight into the fullness of practical living reveals a triadic structure of I and Thou guided by cause, permeated by the body, bound by trust, and inherently moral. A whole person as trusting and trustworthy makes and breaks promises; those are acts of whole living. Each aspect is necessary; neither is sufficient. As independent, extracted from its context, the body would not trust. That is an abstraction and must be avoided. Viewed structurally as I-Thou-Cause and inclusive of nature, the whole triad acts; it trusts. As a distinguishable but not separable aspect of a trusting, trustworthy triad, the body is integral to trusting and trustworthiness. When we break promises, our bodies, habitat, the natural expanse participates in that failure. As distinguished in the whole of practical living, nature participates in triadic trusting, trustworthiness, as well as failing to do so.

How understand the body's participation in triadic trusting? Consider mediation in and among triads. The body, social habitat, and natural expanse are not learned independently of triads and then integrated into them. We learn them through significant persons whom we mutually trust, make promises and keep them. What we learn within triads of mediation we teach others. All learning is mediated. Mediation occurs only within triadic-trusting. Trusting significant others as persons who teach us about our natural world, we trust their teaching about the natural world. The meaning of nature is learned through mediation of triadic-trust and refers to that which we distinguish within living, our bodies, natural habitat, the natural expanse. In that sense, our bodies participate in trusting, in trustworthiness. If viewed independently and objectively, abstracted, our bodies do not trust; they lack the required potentialities, specifically agency. Extracted trees do not promise fidelity; that is not one of their characteristics. Our physical hearts do not promise dependability. In contrast, viewing within the Master Narrative, trusting is an act of a physical, social, cultural whole living person. Within trusting mediation, we learn other characteristics of nature.

Second, nature acts. As integral to whole persons participating in mediation, nature trusts and is trustworthy. Trusting requires agency, the capacity to initiate without compulsion a choice among options. A choice to run a three minute mile finds resistance from a whole person, most notably our bodies. No amount of training overcomes the resistance of the legs, lungs, the bodily center, emotions, and will. The trustworthy natural dependable body will not support that choice. Yet it supports exercise within one's bodily capacities. The natural acts through the whole person. Abstracted from the Master Narrative, nature does not have the capacity to initiate without compulsion a choice among options. However, within the topos, it does.

Third, the natural is malleable; it is capable of being formed or altered by outside forces. Our bodies are malleable. By over eating, the body gains weight; lack of eating, it loses weight. Exercise influences the muscles to grow and expand; no exercise, smaller and contract. The habitat of a society and culture can be formed into artifacts; others not. Wood is malleable, capable of receiving various forms, though some are not as malleable as others, mahogany compared with pine. The natural expanse is malleable, at least some aspects. Cells can be altered, genes structure altered; the planets altered (even if small) by human exploration. However, exploration into characteristics of our bodies, habitat, and natural expanse seeks to discover the hidden, the "other," mystery. Why does nature behave that way?

The way of nature is based in its potentials. Abstracted from other members of a triad, "I" has activity potentials of agency, movement, thinking, willing, sensing, feeling, purposing, making sounds, talking, trusting, etc. "Thou" has the same. It as cause is the ends, purposes, ideals, that "for the sake of which" social action occurs. The natural has potentials of bodies, cultural artifacts, natural habitat, micro and macro natural expanse, genes to solar systems. In contrast, from the topos, as lived nature, each person with personality is numerically one within I-Thou-It, the natural. Persons are natural I's and Thou's bound and stabilizes by reciprocal trust. In that sense the natural has agency. Let me explain.

Begin with a person, singular, numerically one. Potentials of I develop in interaction with potentials of other members of a triad. For example, a person's agentive potential develops in relation to its other activity potentials. Agentive potential means the potential to act, to initiate an action without being controlled, compelled by a power other than its own. Agency manifests as the development an activity potential. A person's activity potential of hearing is developed in relation to the potential of her ears and that heard, seeing in relation to eyes and that seen. As potentials develop in relation to each other and to the habitat, a distinctive individual person with a distinctive personality develops. As potentials of a numerically one individual develop in internal relation with each other, a distinctive agentive person with personality develops, a whole member of a triad. But that is only one member of a triad, viewed in isolation, and an incomplete picture of the numerically one I or Thou.

Each potential of an individual develops in triadic interacting with potentials of other members of the trusting-triad. Persons can be distinguished by their activity potentials—as causes and body/nature are distinguished by their activity potentials, and by those distinguished from others we meet in our living, our family dog, daisies in the front yard, house we live in, school we attend, church where we worship, natural habitat of our living. Persons bring their potentials to the triad within which they act and creatively find their own personalities, organized societies (cultures), solidarity through mutual trusting and causes and stability through institutions, The Personal, and their place and role in the Dance, achieving self-knowledge.[13]

How does It as cause and nature interrelate? It is usually thought that causes or purposes are central to individual and social action. Under the action-movement distinction, causes are thought of as mental, not physical. However, insofar as causes are held by persons, causes are developed in the triadic interactive development of potentials of natural persons. No brain, no cause; no personality, no cause. However, persons have the capacity of thinking and choosing among genuine alternatives. As activity potentials, thinking and choosing are distinguishable characteristics. As developed, thinking and choosing are social actions permeated by the various activity potentials of an individual in interaction with those of other members of the triad, both potential and developed, including the natural. How are these characteristics related to other members of the triad? What is their place?

Place

First, each of the distinguishable elements of a triad, I, Thou, and It and the natural is required for a triad; each, a *sine qua non*. Through mediation of trusting triads, I or Thou learn to distinguish the natural and its characteristics. Ironically, they learn that no triad exists apart from nature. Triads cannot be distinguished without nature.[14]

Second, the natural is present in all dimensions and activities of a triad. Though not sufficient to account for triads and their activities, the natural permeates every dimension of triadic actions. Living, walking hand in hand with one's love, going to the grocery store, lifting weights, playing the cello, teaching a student to fly, writing a book, keeping promises—all involve arms, legs, head, torso, blood, brain, heart, purpose, intention, planning—all are triadic in structure; each distinguished member of the triad having a place, specifically lived nature. More broadly, lived nature is formed and habituated by a society and culture in a natural habitat. Each lived action in and of a society with a culture is natural. Social relations culturally structured are the living within and of a habitat, forming it and being formed by it. Living reveals a triadic structure permeated by the natural as body, as habitat, as natural expanse from genes to distant galaxies. The natural is integral to each triad, as are I, Thou, and It as cause. What is the role of the natural in triadic trusting, in social action?

Role

By role we mean the part I, Thou, Cause, play in a trusting triad, in social action of society and culture. Consider role as contributing potentials to a triad, to society, to culture. Each member performs its role by contributing and developing its activity potentials in interrelation with different members of a triad glued by trust. Further, they form a *nexus* that has its own potentials. As the natural is inherent to individual members of the triad, it is also inherent to the *nexus* of an interacting triad. *Nexus* is the locus of interacting members of the triad, of I and Thou, cause, and body/habitat/nature. *Nexus* has activity potentials individual members do not, though there would be no *nexus* apart from the triad and its potentials. Each activity potential of a *nexus* involves the natural. Whether a primary or secondary institution, it forms within a *nexus* that in turn is formed within a triad one element of which is It as natural. Here arise culturally organized societies with solidarity and stability. Culture rests neither in Idealism nor Naturalism, but within triadic trusting that involves I, Thou, and It understood as cause and the body, habitat, and the natural expanse.

As we shall point out later, social action integrates I-Thou-It. It is not distinguished by action vs. movement, connected in some way into groups. Avoiding Being and Rationalism, think of social action within the master narrative of embodied Persons-in-triadic-trusting-relations.

Place of Science

What is the place of science as a discipline in this scheme? Armed with skepticism and objectivity, the emerging sciences were driven by curiosity and human need, especially living bodily. Illness strongly encourages the development of science. From Hippocratus in fifth century Greece to the present, difficulties of the lived body motivated students of the natural world to find cures for diseases. The Black Death of 1348–1351 encouraged development of medicine, for example. Recently, social and cultural interrelationships with habitat encourage the development of social and natural sciences, ecology, for example. The results are impressive. The power of scientific method in the hands of scientists guided them to important understandings of the natural world. Under the influence of technology, the quality of human living in society, culture, and habitat has increased.

That is achieved by both distinguishing for intense study aspects of our bodies, habitat, natural expanse and expecting a method to provide objective, impartial views of the natural world. Each science seeks to provide a rich, full understanding of its area of focus, providing knowledge to aid bodily living, society, culture, and habitat. No science focuses on the whole of nature. Each science is limited. Each assumes both what is believed to be true about nature and its connection to human ability to comprehend it. Consider two assumptions, the Law of Nature and the Uniformity of Nature. What is a law of nature? It "is a description of what actually takes place."[15] Law of Nature refers to the total range of what actually takes place. Yet, as Kemeny notes, "... we find that most laws that could conceivably be created for the universe will forever lie beyond our limited human possibilities."[16] The Uniformity of Nature assumption we are told is that "nature tomorrow will behave just like today,"[17] assuring us that Background is a reliable guide into Foreground. That terminology is untenable; it is false. Underlying that understanding is the assumption that nature behaves like a human being.[18] Humans change; we want to prevent nature from doing so. The point of the uniformity of nature is clear. If law is an accurate description tomorrow, it is an accurate description today. Yet, the life of humans plays a part in scientific knowledge. Even if we conceive of the simplest possible Law, one that covers the complexity of laws, "it will have to be in the form that human limitations and the complexity of nature are such that it is possible for human beings to learn about nature."[19]

Though pressing its horizons, no science transcends them. Not only limited, sciences are social action.

Science is an activity within, supported by, and variously related to institutions, including families, religion, and schools. From the Middle Ages through the modern period, science has been guided by the state and the economic order.[20] During the early Modern period science was the activity of individuals outside established authority, especially the church. The sciences focus on the natural, distinguishing within it for investigation, for example, the heavenly bodies for astronomy, motion for physics, development of plants and animals for biology. They seek to do so impersonally, objectively, without bias from culture, religious, or personal preference. That is, they attempt to stand outside triadic-trusting and mediation. Nevertheless, reflection occurs only within the context of triadic-trusting and is mediated by it. No impersonal stands apart from the personal, from persons in triadic-trusting. Scientific objectivity is rooted in triadic-trust and deeply moral. Ironic. Focusing objectively on the natural world assumes triadic-trusting and the accompanying moral structure. There can be no separation of parts from wholes, as in S-P logic; distinctions can be made only within the Master Narrative, triadic-trusting. The natural may appear to be impersonal, beyond the influence of I, Thou, society, and culture. It is not. It is meaningful to us only in context of triadic structure of moral social, cultural living. Science works within the Master Narrative.

DUALISM REVISITED

Dualism persists. One could ask for the relation between nature and purpose, or nature and mind, or how can two reals unlike each other interrelate. Asking persists; but it is only the rear guard action of an exhausted master narrative. Consider the impersonal vs. personal (as in modern mind-body problem); free vs. determinism; agentive vs. non-agentive; and rational vs. non-rational (emotions, passions). Each isolates two aspects of the whole person and finds their relationship problematic. However, in each case, the aspects are rooted in the activity potentials of natural I-Thou-It; and their role in the development of the whole person is ignored. The engine driving choosing between contrary aspects and then forging their relationship to form a whole is the metaphysics of Being and Rationalism. Their differences highlighted, the search begins for one principle to explain and relate the differences. Example, the free will vs. determinism problem places in bold relief free choice of the mind and determinism of the body and then searches for the one principle that would properly relate them, such as reducing them to mind, to body, or to some rational transcendent principle. Once cultural dyadic objectivism, cultural monadic subjectivism, the metaphysics of Being and Rationalism, and the Master Narratives within which they find their authority are recognized as exhausted, it is possible to take a fresh look. Beginning anew with the fullness of practical living and its trusting-triadic structure, what has been formally forced by culture and philosophy into Being and Rationalism can now be seen as aspects of trusting-triads. Now we see the futility of asking certain types of questions and the fruitfulness of asking others.

CONCLUSION

After finding and describing the triadic structure of ordinary living, we creatively found the Master Narrative, Persons-in-trusting-triadic-relations. Within that *topos* we considered the issue of the relation the body to what am I, what am I to be and do; of trusting triads to their natural environment and found that triads of trust are inherently natural. Triads of mutual trust are not separated from the body as mind-body or action-movement. We found such dualisms cul-de-sacs. Persons in I-Thou-It triads are also bodies living in habitats situated in a natural expanse. Thus, we speak of whole persons, within which we can distinguish activity potentials, bodies, personalities, trust, background and foreground, our second nature, and causes or purposes. Knowing ourselves as whole persons, we are coming to what we are. We also find in trust the basis for the life good to live, or what we are to be and what we are to do. Whole persons live in mutual trust with each other and with other triads in environments. They are society, culture, and the ultimate environment, the Personal. They provide for the knowledge and development of whole persons. Turn to society and culture.

Notes

1. Pierre Hadot, *The Veil of Isis. An Essay on the History of the Idea of Nature* translated by Michael Chase (Cambridge, MA: Harvard University Press, 2006), 1.

2. The degree and range of neo-platonic influence on Augustine remains under dispute. That Augustine was influenced by neo-Platonism is indisputable. For a helpful discussion of that influence, see Carl Vaught, *Encounters with God in Augustine's Confessions, Books VII-IX* (Albany, NY: State University of New York Press, 2004.), 42–56.

3. See Book Two in Augustine, *On Free Choice of the Will* translated with introduction and notes, Thomas Williams (Indianapolis, IN: Hackett Publishing Company, 1993).

Persons and Nature

4. Interestingly, the distinction between nature as *phusis* and nature as created order continues into the modern world but is ignored as rational reflection and science ignore historical background in the interest of establishing a new order, the Modern World along lines of the Emerging Self and science. Abramic creation remains in Descartes' two created orders, as Greek *phusis* remains in Spinoza. *Phusis is natura naturans,* and the objects formed are *natura naturata.*

5. What we call old individualism first arose the West in the Greek polis in the fifth and fourth centuries BCE. Autocratic rule shifted to democratic as political debate and rhetoric grew in influence. This kind of individualism developed within cultural dyadic objectivism. Representatives include Socrates, among philosophers, and Demosthenes, among rhetoricians, and Hercules, among mythical heroes.

6. William C. Dampier, A *History of Science and Its Relations with Philosophy and Religion* (Cambridge, UK: Cambridge University Press, 1961), 128–129.

7. Dampier, *A History of Science*, 119–120.

8. See F. M. Cornford, *From Religion to Philosophy*, (New York, NY: Harper and Row, Publishers, 1957), 124–127. "The work of philosophy thus appears as the elucidation and clarifying of religious, or even pre-religious, material." Cornford, *From Religion to Philosophy*, 126. Cornford assumes modern dualism, ". . . each of us lives imprisoned in a world of his own, centered about his own consciousness, with sensations, feelings, and images which exist in no other brain but his, we are convinced that all these words somehow fit together into one and the same world, and all possibility of communication rests on the trust of that conviction. It is this common world that the philosophies seek to account for and explain; and, as we have tried to show, what at first seems most significant in that cosmos is of religious, and therefore of social, origin—a product, not of individual invention, but of collective mentality. When the individual intellectual gets to work upon it in what is called philosophic speculation, it hardly succeeds in introducing any new conceptions, but merely analyses the content of its datum, and deduces from it diverging systems." (Ibid., 126–127.) So, why begin there? Specifically, ". . . reason itself, in which the philosopher trusted, had inherited its claim to immediate and certain apprehension of truth from the prophetic faculty of the inspired sage . . . a philosophy may be eminently rational, and yet take its premises . . . and deduce a whole system of the universe without feeling the need to check its conclusions by any close study of observable facts." F. M. Cornford, *Principium Sapientiae, A Study of the Origins of Greek Philosophical Thought* (New York, NY: Harper and Row, Publishers, [1952] 1965), 159.

9. For clarity we shall continue using *nature*, though without adopting its metaphysical interpretations in Western Philosophy.

10. We agree with Borden Parker Bowne; dualism must be rejected in favor of living as whole persons, though we develop that insight in different ways. See Herbert W. Schneider, "Introductory Essay: Bowne's Radical Empiricism, in Warren E. Steinkraus (ed.), *Representative Essays of Borden Parker Bowne* (Utica, NY: Meridian Publishing Company, n.d.), xi–xv. Also see Borden Parker Bowne, "The

Significance of the Body for Mental Action," in Steinkraus, *Representative Essays*, 16–23.

11. See Melville J. Herskovits, *Cultural Anthropology*. Abridged revision of *Man and His Works* (New York, NY: Alfred A. Knopf, [1947] 1960), chapter 6, "Habitat and Culture."

12. Think of bodies as our bodies, the bodies of I and Thou in triads; the natural world distinguished by similarities and differences, Aristotle's early taxonomy, such as the physical and biological; the natural expanse of the micro level observable through electron microscopes as well as theoretical entities such as quarks and the macro level observable through the Hubble telescope (awe inspiring size and power).

13. Though tempted to seek the unity and identify of individual persons, be careful. If one seeks a unifying essence of a person, one works with within the metaphysics of Being, continuing the one-many problem. Seeking identity through change again manifests the influence of the same metaphysics and the permanence-change issue of the Greek physiologists. Both begin within metaphysics and account for wholeness of living. In contrast, begin with wholeness of living and penetrate it to mystery; the approach here. Unity and identity are found within the wholeness of living.

14. Cf. Vine Deloria, Jr., and Daniel R. Wildcat. *Power and Place, Indian Education in America* (Golden, CO: American Indian Graduate Center and Fulcrum Resources, 2001).

15. John G. Kemeny, *A Philosopher Looks at Science* (Princeton, NJ: D. Van Nostrand Company, Inc., 1959), 38.

16. Kemeny, *A Philosopher Looks at Science*, 38.

17. Kemeny, *A Philosopher Looks at Science*, 59.

18. Kemeny, *A Philosopher Looks at Science*. 60. *Phusis* in ancient Greek religion was thought of in god terms, where gods were thought to posses human qualities. For example, Plato views *phusis* as mind and organic body, where mind governs body.

19. Kemeny, *A Philosopher Looks at Science*, 63.

20. See Michael Polanyi, *Science, Faith and Society* (Chicago, IL: University of Chicago Press, [1946] 1964).

Chapter 5

Society and Culture

Whole persons, who achieve self-knowledge, live in stable, solidar societies with organized ways of life, cultures. They form our emotions, attitudes, thoughts, actions, and habituate our behavior as well as protect us from each other and the uncertain forces of nature. However, suspicion weakens our cultural shell by questioning the connections between background and foreground and the authority on which they rest. Critical questions raise four issues that drive to the core of society and its organization: (1) can other persons be known, (2) can individuals act together, (3) what provides solidarity for a society/culture, and (4) what stabilizes social solidarity? Answers will show how persons-in-trusting-triadic-relations as authoritative master narrative guides to satisfactory answers and provides for self-knowledge. We shall argue that society with an organized way of life that continues over time and possesses solidarity and stability, rests in triadic-trust and institutions. If that claim can be adequately supported, the grip of suspicion loosens, and the possibility of self-knowledge is strengthened

To begin, consider the possibility of society by addressing the first two issues. Both arise from the continuous influence of cultural monadic subjectivism, the assumption of modern dualism, and Rationalism's commitment to the conceptual universal. If only the individual knows and acts, two requirements for a society become questionable: knowing other minds and acting in social concert with other persons. The triadic structure of the fullness of practical living, rejection of dualism, whether ancient or modern, and Triadic-Trusting, the Master Narrative, allow us to set aside those former obstacles to establishing social solidarity and stability. Turn to the first requirement, knowing other minds.

128   *Chapter 5*

SOCIETY

Social Knowing

The Other Minds Problem

Can we know other persons? If not, we would know no one with whom to relate, much less identify the tie binding us. Our discussions of triadic mediation lay the basis for setting aside the other minds problem, at least in its modern form. Let me explain. The modern importance of the problem of knowing other minds, that they exist and what they are thinking, sensing, feeling, and desiring, lies in its impediment to any social theory including the basis of social formation, solidarity, and stability. Foundationalists, working in seventeenth and eighteenth century Europe who rejected medieval Order, were beneficiaries of the Renaissance Master Narrative, Emerging Persons. Driven by the demand to answer skepticism, they generated a barrier to building bridges to other persons. Descartes' radical skepticism authored solipsism and with it the other minds problem. Alone in the opaque chamber of skeptical doubt, one has only one exit. In some manner, she must move through the wall of experience to that to which it refers. Unable to get outside of one's experience, can one nevertheless do so?

Consider the skeptic's formulation of the other minds problem.

(1) Any conscious undergoing of an experience is an idea.... [Ideas] are data present for a conscious subject and may be called mental events.
(2) As mental events they are modifications of an individual mind and, consequently, subjective.
(3) Also, mental events *are* because an individual mind has them. It is correct, then, to say about mental events, *esse est percipi*.
(4) Mental events and physical behavior are different things. I know this because I can have a headache and successfully pretend not to have one, or I cannot have a headache and successfully pretend to have one. Indeed, other persons can be successful in their pretense of having or not having pain or other sensations.
(5) Mental events and physical behavior are contingently related, not logically or causally related.
(6) Every act of knowing begins and terminates with experience, that is, with the kind of subjective data identified in proposition (1).
(7) A necessary condition for knowing either that another person exists or what he experiences is either that I experience his experiences directly or that I infer by some reliable method that he exists and that he is having certain kinds of experiences. It is logically impossible directly to

apprehend another's experience. If I did, it would then be mine and not his, and his would be his and not mine. Furthermore, there is no method that is perfectly reliable by which I can make correct knowledge claims about other minds.[1]

Those accepting Descartes' radical skepticism struggle with the intractable problem of knowledge of the external world. In the early years of modern social theory, Cartesian solipsism prevailed. Finding intersubjectivity an intellectual cul-de-sac and wanting to set their discipline on the solid grounds of science, they turned to what is observable, to some form of behaviorism. Yet, that approach fared no better. They could find no explanation for such everyday phenomena as refraining. To help, they reintroduced subjectivity, only to find the other minds problem a thorn in their side they could not remove.[2]

Faced with intractable Cartesian solipsism, some social theorists turned to the argument by analogy. Schutz is one who did, calling it simultaneity.[3] Our outer lives are a "field of expression" of our inner lives, our bodily presence. If my friend's bodily movements parallel mine I sense the simultaneity, sense the "other person's stream of consciousness is flowing along a track that is temporally parallel with" my own.[4] This allows a view, though indirectly, of the subjective life of another person. Interestingly, this means that we can "know other people better than we can know ourselves. For we can 'watch' other people's subjective experiences as they actually occur, whereas we have to wait for our own to elapse in order to peer at them as they recede into the past. No man can see himself in action, any more than he can know the 'style' of his own personality."[5] Unfortunately, the skeptic's argument rests on a search for certainty, and Schutz sidesteps it. For skeptics, the argument by analogy is untenable. One may believe that the experience of others runs simultaneously with one's own, but what evidence could one cite to show that it does? Only by directly apprehending another's inner life could one do so. That is impossible. Unable to show (providing unimpeachable evidence) the characteristics of the inner life of another, claims regarding the existence or content of other minds are only conjecture. What is one to say about that quandary?

Consider the other minds problem as an antinomy. We know that other minds exist and their content, and it is false that we know other minds exist and their content. The evidence of everyday life favors the left side of the disjunct, and the philosophical demand for evidence supporting any claim about other minds favors the right side (note the skeptical argument above). Both sides are true, but they cannot be, they are contradictory. Thus, we are faced with an antinomy. Resolving an antinomy requires that either side of the disjunct be shown to be false, or showing that the antinomy rest on unacceptable assumptions. The debate has raged over the skeptic's argument supporting the right side of the disjunct. That philosophical energy, however, has been misdirected. The issue lies elsewhere in the assumptions generating the problem. They are found in the belief that since the knowledge of the past can no longer be accepted, resting as it does on tradition, only certainty can suffice. Rejecting the Background, any step into the Foreground must be taken thoughtfully. Descartes' approach is well known. Only certainty can replace tradition. Accepting the demand for certainty, he employed methodological skepticism, or radical skepticism, to silence warnings of the skeptic as the first steps were taken to find a solid foundation for knowledge. That approach led Descartes to the certainty of the thinking thing. Unfortunately, nothing else could be known with certainty, and the difficulties of showing that we are not alone in the world loomed large.

Why assume with foundationalists skepticism's demand for certainty? Careful description and analysis of everyday living reveal its triadic structure, I-Thou-It in which all knowing there is believing, and in all believing there is knowing. Descartes' formulation of methodological skepticism rested on patterns of reasoning he learned from others in whom he placed trust. He did not invent logic. Though he had the potentiality to think logically, the development and fruition of that potentiality took place under the tutelage of parents, friends, and teachers, who habituated him into the tradition of Aristotelian logic. He would not have been able to formulate the problem in the way he did without having his mind formed in just the way his was. Prompted by current pyrrhonist skepticism, he accepted the demand for certainty that rested on a tradition passed on by individual persons in whom he placed his trust. This does not mean certainty rests on tradition. Rather, both tradition and certainty are pervaded by believing the language of our society learned from those we believe, trust.[6]

The other minds problem could not arise apart the assumption of sharing with other person's beliefs, concepts, arguments, purposes, and *topos*, Master Narrative in the sixteenth and seventeenth centuries. Descartes thought amid an I-Thou-It triad. His knowledge was mediated by a society and culture, triadically structured and unified by trust, persons, freedom, promise keeping, ought, transcendence, and *kenosis*. Ironically, he could advance his argument, *cogito ergo sum*, and its solipsistic consequence only amid triadic trusting. Thus, to understand knowing, start with the triadic structure of the fullness of everyday living to knowing, not with the assumption of radical skepticism. Modern philosophy, driven by the radical skepticism Descartes assumed, reverses the starting point for philosophical thinking. It begins with the problem of knowing set by the assumption of skepticism and the demand for certainty, proceeds to solipsism, and then to the problem of knowing the external world, including persons in society. Social Personalism, after postmodern philosophy and its devastating critique of modern philosophy, freed from the core of ancient, medieval, modern and its ever present impersonalism, moves from the fullness of practical living to understanding knowing and acting within that relation. Setting aside the other minds problem, the issue of acting together arises.

Social Action

Recognizing we know other minds, we can seriously consider how persons form a society. Persons-in-trusting-triadic-relations are more than a relation of knowing; it is a relation of actions. In the modern period from the Renaissance to the present with growing cultural monadic subjectivism, actions are individual. If so, social relations and organizations present a problem. Can individuals act together to form a social organization? Can one individual, say a King, be the will of a nation? Can a King be the nation? Natural persons have the capacity to will, but social organizations do not. Social actions, particularly institutions such as political, religious, educational, media, regulative, economic, and family stifle the freedom of individual action; they are necessary, but their power and influence must be constrained.[7] If so, and assuming the Master Narrative of Emerging Persons authorizing and legitimating individual freedom of action, how account for persons working together; for solidarity; for the stability of social actions, institutions? Under Emerging Persons, individualism, it is difficult to do so.

To begin, consider the meaning of "action." First, what is action?[8] Within whole persons and the fullness of their practical living, and in light of their I-Thou-It structure bound and stabilized by trust, some helpful distinctions can be made. Though useful, these distinctions do not necessarily carry with them mind-body, or action-movement dualism. The following definition is helpful. "For every person S and every action a, S performed if and only if: (i) there is a b such that b is the appropriate bit of bodily or mental behavior of S or there is a b such that b is the appropriate bit of bodily or mental behavior of S and the appropriate effects of this bodily or mental behavior; (ii) b occurred; (iii) there is a v such that v is a volition of (person) S and v caused (behavior) b; and (iv) c occurred."[9] Defined in this manner, an action is performed by an individual whole person, and within it no social action is possible. How can a holder of modern individualism and dualism give an account of social actions, actions that could explain how social solidarity and stability can be formed?

Distinguish between natural action and artificial or nonnatural action. Natural action is performed by a whole person, such as Jack Hansen; an artificial action is performed by an individual on behalf of a group of persons. For example, the President of General Motors acts in behalf of General Motors. However, artificial action as acting on behalf of a group does not explain the presence of the group, on what basis they relate to each other in solidarity and stability. We may say that only self-interest and external forces form societies, but they cannot account for fellow-feeling, solidarity, and the stability over time. Note that one other action is institutional, action performed by institution. Later we will discuss institutional action.[10] How solve this seemingly intractable problem?

Actions by whole natural persons lie at the root of any view of action. The performance of an action always occurs in an I-Thou-It, natural, trusting-triad, that in turn lies in a, social, and cultural context. Actions as contextual are multidimensional, including natural, artificial, purposive, interpersonal, institutionally structured, temporal with a Background and Foreground, at least. We claim that knowing is an action, and all actions are social. Thus, though individual natural persons have the potential to choose freely, non-compelled, among genuine options, they do not carry out or perform an action in isolation from other persons and uninfluenced by a body, society, culture, and habitat. Are those claims true? Further, how infer from the promise that individual knowing is an action the claim all actions are social?

Consider two lines of argument. First, consider knowing. Earlier in the discussion of mediation we found that each act of knowing, though performed by an individual, is an act of triadic-trusting. Triadic-trusting is a social action. So, each act of knowing is a social action. Turn to a second argument. Actions have two important dimensions that can be distinguished but not separated. Distinguish between potentials of an individual actor and actions performed by that actor. A potential of a person is what that person can do when called on. Potentials include capacities of an I to deliberate among options, to initiate, and to carry out non-compelled movements with regard to an It in concert with Thou. Potentials may or may not be acted upon. The capacity for free actions allows a person to make a choice, but powers or events beyond the individual's control may hinder carrying out the choice. A person may choose to walk freely in the family's neighborhood, but prison bars may prohibit him from doing so. In choosing, a person can be said to have will *agency*, but in carrying out the choice the person, hindered by prison bars and external forces, lacks will *power*. Though that distinction is meaningful, it would be odd to choose to go for a walk in the family's neighborhood and unimpeded not do it. Odd, yes, but the distinction nevertheless holds. There is a distinction between choosing to do x and doing x. For our purposes, that is satisfactory.

Now consider actions, as will agency or will power. Both are actions. That is, they are choices, but one is not carried out and the other is. Further, actions always occur within society and culture and are deeply influenced by them. For feral children, it is reasonable to say the range of their will agency and will power is limited by the narrow range of language and genuine alternatives derived from the rich possibilities of a society and culture. Otherwise, each person is born and reared within a society, under a Master Narrative, structured by social institutions that possess solidarity and stability. There are no totally isolated actions. In addition, the triadic relation has potentials of its own. We shall see that triadic relations occurring with regard to norms and within a habitat have a nexus with potentials that range from momentary associations to highly stable and long lasting institutions we call secondary institutions. The upshot is that though there is a sense in which all actions are performed by individuals, they are so only in the sense of choosing on the basis of the potential of whole persons in a triad. As performed, actions of whole persons are always natural, social, and cultural.

Thus, the activity of whole persons can be distinguished in the following manner. All actions are natural social actions. Though they originate in the potentials for non-compelled choice, actions are carried out in a triad-trusting environment; actions are social. Social actions have these central characteristics: they are non-compelled activity; mediated through triadic-trusting of society and culture; habituated into social/cultural trust and patterns; understood within the *topos* of the book of knowledge of a society and culture, specifically it's authoritative Master Narrative that legitimates solidarity and stability of a culture and our second nature. Recognizing we know other minds and that knowing is an action, we argued that action is social action. At the doorstep of society with an organized way of life, a culture, questions three and four arise. Third, what tie provides cohesion allowing triadic actions to be social; that is, what ties actions of I-Thou-It allowing the triad to be a society? That tie discerned, the fourth question presents itself. What stabilizes solidarity of actions in a triad? Turn to the third question, what binds actions of whole persons into a society and provides solidarity for triadic action?

Solidarity

Before proceeding, what is solidarity? It refers to the ties that bind people to one another and allow a society to form. Ties range from kinship in simpler societies to interdependence in more advanced ones. The search for those is the province is sociologists. We are interested in the character of the tie. We claim ties binding any people into a society, simple or advanced, are triadic in structure and stabilized by reciprocal trust. The triad is I-Thou-It, and trust binds I-Thou-It, without which I-Thou-It could not be identified as a triad. Trust is the glue, *sine qua non* ingredient binding each I-Thou-It into a micro-society. As we have seen the unity, the solidarity of persons is the act of believing the body of knowledge of my society; more, it is acknowledging and trusting persons within the society who convey that knowledge. It is the glue, the core of the fellow-feeling we know as we go about our lives. Specifically, it is triadic-trusting. It is I-Thou in the mutuality of trusting regarding It; I trusting the person Thou, regarding It, the book of knowledge, thou teaches. What does this have to do with solidarity? It speaks to its core. How understand triadic trust?

To locate the root of social bonding, solidarity, appeal to the I-Thou-It triad. There find five elements: goals, causes or purposes; common problems in the Background and Foreground; solutions to common problems; common history; and Background providing guidance in the Foreground. In addition, these share a temporal pattern, past, present, and future as well as coterminous present. Consider each.

Common goals bind as persons knowing them act with reference to them. A college athletic team will serve as an illustration. Knowing the goal of defeating its arch rival on Saturday, a football team finds itself united. As the coaching staff leads the team to understand the problems the opposition presents, the team analyzes the challenge it will face on the field. Finding solutions to the problems presented by the opposition prepares the team to face the challenge with reasonable expectation of victory. Each team member must grasp what he must do, how it fits into the game plan, and prepare to execute the plan. Also, teams are united by a college with a history. A player recruited by a college with a history of high academic standards and sound football program could accept the invitation and scholarship support to play football. He knows what playing at that college demands of players; with his teammates he accepts the challenge. Finally, he has confidence the college and his Background will guide him successfully into the Foreground of four years of learning and playing football. He talked with former team members and understanding their views agree with what he learned about the college academically and athletically, he joins the team. His social bonds extend beyond the present team members to those in the past. He is part of a tradition of academic excellence and athletic success. True of a football team; true of persons in a society.[11] Yet, are these adequate bases for social bonding that escape suspicion? They are not.

Each element is thought to rest on knowing goals, problems, solutions, common history, and the reliability of the Background as a guide into the Foreground. For and organized society, its bond lies in its Book of Knowledge. If knowledge loses its criteria for acceptable evidence and inference, it loses ties connecting evidence to claim, skepticism develops. Authority legitimating connections dissipates, and knowledge loses its reliability. Suspicion arises. However, knowing rests in accepting the authority of the significant others teaching the knowledge. Look carefully. Accepting *what* the authority teaches rests on trusting the persons, the significant other, and the authority from which one learned. Social bonding rests in trusting the person or persons who teach knowledge. At root, the tie that binds is not knowledge. It is found in mutuality of triadic trusting of persons or society who teaches what it knows. Triadic trust ties, binds persons to each other both in the present and through time.

Though all learning presupposes an initial addressing and believing, the solidarity of the Background places mutual trusting in the relationship. Solidarity among the members of the triad, I-Thou-It, is dependent on the unity of the Background and Foreground, and those in turn are dependent on the integrity of society, resting in triadic trusting.

Before moving to stability, recall that triadic-trusting is mutual promising to keep fidelity among persons. Promises can be broken. If so, persons are free to choose among genuine options. Promise keeping places one under the moral obligation of fidelity. Also, persons in their freedom and moral life are transcendent to any attempt to capture them in a conceptual net. Persons-in-triadic-trusting-relations, the Master Narrative, essential to social action, are a moral relation. Solidarity is moral.

CULTURE

Stability

Turn to the last question, what stabilizes the solidarity of social action? Triadic trust provides social solidarity; can it stabilize solidarity? No one doubts that continuity through change is present in human social life. But, what is it, and how account for it? A straightforward answer is that institutions stabilize our second nature.[12]

Before we proceed, what do "stability" and "institution" mean? Various definitions of "institutions" have been attempted. For example, Marcus Singer says, "An institution can be thought of as (1) a relatively permanent system of social relations organized around (that is, for the protection or attainment of) some social need or value; or as (2) a recognized and organized way of meeting a social need or desire or of satisfying a social purpose."[13] Emphasizing the place of norms in institutions, Parsons says, "Then in looking for the field of empirical facts with which the theory of institutions should be concerned, I should concentrate on those uniform modes of behavior and forms of relationship which are 'sanctioned,' that stand in some kind of significant relation to normative rules to a greater or lesser degree approved by the individuals subject to them. . . . It is in the particular feature of being related to norms that the institutional aspect of these uniformities lies."[14] Though other definitions are available, from these general characteristics emerge. Institutions are relatively permanent social relations, sanctioned by approved norms that satisfy a social desire, need, and/or purpose. What is the place of institutions in our lives?

To answer that question, distinguish among habitat, culture, and environment. By habitat we mean the natural setting of human existence, "the physical features of the region inhabited by a group of people; its natural resources, actually or potentially available to the inhabitants; its climate, altitude, and other geographical features to which they have adapted themselves."[15] By culture we refer to "that part of the total setting that includes the material objects of human manufacture, techniques, social orientations, points of view, and sanctioned ends."[16] And by environment we refer to "man in his natural and cultural setting."[17] To summarize, institutions are relatively permanent social relations, sanctioned by norms that satisfy a social desire, need, and/or purpose and are situated among the ecosystem, our normative beliefs, and ourselves.

It is reasonable to say, then, that a social group shares a way of life that identifies the group and distinguishes it from others. That way of life is its culture. Central to any culture are norms, ideals that guide its common life. These include techniques for securing food from the natural environment and for manufacturing products, beliefs and practices that guide and govern the distribution of goods and services, a web of rights and responsibilities, reproduction and care of children, regulative relationships between groups and among individuals as well as other societies, transmitting the cultural skills and knowledge to the younger generation, a belief system that explains the nature of the universe and the place of persons within it, and a language to accumulate and transfer knowledge. As these social activities become shared, we bond with other members of society, solidarity; as they become recognized and formal, they also become formal and stabilized. We have seen that that felt and recognized unity, that solidarity is trusting. These stabilized patterns are institutions. That is, they stabilize the solidar of a society.

Next, what does the word "stability" mean? The word stability is derived from the Latin word *stabilis*, standing firm. A stable life, whether of an individual or of a society, maintains equilibrium and is self-restoring. It is dependable, predictable, rights itself under pressures that tend to move it off course, and continues a course of action when faced with unacceptable alternatives. The members of a society continue to abide by the solidar and the central norms around which the way of life of a people, a culture is formed, that is, the moral life of a society. For example, individuals living according to the norms of a society and following its institutional patterns, must exercise judgment or *phronesis*/prudence. Having freedom of choice, we do have alternatives. Cultural, institutional habituation seeks to form persons to keep promises, follow rules, and keep commitments, that is, to act morally. That "keeping" is a life that is stable. Acting morally, we make a mark in our relation with other people and the natural world. We sometimes call this "mark" our cultural character. In light of these distinctions, we restate the question. In the dimension of human social existence that involves trusting, oughting, and transcending, what guarantees its continuity, its standing firm, its capacity to right itself, and its dependability through change? Or, what stabilizes the culturally habituated moral life?[18]

Question

With these definitions before us, return to the issue. How account for a society's continuity through change, its ability to stand firm, to right itself, to be dependable through time? We determined that the solidar of our second nature is trust. We do not simply trust, however. We continue mutual trusting structured triadically; it is temporal action. What accounts for the continuity of the solidar of trusting and its moral dimensions? The issue is to account not only for the continuity or stability of social acting, but also, and more fundamentally for the stability of solidarity. No one doubts that continuity through change is present in human social life. But, what provides for it? The traditional answers include the suprastructure of Being and Rationalism that undergird and connect the Foreground of social goals, problems, approaches to achieving them, and criteria for a satisfactory solution; to the Background with common history and common habituation. In contrast, we contend that stability is dependent on stable connections through time, especially between Background and Foreground. Those stable connections are institutions. We find their root in interpersonal, triadic relations of mutual trusting.

Two issues linger. If institutions provide stability for the solidar of trusting, how can they provide for and maintain the freedom of individuals to accept, modify, or revolutionize their society as well as the order that holds individuals responsible for their actions? The problem of social order and human freedom is deeply puzzling for any society. To begin our search, we ask whether institutions are found, made, or both found and made?

Answers from History

Historically there are two sources for answers, dyadic cultural objectivism and monadic cultural subjectivism. According to the latter, societies, their culture and institutions are made by individuals who share a commonly agreed on way of life and seek to achieve its goals through stabilized patterns. A society ultimately rests in the individuals composing it. The grounds of stability lie there. That is, the infrastructure of individuals alone, whether physical, psychological, or linguistic, sufficiently account for the institutions that stabilize social action. According to the former, humans find a transcendent structure, such as a moral order, the commands of some god or gods, Fate, or Reason under which persons live, and appeal to it to stabilize and form their way of life in society. The grounds lie in the superstructure, such as the Absolute, Reason, God, Eternal Forms, or Nature. We could appeal to a superstructure or an infrastructure to account for the institutions of a society that stabilize it through change. As we have seen, the anomalies within each weaken its answer to the problem. Also, both rest on exhausted authoritative Master Narratives that lack power to bestow legitimacy. Reconsidering the fullness of everyday living, we find it is triadic in structure with mutual trusting the solidar. How then are institutions related to trusting and how do they stabilize trusting? What stabilizes trusting? We shall present a third alternative and argue that it avoids the difficulties of both and offers a more plausible account for stability of the *nexus* of the triad along with its solidar.

We turn now to examine how, if at all, institutions and the triad are related. Is it possible that within triadic trusting we can account for institutions and their stabilizing solidarity?

Triads and Institutions

Consider the members of the triadic relation, I, Thou, and It. Each individual I and Thou is numerically distinct and triadically related both to other individual agents who possess will agency and to the It. Though we can distinguish each individual person within a triad, we cannot separate them. Anything that can be said about each person, anything that each person becomes, occurs within and is deeply influenced by the other members of the triad.[19] Whatever is said about individuals occurs within a triad.[20]

Consider next the internal relations of the triad.[21] First, the triad is intrinsically situational: the It indicates both a habitat and a culture, while the I and Thou indicate psycho-physical beings related to those environments. Second, relations within the triad are stable, enduring, and maintained and others are not stable, enduring, or maintained. Two examples are an Oxford college and a momentary association such as giving directions to a stranger.

Why are some relations within the triad stable, enduring, and maintained and others are not? Consider the elements within the triad. Recall not only the possibilities I, Thou, and It bring to the triad but also the needs, purposes, and agencies of I and Thou as well as the exigencies of the It. In so far as I-Thou-It are natural triads, they operate, as best we can tell, according to the laws of physics and biology; thus, there is a kind of permanency, a high degree of stability in these relations [gravity, for example]. Undergirded by that natural context, each element within the triad both undergoes and acts on the other members of the triad. Limited by habitat as well as freed by its value possibilities, I and Thou intend to achieve common purposes, satisfy common needs, and collectively live according to norms built into purposive action. Institutional structures arise, stabilize, and remain within the I-Thou-It triad on the basis of the orderliness of the habitat and natural expanse as well as shared needs, purposes, and norms. If there were no interaction within the triad there would be no shared norms, a solidar, or social structures, stable or otherwise. Where there is norm governed interaction within the triad to satisfy social needs or purposes there are stable, enduring structures, institutions. How does such interaction generate institutions? It occurs with and on the basis of the nexus. Let me explain.

Institutions that develop in any society rest on shared needs, the activity potentials of each member of the triad, and causes, that with regard to which persons act. The I and the Thou of the triad, bring to the triad needs for food, shelter, clothing, regulation for competing needs, organized understandings of the religious, child bearing and rearing, passing on the ways of society's culture, and communication.[22] In a triad, I, the Thou, and the It interact to fulfill their needs guided by shared norms, or causes. In triadic interaction a second group of potentials arise, potentials not found in individuals and not found beyond the triad. The interaction has a focus we call the nexus. As triadic interaction occurs, pattern potentials appear that are located neither in the individuals participants of the triad nor external to the triad. They appear only in the nexus. The patterns are the potential ways of meeting the needs of the members of the triad and are required for the triad to continue. The interaction has a focus we call the nexus. In that focused interaction, seven stable social patterns emerge appearing within the triad and nowhere else:

economic, political, religious, productive, education, regulative, and communicative. These triadic potentials are not found a priori but through observing cultures, finding their societies structured in triads.

Here we find the basis of social difference and interdependence. Each I and Thou of the triad brings to the nexus "bents," or "talents." Those talents are limited. No one member of the triad can care for all her needs. For example, no one can be her own educator, can provide for all her economic needs, be her own priest, be her on media, set up her own regulations, be her own government. No one is isolated from all others and is talented enough to do everything. The only way one's needs can be met is to depend on others. The I and Thou bring their inherent interdependence to the nexus of the triad. Here we find in the nexus the basis for social differentiation, both horizontal and vertical. In our discussion of solidarity we found the basis of social unity. Here we find the basis of social differentiation.

On the basis of and within the pattern potentials of a nexus a particular society forms specific, concrete institutions. In America they are capitalism; representative form of democratic government; Baptist church; nuclear family; universal formal education K-12, technological schools, colleges, and universities; a constitution; and mass media. Each institution develops on the basis of trust and is differentiated by the talents, giftedness of the members of the triad. Such institutions stabilize social action, including trusting, oughting, and transcending.

These patterns are present only in the nexus of the interacting triad and cannot be reduced to the components of the triad. We shall call these "primary institutions."

Primary Institutions as Pattern Potentials of the Nexus of the Triad

Now we face a problem. Institutions form, decay, and die as new ones take their place. For example, in the West the extended family of the ancient world has been replaced in the modern world by the nuclear family. Though individual institutions last for awhile and die out, they are replaced by others of the same type. That is, though the extended family rarely exists, the nuclear family has taken its place. And both are types of family, of the reproductive institutional structure. Now, how account for the continuity of the type, such as the reproductive institutional structure, as well as the changeableness of the token, the individual instances of family structure?[23]

Consider primary institutions. They are stable, enduring, norm governed social pattern potentials of the triad undergirded by physical laws. The I, Thou, and It interact on the basis of the natural possibilities [including their own bodies, needs, and talents], value possibilities [purposes and goals], and the potentialities each brings to the triad.[24] As the interaction occurs, it has a focus. The focus is present only in the interacting connection and is not reducible to the individual participants in the interaction. We shall call this focus of interaction a *nexus*. As the triadic interaction occurs, pattern potentials appear that are located neither in the individual participants of the triad nor external to the triad. They appear only in the nexus. These patterns are the potential ways of meeting the needs of the members of the triad and are required for the interaction to continue. For example, the possibility of communication occurs only within the triad and is required for the interaction to continue. Without the possibility of communication between I and Thou regarding an It, their social interaction would be severely limited. For I and Thou to relate to each other with regard to an It, they must be able to communicate with each other, to share information, knowledge, methods, procedures, and criteria. It is conceivable that an interaction could occur without communication; however, that would be only within the ecosystem (if at all). As one considers the life of the triad, particularly as it continues beyond its present members, it must be possible to teach members the ways of living generated within the triad, that is, their culture.

Further, the potentiality of communication would make possible education, whether informal or formal. In this sense the potential of education is intrinsic to and maintained within the structure of the triad. Here we find a pattern potential of the triadic relation that is not reducible to the individual members of the triad.

Finally, in general each I and Thou possesses the same needs. But each brings to the nexus "bents," or "talents." Furthermore, no one member of the triad can care for all her needs. For example, no one can be her own educator (even an autodidact can do so only on the basis of previous learning that was not self-taught), can provide for all her economic needs, or can be her own priest. The members of the triad are interdependent. Here we find in the pattern potentials the basis of social differentiation, for social hierarchy. In our discussion of solidarity, we found the basis for social unity, for our horizontal relationships. Here we find the basis for social difference, our vertical relationships.[25]

At least seven pattern potentials appear in every society: economic, educational, political, reproductive, religious, regulative, media and communicative.[26] The specific institutions a society forms varies with the possibilities of the habitat and the potentials of the members of the social group to transform the habitat to meet their needs. They could choose a barter system, capitalism, or some other specific economic system. Pattern potentials that arise only in the nexus of the interacting triad are primary institutions, or institutional types (in contrast to universals). The specific concrete institutions a society develops on the basis of and guided by the pattern potentials of the triad we shall call secondary institutions, or institutional tokens.

Creative-Finding Secondary Institutions

What then is a secondary institution? It is a specific, historically concrete, relatively permanent pattern of social relations, (vertical and horizontal) sanctioned by norms that satisfy specific social desires, needs, and/or purposes. A particular school, say Furman University, is a secondary institution. But what is the relation between a primary and a secondary institution? A secondary institution is a particular pattern of relationships made out of the possibilities of primary institutions.[27]

We claim that secondary institutions are the numerically distinct, specific constructions made as we creatively find and explore the possibilities of primary institutions. In our daily lives we consciously intend little of what actually occurs. For example, as we pay tuition at Furman we sometimes do so with cash. As we look into our purses or billfolds, we consciously identify the bills we need and hand them to the bursar, who hands us our change, if any. In this transaction we do not consciously intend the full range and multilayered complexity of Furman as well as its place and function within the American economy. We participate in the institutional life of Furman, yet we are consciously aware of and intend only a small part of it.

Institutions and Trust

By connecting Background and Foreground, primary and secondary institutions stabilize society through time. The claim here is that trust is the root of institutions stabilizing power. But is that true?

It is not hard to find trust here. As we consciously matriculate into Furman's life, we know that we are obligated to pay tuition and fees, which imply a "holding for true" accompanied by some justification. But that transaction and its implications occur within a framework of trust in other people, the college, the economic system, and the natural environment. And that framework is the background. Also, the background is at least institutional in structure, though it may be more.

To locate the place of trust in relation to institutions, we need to keep in mind the distinction between the activity potentials of the individuals and the pattern potentials of the nexus found only in the triad. Think of belief as an activity potential. Without that potential individual humans could not trust. Trees do not seem to have it, but many animals do. However, without the triadic interrelationship it would make no sense to mention trust, the recognition of an object or cause, and acknowledgement of a person in which confidence is placed or not placed. This means that trust can appear only within the potentials of the interrelationship among the members of the triad. It is here that primary institutions appear structurally possible (the range of these structures is limited by the individual potentials and relational potentials), and the possibility of trust can be made a reality. That is, if an individual remained alone, no trust could be formed. In the potentials of the nexus and the constructions made within and the basis of those potentials, we find trust as the unifier of concrete institutions.

We may add at this point that trust undergirds, permeates, and unites institutions; ethics does as well. Mutuality of trust, as we have seen, implies an obligation to keep promises, the promises to be trustworthy. In the freedom of each I and Thou to choose and keep promises, we also find transcendence of the Thou and I in their mutual relation. This also means that in our mutual promising to maintain requires a renunciation of my own self-interests for the sake of fidelity, trust. Implied in trust is *kenosis* (renunciation of selfishness) for the well-being of others, for the care of others.[28] From this we can conclude that institutions resting on trust, rest on the ethics of obligation, transcendence, *kenosis*, and concern for the well being of others. Social stability, in so far as institutions provide it, it is ethical. Ethics does not rest on social stability. Indeed, trust is found at the roots of potentials of the members of the triad and continue from primary institutions through secondary ones.

Lingering Questions

Return to two lingering issues that arose from searching for the stabilizers of social action. Earlier we asked whether institutions are found or made, and how can a society maintain order and yet hold to individual freedom?

Are institutions found or made? That secondary institutions are made is clear. But whether primary ones are made or not is problematic. Let's frame the issue as an antinomy. Consider the conjunction: primary institutions are made and primary institutions are found. Each claim is true. Any examination of the natural world, either by a physicist or a biologist, would supply adequate evidence for the truth of the left side of the conjunct. Searle drives his stakes here, Dewey would as well, and most modern sociologists seem to agree as does Berger, for example.[29] However, the right side of the disjunct is true as well. Any record we have of what we would call persons indicates that they both are born into and learn in social-physical contexts. That includes forming and learning language. In that sense humans find institutions pre-existing, in some sense, their existence as humans. Thus, both claims are true, but they cannot both the true; they are contradictory. Hence, the antinomy.

Our short study reveals that the approach taken by two metaphysical world-views that attempt to be exclusive is to attack the other conjunct of the antinomy in an attempt to show that it is false and that their side is true. We find each is a limited ontology and return to the puzzle of the antinomy. Returning to experience, not from the point of view of the methodological skepticism of a Descartes but from that of radical empiricists such as Borden Parker Bowne, we search for structures that are implicit in the fullness of practical living and manifest themselves within it. We learn that living is essentially triadic, always involving I, Thou, and It. Further reflection helps us realize three important aspects of interactions within triads: (1) each of the three elements brings to the triad dispositions or potentialities, if you will, that allow for the formation of human social life, and (2) the interaction of the potentialities/dispositions are developed in terms of the natural capacities [natural law of gravity, life needs, for example] of all three and the normative life of the I and Thou in relation, and (3) the interaction necessarily involves communication among the three. Together, these provide for stability, endurance, and maintenance within the framework of the triadic structure, the condition for the continuation of the structure itself. Within triadic structure we find primary institutions.

Institutions are not only found, they are also made. They are made in the sense that they arise only within the interaction of the triad. They are potential within the triad. They come into existence, move beyond potentiality, through the creative finding of I and Thou in relation to the It. Here we find not only primary institutions but also secondary ones. Education as an enduring and stable social structure is creatively-found. Thus our answers to two questions Searle raises. There are primary institutions that are found and secondary institutions that we make.

Also note that societies stressing order risk limiting individual freedom; those stressing individual freedom risk disorder. We have shown that our second nature requires both a solidar and stability to meaningfully relate the Background and the Foreground. That raises the question of the place of individual freedom and social order in our second nature. Succinctly, individuals, though intrinsically social, can act contrary to their second nature, their solidar, and their stabilizers. Each numerically distinct, naturally "bent" individual has the potential to initiate action, to imagine possibilities, and to reflect on their implications. In that sense the individual person though formed in the triad is nevertheless free. The person can imagine, reflect, and act in ways contrary to the culture; but it will always occur in a society with a culture. Such freedom is not eliminated by the order of a culture. But it is always formed and informed by that culture. As Martin Luther King, Jr. attacked racism in America and occasionally acted contrary to established law, he did so as an American. We are culturally influenced but not culturally determined.

CONCLUSION

Self-knowledge does not occur in a vacuum. It is gained and lived in an organized society. That raised four questions: how can persons know each other, act together, bond into society, and stabilize their bonding over time? Answers that appeal to Order and Emerging Persons, cultural dyadic objectivism and cultural monadic objectivism, grounded in the Metaphysics of Being and Rationalism are weakened by their own internal anomalies and suspicion, lost their authority, legitimacy. In persons-in-triadic-relations-of-mutual-trust, an embodied narrative almost ignored by the exhausted authority of contemporary Western individualism and science, we found a *topos*, a perspective with rich possibilities for guiding us to self-knowledge.

The Master Narrative, persons-in-triadic-relations-of-mutual-trust, guides us to understand properly social action. Answering the other minds problem, trust provides the tie required for solidarity. Triads are composed of I mutually trusting Thou regarding a Cause, an It. There we find all humans living in mutual trust, ought and transcendence. However, persons may break a specific promise, may act in an untrustworthy manner. We found that ironically, breaking secondary trust can occur only within primary trust of social solidarity.

We also asked what stabilizes solidarity and learned that the basis for stability is found in the triadic relation itself, specifically in the *nexus*. There we found pattern potentials that when acted on form the seven basic institutions of society. We also learned that primary institutions are rooted not only in trust and in the causes of society but also in the needs I and Thou bring to the triad as well as their "bents," "giftedness," and "talents." As potential, we can act on them and form concrete institutions of a society at a particular time and place.

Living in a social, cultural context, we learn more about ourselves. Aware of ourselves as persons living as members of a culturally organized society, we also learned to speak of ourselves as whole persons living in a culture situated in a natural habitat. Body, habitat, the natural expanse play a central role in whole persons living in triads of trust but also in societies with cultures. They play a central role self-knowledge. We contend that the natural lives and passes through the pores and interstices of persons, societies, cultures as thoroughly it does through I, Thou, and Cause. Being natural does not mean distinctions are not made; they need to be made, and are worthwhile. But distinctions must be made by whole persons living together in reciprocal trust or distrust for the well-being of each person.

As we learn what we are, we also learn what we are to be, and what we are to do. We are, at least, whole persons guided by the moral structure of mutual trust to seek the well being others and ourselves. To do that, we create institutions to care for each other, feed the poor, shelter the homeless, and enfranchise the disenfranchised; that is, to love mercy and act justly. But, what authorized, legitimates both what we are called to do and the patterns within which our callings are carried out?

The *topos,* the Master Narrative, also points to the Personal. Through the Master Narrative, we come to acknowledge and trust the Personal. Why believe that insight? What does the metaphor "The Personal" say about The Personal, the Presence? In what way does the Personal as authority legitimize the connections between background and foreground that make it possible for us to be and to do what our self-knowledge requires?

Notes

1. Thomas O. Buford, ed., *Essays on Other Minds* (Urbana, IL: University of Illinois Press, 1970), x–xi.

2. Some whose work is affected by this quandary are Peter L. Berger, Mary Douglas, Michel Foucault, and Jurgen Habermas. See Robert Wuthnow et al, eds., *Cultural Analysis* (Boston, MA: Routledge and Kegan Paul, 1984), 246.

3. See Alfred Schutz, *The Phenomenology of the Social World* (Evanston, IL: Northwestern University Press, [1932] 1972), chapter 3, 97–138.

4. Schutz, *The Phenomenology,* xxv.

5. Schutz, *The Phenomenology,* xxvi.

6. Frederick Will argues in a similar manner that it is odd to attempt to understand human knowledge by divesting "oneself of as much of this knowledge as one possibly can and then see how much of it, starting form new sure beginnings, and proceeding by new sure steps, can be regained." Frederick Will, *Induction and Justification: An Investigation of Cartesian Procedure in the Philosophy of Knowledge* (Ithaca, NY: Cornell University Press, 1974), 161.

7. In the ancient and medieval worlds under the Master Narrative of Order with power moving from top down, it was assumed that the lower in the natural world and in humans, their bodies, their desires must be constrained and formed by powers external to them, political and educational. Only through formative constraints can the intellect begin to perform its proper function, guide persons by acting prudently to form the virtue of prudence. Augustine's descriptions of beatings in school are an example. The Renaissance slowly replaced Order with Emerging Persons. Under the influence of modern science, political freedom after the Magna Carta, and modern dualism articulated by Descartes, the emphasis shifted to individual person's freedom to act unconstrained by institutional power, other than what the individual authorizes. The problem arose under dualism whether knowledge and action could be other than individual. The benefits of the new Master Narrative generated major obstacles to forming societies, knowing other minds and on what basis form solidarity and

stability of a society with a culture. The problem of legitimation arose for Emerging Persons. Indeed, both Order and Emerging Persons implode through internal problems they generated for themselves.

8. Myles Brand (ed.), *The Nature of Human Action* (New York, NY: Scott, Foresman and Company, 1970), 6, 8. For reasons to be stated later, we recognize that freedom is central to action and that action is central to the nature of persons. With significant modifications mentioned later, we adopt a voluntarist, triadic view of action. Other philosophers have focused on it, and the result is a wealth of literature. Alfred Schutz in *The Phenomenology of the Social World* investigates the actions of people through an analysis of the concept of meaning and a rich description of the lived experiences of other people. Also, sociologists have long recognized the place of the concept of action in their theories. The work of Talcott Parsons is a good example. See "Prolegomena to a Theory of Social Institutions," *American Sociological Review* 55 no. 3 (June 1990): 313–345.

9. From Brand, (ed.). *The Nature of Human Action,* 6, 8.

10. Natural and artificial actions are well established in the literature. See Mary Douglas, *How Institutions Think.* Syracuse (New York, NY: Syracuse University Press, 1986), and Elizabeth Wolgast, *Ethics of an Artificial Person, Lost Responsibility in Professions and Organizations* (Stanford, CA: Stanford University Press, 1992). The definition of action offered above refers to natural action. Artificial action was offered by Hobbes in his discussion of state action. Institutional action is triadic action developed by Thomas O. Buford, *Trust, our Second Nature, Crisis, Reconciliation, and the Personal* (Lanham, MD: Lexington Books, 2009), 89–91.

11. For a twentieth century attempt by an individualist, consult William Ernest Hocking's theory of will circuits, especially *Human Nature and its Remaking*.(New Haven, CT: Yale University Press, 1918), and *Man and the State* (New Haven, CT: Yale University Press, 1926). For an essay on will circuits in Hocking's thought consult, Tom Buford, "Institutions and the Making of Persons: W. E. Hocking's Social Personalism, " in *A William Ernest Hocking Reader*, with Commentary Edited by John Lachs and D. Micah Hester (Nashville, TN: Vanderbilt University Press, 2004), 290–304.

12. This point was recognized early in the twentieth century by Charles Horton Cooley. "An institution is simply a definite and established phase of the public mind, not different in its ultimate nature from public opinion, though often seeming, on account of its permanence and the visible customs and symbols in which it is clothed, to have a somewhat distinct and independent existence. . . . Language, government, the church, laws and customs of property and of the family, systems of industry and education, are institutions because they are the working out of permanent needs of human nature." *Social Organization* (New York: Scribner's Sons, 1909), quoted in Edgar F. Borgata and Henry J. Meyer, eds., *Sociological Theory, Present-Day Sociology from the Past* (New York, NY: Alfred A. Knopf, 1956), 252.

13. Marcus G. Singer, "Institutional Ethics*,*" in *Ethics*, A. Phillips Griffiths, ed., Royal Institute of Philosophy Supplement, 35 (Cambridge, UK: Cambridge University Press, 1993), 227–28.

14. Talcott Parsons, "Prolegomena to a Theory of Social Institutions," *American Sociological Review* 55 no. 3 (June 1990): 320.

15. Melville J. Herskovits, *Cultural Anthropology* (New York, NY: Alfred A. Knopf, 1960), 95.

16. Herskovits, *Cultural Anthropology*.

17. Herskovits, *Cultural Anthropology*.

18. "Moral" refers to the central norms and patterns of behavior of a society. "Moral" is not the same as "ethical." Moral refers to what is the way of life of a society, and ethical refers to what ought to be their way of life.

19. Each person brings to the triad activity potentials, at least, that allow her to develop. However, the particular personality she becomes occurs in the triadic context. It is crucial to distinguish self, personality, and person: the activity potentials, the way the activity potentials develop and take form in the context of Thou and It, and the one whose these are. See Peter A. Bertocci, The Person, His Personality, and Environment," *Review of Metaphysics*, no.32 (1979): 605–621. See also Niebuhr, *Faith on Earth*, and Josiah Royce, *Outlines of Psychology: An Elemental Treatise with Some Practical Applications* (New York, NY: The Macmillan Co.), 1911.

20. The triadic relation can be conceived graphically as a triangle, with I, Thou, and It appearing as the three points.

21. Cf. Theodore R. Schatzki, *The Site of the Social* (University Park, PA: The Pennsylvania State University Press, 2002).

22. That humans have needs is well established by Gordon Allport, *Pattern and Growth in Personality* (New York, NY: Holt, Rinehart and Winston, 1961); Paul Ricoeur, *Nature and Freedom: The Voluntary and the Involuntary*, part I, trans. Erazim V. Kohak (Evanston, IL: Northwestern University Press (1950) 1966); and Peter A. Bertocci, *Introduction to the Philosophy of Religion* (New York, NY: Prentice-Hall, 1951), 191–222. Bertocci's discussion of needs distinguishes between primary drives (physiological) and native mental motives, as well as their interconnectedness. Their place in institutions is noted by James K. Feibleman, *The Institutions of Society* (New York, NY: Humanities Press, [1956] 1968).

23. Cf. Carle C. Zimmerman, *Family and Civilization* (Wilmington, DE: Intercollegiate Studies Institute, (1947) 2008).

24. "Potential" is what can be done when the occasion calls for it.

25. See James Alexander, *The Civil Sphere* (New York, NY: Oxford University Press, 2006), 206. He says that "In social systems . . . every actor occupies a dual position. He or she is a subordinate or superordinate actor in a whole series of vertical hierarchies and, at the same time, a member of the horizontal community of civil life."

26. This list is from Alexander, *Civil Sphere,* 203–204. They are derived from empirical studies of societies, not logically deduced from axioms. .

27. This discussion of institutions as they appear in the triadic relation gains strength through building on the insights of dyadic cultural objectivism and monadic cultural subjectivism. The former recognizes that humans find themselves enmeshed in a society; humans are inherently social beings. They need stable horizontal and vertical structures in which to live. The latter recognizes that humans through their

imaginations, power of rational reflection, and free will can and sometimes must challenge and change established vertical and horizontal institutional relations that fail to meets their needs. Humans need the freedom to modify or revolutionize those social patterns that are not responsible and that are unfair. However, the weakness of the former is its resting social structures in a rationalistic, hierarchical metaphysics that limits freedom, social alternatives, and human growth and development. The weakness of the latter is its tendency to reject all social structures that do not meet one's specific interests and needs. Such a view taken to extreme can result in disorder. The view outlined here provides for social order in the patterned potentialities of the triad and for human freedom, imagination, and reflective thought in individual potentials and capacities the I and Thou bring to the triad. Further, this view is a type of "natural law" theory, if one interprets the word "natural" to mean what is inherent to the triad relation, the pattern potentials. Pattern potentials are not the universal, eternal possibles of reality, Plato's eternal forms or the eternal forms of the mind of God, that "receive existence as the demiurge or God in its goodness persuades the Receptacle to take unto itself their likeness, creating the best of all possible worlds. They exist, however in the pattern potentials of the nexus of the I-Thou-It triad.

28. Cf. Virginia Held, *The Ethics of Care, Personal, Political, and Global* (Oxford: Oxford University Press, 2006). She recognizes that care is a value and a practice, and she finds trust to be essential to practice. Her analysis, however, assumes an individualism and though she sees it as developing within social relations, she does not account for those relations. We do so by appealing to the triadic structure of experience and the centrality of trust to that relation. That is, she needs a social Personalism to account for the ethics of care.

29. Peter L. Berger, *The Social Construction of Reality; a Treatise in the Sociology of Knowledge* (Garden City, NY: Doubleday, 1966).

Chapter 6

The Personal

The Personal is the Ultimate Environment of triads, society/culture, and nature. Our search for self-knowledge led to investigating environments on which we depend and that contribute to what we are, who we are to be, and what we are to do. Rejecting the failed master narratives Order and Emerging Self, grounded in being and Rationalism, we turned to the fullness of ordinary living. There we found potentialities of persons, causes, and bodies realized in triadic social structures bound and stabilized by trust for the sake of the well-being of whole persons and their environments. Each environment glued by trust, sustains us, and points beyond itself to the Master Narrative, Persons-in-triadic-trusting-relation. The Master Narrative, the *topos* within which we live and know, points to that on which it depends, the Personal. The Personal participates in triadic relations, mutual trusting, does not act treasonously, desert, lie, or break promises. Finally, as addressed by the Personal, we respond by acknowledging as Personal the one calling us. In that response, we mutually trust each other and assume the responsibility of the moral requirements of promise keeping. In that relation we come to know what we are, whole persons

Why believe that insight? First, recapitulate the discussion to this point.

RECAPITULATION

Suspicion destroys hope for achieving self-knowledge through either Order or the Emerging Self. It severs connections binding our background and foreground required for social and personal solidarity and stability. In the present so-called Post Modern world in the West, options present themselves.

They range between two poles, Order of Cultural Dyadic Objectivism and the Emerging Self of Cultural Monadic Subjectivism. The former, from the ancient and medieval worlds, focused on the structure of social life and finds in Order its solidar and stabilizer. Individuals were defined by that structure and allowed little room for growth outside of it. That is, their place in the hierarchical structure of society limited their social space. Whatever growth opportunities they possessed lay in the religious realm, their relation to their God or gods. Social structures provided both solidarity and stability. While those structures were subjected to critique and change, ancient and medieval societies appealed to a metaphysical order to undergird their weakening or destroyed social solidarity and stability. Turning to the metaphysics of being understood through Rationalism, they believed that God or Being grounds social unity and stability.

In the Renaissance and early modernity, Cultural Monadic Subjectivism rejected the grounding of society, its solidarity and stability, in being and the power of rationalism to grasp it. Affirming the freedom of individuals to make their own way in society, the Cultural Monadic Subjectivist attacked the rigid social and cultural structures of the past and demanded freedom to choose solidars and stabilizers. These the Subjectivist found in the individuals themselves, in their nature and most cherished values.

Unfortunately, neither approach adequately provided for the unity and stability of triadic action. The cultural dyadic objectivist overemphasized the social aspect of triadic action to the detriment of the individual persons in the triad. And the cultural monadic subjectivist overemphasized the individual aspect of social action to the detriment of the social unity of triadic action. As we have seen, any position between these two poles is beset with the same problem. What is that problem?

The problem lies in grounding Master Narratives and self-knowledge in being as illuminated by the tradition of Parmenides and Heraclitus, and in attempting to understand both the solidar and the stabilizer of society within the One Many problem generated by being. Dyadicists appealed to the One and attempted to account for the many in terms of it. Spinoza is a modern example. The Subjectivist appealed to the many, attempted to account for their unity in terms of them. Leibniz is a good example. Unfortunately, framing the problem in that way leads to the violence of metaphysics, to the violence of the person, to the denial of the meaning of individual personhood, as well as to the failure to grasp social action as the faithful triadic relation of trust, values, cause, and Cause. Succinctly, self-knowledge cannot be adequately attained through impersonal being.

We must move beyond Being and Rationalism to ground any master narrative authorizing and legitimating self-knowledge, social action, its stability and solidarity. This issue lives at the root of western culture, as Heidegger and Wittgenstein pointed out. Both encouraged us to move beyond being. If we do so, what unifies and stabilizes culture, society, the lives of persons, triadic action?

If we move beyond the deep, all pervading but now impotent Rationalism of our cultural Background, are we left directionless to face and live into the future? We are not. Within the Master Narrative of persons-in-triadic-trusting-relations, the Personal comes into full flower and provides direction to living lives good to live.[1]

Each step in our discussion points to The Personal. Lost under suspicion, we turn to our past and find in the Abramic tradition something personal that is also social. Though submerged by the ancient and medieval Order of social, natural hierarchy and by Renaissance Emerging Self of isolated individuals seeking social connection, it continues. "Something personal" suggests The Personal.

Looking fresh at the fullness of our practical living, we find an underlying structure, I-Thou-It triad bound and stabilized by trust. Personal living is always communal. That suggests the Master Narrative, Persons-in-triadic-trusting-relations. We live in environments, though not limited by them. Triadic structures point beyond themselves to social action, society, culture, and the natural (personal bodies, habitat, and the natural expanse). Meanwhile, "something personal" continues, suggesting the Ultimate Environment, the core of the *topos*, the perspective, the Master Narrative, the Personal.

The Personal as grasped by us is triadically mediated. It is grasped as participating in each triad, yet it is also mysterious other. The Master Narrative the most complete *topos*, is an interpersonal way of grasping The Personal. Further, The Personal is faithful, trustworthy, creator. As Creator, The Personal creates *ex nihilo* the underlying structures of trust that provide for solidar and stable connections between Background and Foreground. Being created by the Personal, connections between Background and Foreground gain their legitimacy and disperse the threat of suspicion. In the Personal, we know what we are.

Returning to the insight, why believe it?

EMBRACING THE INSIGHT

It can be argued that we should embrace claims only on solid evidence. Some justification is required. It can be argued that the Master Narrative is a linguistic device referring to the Personal. It is not the Personal, unless the Personal is metaphor and nothing more. The Master Narrative unveils what is there, but is what is there the Personal? Responding, two approaches are possible. On the one hand, relying on the metaphysics of Being and Rationalism, we could appeal to an argument. On the other, relying on metaphorical insight, we could seek to be eloquent, tell the most complete story. The latter approach is inside, interpersonal, metaphorical; the former is outside, objective, critically reflective, observational, and impersonal. Yet, arguments assume inside, interpersonal relations of mutual trusting. They are ironic.[2] In addition, the question of the existence of The Personal raises the other minds problem. Are there minds other than my own; if so, how can that be known; and how can we know their content? Consider first the argument and second the other minds issue.[3]

Argument

Here is an argument structured in the manner of logicians; premises logically imply the conclusion.

P1 *Actions are agentive, free, temporal (including a Background and Foreground), triadic in structure, governed by a cause (an end), and occur in a world that is friendly to them.*

Agentive refers to the capacity of persons to initiate non-compelled movement. That is, persons can perform actions. As free, they face in the Foreground genuine alternatives, and their choice is non-compelled. They could have done otherwise. Actions are performed in triads of mutual trust. As such all social actions are moral; they do or do not care for the other with regard to their needs and social purposes. This is clear from our discussion of Solidarity. And from our discussion of Stability, actions are performed by institutions, in the special sense we developed. There are no non-triadic actions. Further, actions, as triadic, are performed with reference to a cause, an end, an ideal. Actions are governed by regnant ideals. Finally, actions are performed in a natural and social world that is friendly to them, in the sense that they support them and is amenable to achieving the various options available for choice.

P2 *Actions are supported by warrants and backings.*

In traditional arguments, the truth of a claim (the conclusion) rests on the truth of other claims (evidence) that truth-functionally imply the claim and on the relatedness and relevance of the evidence to the conclusion. But why believe that evidence is related to that claim? On the basis of warrants. That is, the warrant justifies the connection between the evidence and the conclusion. But then, why believe the truth of the warrant? We appeal to a backing to support the belief in the truth of the warrant. Clearly, this is logically an infinite regress. But, as we proceed, we shall seek some stopping place, some backing that can be shown rests on no further backing, but is the Backing, beyond which we cannot reasonably proceed. At that point, we are in the field of Metaphysics.[4]

Consider this example. A particular person's behavior we witness has certain characteristics: agentive, free, temporal, triadic, norm governed, supported by the social/physical environments. A friend tells me that that behavior is an action. Queried, he answers, "I have seen that behavior before, and it is an action." If I press the discussion and ask why those characteristics are connected to action behaviors, he appeals to a reason for connecting them in just that way. He appeals to a warrant. All actions are agentive, free, temporal, triadic, norm governed, and are supported by the social/physical world in which they occur. If pressed for a justification for that generalization, he appeals to a backing. He might reasonably reply that the movement of blood in the circulatory system of the human body and brushing his teeth are different, and the difference lies in characteristics. The circulatory system does not possess them, and brushing his teeth does. The latter is an action, and the former is a movement. And, if pressed for a justification of that belief, he could appeal to his observations of the order and nature of everyday events in his life. And, if pressed further, he would simply say, "That's just the way things are." And, if pressed further, he could simply shrug off the question by saying it is unanswerable. Or he could offer a hypothesis that would best account for "the way things are." Or, he could claim that the reasoning of his argument so far implies an answer. In those two cases, he would seek backing in metaphysics.

P3 *No impersonalism, whether substructure or superstructure, can provide adequate backing for warranted actions.*[5]

Substructure refers to the order of nature to which actions are related and that can, purportedly, account for the nature and structure of actions. And superstructure refers to an order of pattern or form that accounts for the structure and nature of actions. Neither can adequately account for actions nor for the solidarity, stability, and possible reconciliation of fractured solidarity and stabilizers. More important, neither provides an adequate account of trust, the obligation to care for the other, and the transcendence of the other that permeates our second nature.

Consider actions first. According to the substructure, actions are accounted for by appealing to an underlying deterministic or statistical order of cause and effect. That is, to account for event B at T^2 one must appeal to event A at T^1. The relationship could be strong, where it is invariable and uniform, temporal, contiguous, and asymmetrical. A weak form would add, ". . . , unless there are intervening circumstances." Another weak form of causality is the hypothetical. In each case, appealing to the backing of a causal order, an action can be adequately explained. Unfortunately, embedding action in a causal order renders meaningless both truth and error. For example, the determinist argues that we should believe that determinism is true. That assumes we are free to choose between determinism and some other view. However, the determinist argues that all actions, including freely choosing to believe that determinism is true, are but functions of a cause and effect system. That system requires that all choices can be fully accounted for by previous events. That is, all choices are caused by something other than the free, self-initiated, non-compelled[6] cause (free will) of the agent acting. That contradicts an assumption of the determinist who presents arguments to show determinism is true. The determinist must assume the person she is attempting to persuade has a choice between truth and error. Otherwise, why attempt to offer evidence for the truth of the position. If no free choice, there can be no legitimate distinction between truth and error.[7]

The superstructure fares no better. Actions are best explained by appealing to a reality lying beyond them, categories such as "Being, Cause, Identity, Change, the Absolute and the like."[8] Actions are but tokens of one or more of those types. All concrete reality can be accounted for through a deduction from first principles. Here we find subject-predicate logic guiding metaphysical understanding of actions. S-P logic is the form of the backing of the superstructure. In Platonism, for example, specific actions are specifications of the class, Action. Such first principles are expected to account for the orderly change of actions, for example. But they cannot do so.

First principles such as being are necessary, immutable, and eternal. Actions are the behavior of agents; they are freely chosen and are temporal in structure. The temporal relation between Background and Foreground in a trust based triad requires solidarity and stability for the social/personal identity of our second nature. Actions are contingent, mutable, and temporal. Thus the issue is clear. How can two things totally unlike each other be related? If their relation is logical, that leaves unexplained the temporality of action. The superstructure purchases solidarity and stability at the cost of being unrelated to the action it is called on to explain.

If actions have whatever reality they possess through being embedded in eternal forms, they lose their moral significance. All good and evil must rest in the First Principles. If First Principles are Good, then evil must also be a good, a contradiction. To claim with Augustine that evil is the absence of the Good makes both evil and good actions unreal to some degree. But they are real, at least to the extent that we can be held responsible for them. If being responsible is likewise unreal to some degree we soon discover that life itself is to some degree unreal. If so, the pressing reality of problematic actions that drove us to search for explanation has lost its urgency. Our actions have become abstractions in relation to the reality of First Principles. Ironic.

No form of impersonalism can adequately account for the Personal, the life of persons in society. Whether one appeals to the micro of the physical or the macro of Being (understood in the lineage of Parmenides), neither possesses qualities that can account for action. Neither can they account for the characteristics of the triadic structure of social action, at the root of which is trust, obligation (caring for the other), and transcendence; for the solidarity and stability of social action that rest on that ethical base and that are designed to care for the other; nor for the possibility of reconciling fractures in solidarity and stability obligated by the transcendent obligation to care for the other, the Cause. If our second nature is social actions in triadic relations of mutual trust, obligation, and transcendence, where triads are solidified by trust, care for the other, and transcendence goals and structured by both primary potentials and secondary institutions, the impersonal possesses nothing within itself to account for trust, care for the other, and transcendence and for solidarity and stability that rest on the ethical triad.

Neither can the impersonal be the continuant through actions, accounting for stability. It cannot enter into a trusting relationship that unifies persons in the triad and obligates them to seek through stable structures (institutions) to care for the other. Acting persons in triadic relations, unified by trust and the cause of mutually caring for the other as each renounces selfishness, form stable patterns to meet those needs. Those patterns may appear to be impersonal, as the U.S. Constitution. That could be due to their stability; but those are formed by and depend on triadic action rooted in trust and its ethical dimensions. Finally, the impersonal cannot account for the ends of actions, the cause in triads. Those are values, ideals, meaningful and functional only for purposive agents in a triad of trust. Potassium pumps in the brain function; they do not choose ends and work to achieve them

Succinctly, no impersonalism can account for unity within and among social triads, for the structures that stabilize social action, and for the obligation for self-emptying in caring for the other on which the social triad rests and that permeates solidarity, stability, reconciliation. It is possible to allow the iron cage of technological processes to structure social life.⁹ But those structures seek to replace trust with impersonal, predictable patterns that dehumanize action and turn actions into a compelled causal order.

P4 *The Personal is Faithful, Trustworthy Agent, Authority who as constant, continuant, and cause (Purposive End) solidifies and structures triadic action. This hypothesis best explains, accounts for, and provides adequate backing for trusting interpersonal actions.*

On the assumption that P3 is true, and in contrast to any form of impersonalism, what can be expected from the argument? Building an empirical argument, no direct, rational grasp of the Personal is possible. Yet we are not without options. We can advance the structure of the master narrative and persons in community related in triadic-trusting as a *hypothesis* to account for that relationship.¹⁰ The best explanation is the Personal. If so, as trustworthy Agent, the Personal creates persons in triadic relation and trustworthily sustains solidarity and stability to achieve the Cause of self-renunciation and caring for others. Given the truth of the premises, the conclusion can be inferred, embraced.

Therefore, it is true that only the triadic interrelation of persons, specifically The Personal and persons in relation to a Cause, can adequately account for the unity and stability of our second nature.

Irony

That argument is ironic. It asks us to believe the claim is true on the basis of premises implying the conclusion. We are asked to believe that The Personal exists, that The Personal is moral, the causal Agent and the Cause of social relations, and that the relation between them is mutual trust. That is, we should believe in a trusting relation with The Personal, the interpersonal core of the insight, on the basis of a rational argument whose backing lies in fundamental rational principles.

Ironically, rational arguments receive backing, the connection among premises and conclusion, from the insights of the premises and conclusion. The backing rests on trust within the interpersonal relation we call the triad, and on trust in a reality that is friendly to us and is faithful and trustworthy, The Personal. Even if we were to choose some form of impersonalism, whether infrastructure or superstructure, we would assume it is trustworthy. We trust it. It appears that here we find an interpersonal relation with other persons, the Cause, and The Personal. Our formal argument can be formulated only with the backing of triadic-trust, obligation, and transcendence, that is, The

Personal. In that sense the argument is subordinate to The Personal. Before continuing, pause to consider dimensions of that insight.

Implications of Irony

The backing to which we must appeal can be generated from neither Rationalism nor the Metaphysics of Being. It is understandable why philosophers appeal to the metaphor of mathematics in their attempt to ground solidarity and stability. Mathematics is steady and universal amid conflicting religious voices and rapidly changing social conditions. Philosophically, Rationalism, as the extension of mathematics into the metaphysical realm of being, grounds cultural dyadic objectivism. Rationalism and the metaphysics of being are firmly in place. In the Hebrew and early Christian traditions, Yahweh, trustworthy and moral, enters into a trusting, moral relation with finite persons. As that tradition moved into the mainstream of Roman and early medieval life, it called on the metaphysics of Being and Rationalism to provide credibility for its beliefs. Augustine joined the trusting relation between finite persons and the Personal God to being where he found rational support for that trusting relation, an uneasy alliance at best.[11] The irony of Rationalism continued unnoticed. In the modern period with the growth of science and the steady eclipse of religious life, Rationalism became scientific and subordinated the Personal to it. The Metaphysics of Being and Rationalism changed to comply with the new science. New forms of materialism and naturalism appeared. Nevertheless, the Personal, though barely visible in the penumbra of the laser light of rationality and submerged by Universal Being, remained and began to reemerge.

Yet, through this long history, the freedom of persons to make choices and take responsibility for their lives, clearly argued for by Augustine in *On Free Choice of the Will,* continued. As a metaphysic, it emerged in the thought of Jacobi and continued through German and British thinkers to Hermann Lotze and to the United States through Royce, Bowne, and Howison. However, still under the influence of the Spinoza-Leibniz debate, they did not free persons or the Personal from Rationalism and the metaphysics of being. Karol Wojtyla's Personalism remained under the influence of Aquinas and of Max Scheler's value hierarchy of the Great Chain of Being. A.N. Whitehead's and Hartshorne's Personalism was encased in Rationalism and process philosophy. It is only in the mid to late twentieth century that the Personal emerges in a more pristine form, to date, in Mounier, Bertocci, and Macmurray. Yet, they did not consider the irony in their own views. They ignored trust and obligation on which all interpersonal relations rest. It is that trust we have attempted to manifest. We have attempted to move beyond Being and Rationalism and to show the ethical roots of our second nature, Trust and the Personal. From that aside, turn to discussing the relation between the Master Narrative and The Personal.

Other Minds, Again

Since the early modern period of Descartes (1596–1650), epistemic dualism took root in soil prepared by skepticism and modern science. However, any argument for or against knowledge of other minds rests on the prior assumption of interpersonal relationships, specifically triadic trusting.[12] Dualism fares no better regarding the Personal. Persons-in-triadic-trusting-relations reveals unveils in the environments of triadic-trusting. Since all knowing is mediated triadically, what we know of the Personal does not extend to a disclosure of the other.

Recognizing the irony of arguments for the existence of The Personal and the vacuity of epistemic dualism underlying the other minds problem, why embrace the insight provided by the metaphor? That question is important. If we can embrace the insight, we can, through our trusting relation to the Personal, know who we are.

KNOWING THROUGH METAPHOR; MASTER NARRATIVE AND THE PERSONAL

Argument in the mode of logicians purports to show the Personal exists. Ironically, they rest on the backing of metaphor to connect premises and conclusion.[13] That metaphor, we claim, is the Master Narrative and reveals life and its contexts as personal. It also provides for the complete speech, beginning in creative-finding and continuing through the fullness of practical living, of social acting, society and culture, the natural expanse, to acknowledging and unveiling the Personal.[14]

That insight raises three questions. First, what, if anything, should lead to embracing The Personal? Second, how best characterize The Personal? Third, what is the relation of The Personal to triads bound and stabilized by trust, to social action, to society, culture, and the natural expanse, all governed by regent ideals? Turn to the first question.

Embracing the Personal

First, what should lead to embracing the Personal? All arguments backed and warranted by the metaphysics of being and Rationalism, supposedly independent of metaphorical backing, must be rejected. Such arguments require root metaphor to back connections among claims and conclusion. If metaphor leads to embracing The Personal, how can it do so?

Keep in mind that I-Thou-It triads bound and stabilized by trust depend on environments that in turn depend on something not themselves. Practical living has an underlying pattern, I-Thou-It bound by trust and permeated by promising, ought, persons, freedom, *and kenosis*. In turn, it points to the Master Narrative, Persons-in-triadic-trusting-relations. Within the perspective of the Master Narrative, the contexts of triadic-trusting present themselves: social action, society and culture, and natural expanse, and the Personal. The Personal Master Narrative is that in which all possible master narratives find their completion. Each candidate narrative finds its completion in the Master Narrative of triadic-trusting. Finding ourselves inside the Master Narrative, in triadic-trusting-relations, we recognize our insight may extend no further than the Master Narrative. However, the Master Narrative points beyond itself to something faintly sensed, the Ultimate Environment, what is there; insight into its character is gained through metaphor. Seeing, we embrace the insight. Let me explain.

From the perspective of the master narrative, we find environments and learn how they interrelate. Trust is the solidar of social relations. Not a passing emotion or interest, the solidar remains a steady and predictable unifier; the structure of each nexus remains through the temporal span of social action stabilizing it. Found in limited social relations, nexuses live in contexts of more extensive social relations. Particular triadic actions depend on natural habitat, associations, communities, institutions, societies, and cultures. I-Thou-It, triads of mutual trust point to that which is present in each, the Personal.

To clarify, triads of mutual trust point beyond themselves. Trust implies the recognition of persons, their transcendence in their freedom and otherness, and the mutual obligation to care for each other. All social relations are fundamentally moral. In triads, each I and Thou obligate themselves to mutual trusting, to recognize the freedom and otherness of each person, and to seek the cause of caring for each other. Transcendence goes beyond individual triads to communities. The social relation is inherently transcendent as it points to the Personal. Social relations point to society, society to culture, and society and culture to habitat and the natural expanse. The structural interrelations, meaning, and significance of triads of trust and their environments are unveiled as seen from the *topos* of the Master Narrative. The master narrative provides for the most eloquent story, for speaking the truth about that to which it points. How does "speaking the truth" make known the ultimate environment, the Personal?[15]

The master narrative does not unveil the totality of the ultimate environment, but it helps to corner the mystery of it.[16] Through metaphor, the Master Narrative unveils; it "speaks the truth." It tells the most complete speech or story, *vera narratio*. Grassi's insight is helpful; he says, as ". . . metaphorical . . . it shows something which has a sense; and this means that to the figure, to that which is shown, the speech transfers (*metapherein*) a signification."[17] This is familiar. Jane and Dee, best friends, know each other well. Dee's "speech" about Jane could easily be "speaking the truth." Through years of friendship, Dee's stories and descriptions of Jane collectively reveal Jane's personality. Hearing them, we better understand Jane. However, we do not completely understand; they do not capture Jane's other, her freedom, and the deepest elements of Jane's personhood. In the fullness of daily living, we sense something beyond individuals, society, culture, and geographical location, something we learn to call The Personal. Appealing to metaphor, we seek to tell the most complete story; we creatively-find the Master Narrative. Persons-in-triadic-trusting-relations unveil through metaphor The Personal. From the *topos* of the Master Narrative, the environments, the habitats and natural expanse, social action, society, culture are most clearly understood. As dependent, the Master Narrative metaphorically points beyond itself to the Transcendent, The Personal. Grasping presence and absence, we embrace.

Such contextualization could be seen as an infinite regress.[18] It could be seen as a part pointing to a whole, leading us back into discredited Rationalism, Being, and the One Many problem. Environments have environments, but must we be led from one to another to never ending environments? If taken in a logical sense, it is difficult to see how that could be avoided. But, if it is remembered that the *topos* or Master Narrative points to triadic-trusting, to the structure of action, agency as central to action, triads as moral relations obligated by the cause of caring for others, and that the obligation of triads points to a transcendent other, we do not become embroiled in an infinite regress.

Note, finding the backing in triadic-trusting, directs attention to the root of The Master Narrative, creative-finding through *memoria, fantasia,* and *ingegno* exploring the physical sensuous life. Master Narratives are not metaphors embellishing objective propositions. Rather, objective propositions mean within a Master Narrative rooted in the life of whole persons in triadic relations.[19]

Characteristics of the Personal

How best characterize The Personal?[20] It is Thou, Transcendent Other, Faithful Agent, whose agency is self-initiating, original, triadically related to I regarding Cause. The Personal presents a free, self-initiating, trustworthy kenotic agent in triadic relation to other contexts, who trusts, promises, calls forth ought. In its freedom, The Personal cannot be domesticated, controlled, made predictable through a concept. However, as trustworthy, it is predictable. The Personal as Other transcends Being, Rationalism, and other environments. The Personal as Cause, Creator, Sustainer addresses us, calls us to mutual trust and to act on the moral obligation to care for persons and their well being.

The Personal is what is there. We find that as the Master Narrative points beyond itself, unveiling the Personal—Trusting, Trustworthy, moral, Other. That in which we find ourselves is transcendent to triads, social/culture, and the natural yet integral to them. All statements, narratives, speak the Personal though metaphor. However, they are triadically mediated; they mean through triadic-trusting. Never beyond our potential and ability to tell the most complete story, mediation, or creative-finding, the master narrative nevertheless points to and guides our exploration of the Personal.

Environments and the Personal

How best grasp the relation among The Personal, triadic-trusting, social action, society/culture, and the natural expanse? For an answer, consider dimensions of the relation: as participant in triadic-trusting, as the Ultimate Environment in relation to triadic-trusting and other environments, as Other in relation to others, and as trustworthy not anarchical.

Regarding the first dimension, the relation of The Personal to persons living full practical lives, understood as triadic-trusting, is inter-personal. Remember, triadic-trusting mediates what can be said of these relations; our knowledge is always social. Trusting-triadic-relations depend on environments in which they develop and continue. Supportive, nurturing, and trustworthy, social actions, society, culture, body, habitat, and natural expanse acknowledge The Personal. In turn, the Ultimate Environment, though beyond in its otherness, is deeply involved in triadic-trusting. Further, the transcendent ultimate environment, the Personal as Moral is cause, that for the sake of which triads form.

Regarding the second dimension, the relation of The Personal to triadic-trusting and other environments is *creatio ex nihilo*. As Ultimate Environment, The Personal is that on which triads and their environments depend. Persons-in-triadic-relation are born to parents and grows as they trust their parents, communities, society, and culture. Their children live the same pattern. "Depends" is interpersonal, though sometimes thought of as ground. If ground, it is not ontological understood as Being and Rationalism and carries different interpretations. If ontological monism, whether quantitative or qualitative, "depends" implies triadic-trusting, and various environments are ways of speaking of the One ontological impersonal real. More troublesome is the place of freedom of choice in a monistic ontology. If ontological pluralism, whether quantitative or qualitative, the relation noted by "depends" becomes highly problematic. For example, consider the relation between the necessary, immutable, and eternal forms and contingent, changing, and temporal triadic-trusting in Plato; if the problems inherent in relating the two do not, Plato's self-critique should give anyone pause.

In contrast to the metaphysics of Being and Rationalism, "depends" refers to the limited character of triads rooted in trust and directed to moral goods in environments in which they find themselves. Persons, their bodies, their causes, and their relationships have potentialities that develop and grow within the triad. For example, at birth persons are living bodies rich with potentialities called into consciousness by their environments, their significant others. In their growth, their potentialities for reflective thought and freedom of choice among options develop into personalities. They become creative-finders. As such, persons and social action, society, culture, bodies, habitat, and the natural expanse are interdependent. Further, those depend on something beyond themselves, the Ultimate Environment, The Personal. The Personal in its freedom creates *ex nihilo* the potentials of persons; of bodies, habitat, and natural expanse; of triadic-nexus; of relations of trust; and calls them to grow and develop. In the sense of *ex nihilo*, The Personal, unlimited by anything within or beyond its personhood, and out of its unlimited freedom creates potentials in the created and calls them into fruition.[21]

Regarding the third dimension, what is the relation of Personal Other to the created? What is the meaning of "Other"? Within the triad of I-Thou-It, we find "believing in beings who keep faith."[22] Keeping the faith is oughting, accepting the moral obligation to be faithful to the one who is also faithful. In the reciprocal relation of trusting, and responding to the call of another, we recognize the one addressing us as the Personal and through mutual trust bind ourselves to keep our promise to remain faithful. It is the beginning of the formation of the moral subject. It is the first manifestation of "oughting." Pithily, Bowne remarks that ". . . the social order is the only thing which makes individual development possible . . ."[23] Trusting calls forth the potentiality of moral ought. Actualizing the moral capacity of persons implies freedom, memory, trust, self-renunciation for the sake of Thou and Cause, and hope (time and change being common aspects of each), all developed in a stable social, cultural, natural world, in the triadic relation of the potentialities of I and Thou in relation to each other and to a cause.

Here we also find transcendence rooted in trust and ought. Let me explain. In any act of knowing, such as moral knowing, we believe the moral knowledge of our society through persons we trust. As we learn that other persons should be respected, we do so via persons whom we trust. And in trusting, we acknowledge other persons, specifically those teaching the moral lesson. Acknowledging another person with whom one has entered a reciprocal relation of trusting and faithfulness implies the freedom of either member of the triad to violate that trust. It also implies the obligation to tell the truth. To violate a trust is to do what one ought not to do, to tell a lie, to desert, to act treasonously. They destroy trust, fidelity. Further, and here we move closer to transcendence, the freedom of the person to be or not to be faithful. The Other in its transcendence lies beyond the range of concepts or any formulizing procedure. In the triadic relation of trust and ought, persons who call or who respond to a call as moral subjects are mutually transcendent. Their personhood as trusting beings, who in their freedom keep or break promises, lies beyond the totalizing capability of reason. Since metaphysics, specifically that of Being, rests on the rational capacity of the mind, and through concepts seeks insight into reality and to understand its essential nature, we can say that metaphysics is totalizing. According to that approach, all of reality can, in principle, be reduced to metaphysics, whether knowledge, moral actions, art and beauty, or the "fullness of practical living." If the approaches of Rationalism and Being were taken to trusting and oughting of the free person, we should expect to have a full rational comprehension of persons, particularly of moral beings. The triadic relation of trusting and oughting would be reduced to rational understanding, knowledge. The ethical relation would then be a rational relation. Ethics would be a way of knowing.

However, the relation of The Personal to environments and triads rests on a prior and more basic reciprocal relation of believing, trusting, and oughting. As a person responds to a call to know, she responds freely, with trust in and fidelity to a Thou, bound by mutual promising. "You ought" is a call to enter into the reciprocal relation of co-knowers bound by promises to keep the reciprocal obligations of trusting as each makes or attacks knowledge claims within the book of knowledge of a society. In the I-Thou-It relation, neither member can be brought under a concept and fully grasped by it. Each member as free can resist any attempt of the totalizing power of reason, leaving an awareness of an infinite mysterious moral ought. Ethics is more fundamental than any totalizing activity of reason.[24]

The "Other" of members of a triad cannot be domesticated by Being and Rationalism. Free in their reflective ability and in their choosing among genuine options, members are habituated into societies with cultures connecting their Background and Foreground. Preserving freedom, the Personal as agent is related to trusting-triads and other environments as Creator to created. The Personal creates persons in triadic relation of mutual trust, obligation, and caring for each other. That is, The Personal creates in freedom, *ex nihilo*, persons who in the relation of mutual trusting social action are other than The Personal in their freedom, in their potentialities, and in their need. Yet, as Causal Agent and Trustworthy, the Personal sustains the triadic relation and seeks to care for the well being of each person.

Regarding the fourth dimension, does the Creator in freedom creating *ex nihilo* imply anarchy? What constrains and guides the Creator, if rational, ontological principles do not? Does anarchy live at the core of the Personal? For ontological stability amid change, one could appeal to necessary, immutable, eternal principles. The eternal forms and the Good allow Plato to constrain and guide the demiurgos as it persuades the Receptacle to take into itself a likeness of the forms. Giving existence to all the possibles, the demiurgos creates the best of all possible worlds.[25] Being is the ground of the potential. Being and Rationalism provide stability for God who freely creates *ex nihilo*. The conflict between an ontological ordered series, The Great Chain of Being for example, and creation *ex nihilo*, cannot be settled. However, preserving freedom both in persons in triadic relations of trust and in The Personal and rejecting incursions of any totalizing act, specifically Being and Rationalism, we are not bereft of stabilizing options. The Personal and the created order interrelate through trusting-triads. Further, The Personal implies Person; only Person can be The Personal. Person is also Other; we do not penetrate into the final mystery of Person through the metaphysics of Being and Rationalism. Person does not domesticate Other. Mystery remains. Yet, it is corned and stabilized in Faithfulness, in Trustworthy actions. The Personal is Trustworthy. In the Personal, we know who we are.

CONCLUSION

Having considered The Personal as Ultimate Environment, as Authority, we turn to the interrelations of the persons and their environments. Our story is eloquent; it tells the most complete story, one that allows self-knowledge.[26] In triadic relations with the Personal, we know who we are. But, what are we to be, what are we to do? To explore those questions, turn to Dancing.

Notes

1. See Macmurray for a comparable discussion of what we call the Personal. John Macmurray, *Persons in Relation* (London, UK: Faber and Faber Ltd., 1961), 15–43.

2. Led to metaphor, the topos of triadic trusting was earlier established as the Master Narrative.

3. Traditional arguments ontological, cosmological, rational, empirical, ethical are arguments, premises offered in support of a conclusion. They depend on backing for connections, coming to rest on metaphor, story. Since that is the case, the argument offered below, though Personalist, is paradigmatic.

4. See Stephen Toulmin, Richard Rieke, and Allan Janik, *An Introduction to Reasoning* (New York, NY: Macmillan, 1979). In their discussion of warrants and backing, they do not place reasoning in the context of the Background/Foreground, neither do they appeal to metaphysics for support of a backing.

5. Developing an arguments for the claim, traditional language of Personalist, such as Bowne, is appropriate, thus the use of "impersonalism-Personalism" contrast.

6. "Noncompelled" means that the action is initiated by an actor and that the initiation is brought about by an actor, who though influenced, chooses among options. The actor acting freely causes the action to occur, but the cause is self initiation; the self-initiated action does not occur because necessarily caused by some previous event.

7. That argument is an old one. See Borden Parker Bowne, *Personalism* (Boston, MA: Houghton, Mifflin Co: 1908), 159–216.

8. Bowne, *Personalism*, 218.

9. See George Ritzer, "The 'McDonaldization' of Society," *Journal of American Culture*, no. 6/1 (Spring 1983): 100–107, and Thomas O. Buford, *In Search of a Calling* (Macon, GA: Mercer University Press, 1995).

10. This move is made by Edgar Sheffield Brightman in *Person and Reality*. See his discussion , "Metaphysics and the Problem of God," chapter 16, 300–321, *Person and Reality, An Introduction to Metaphysics,* edited by Peter A. Bertocci, Jannette E. Newhall, and Robert S. Brightman (New York, NY: The Ronald Press, 1958).

11. Debating the place of Being in Augustine's thought continues. Vaught subordinates Being to God and faith; Buford argues for an uneasy marriage of Being and Person. See Vaught's three volume study of Augustine's *Confessions. The Journey toward God in Augustine's Confessions, Books I–VI* (Albany, NY: State University of New York Press, 2003); *Encounters with God in Augustine's Confessions, Books VII–IX* (Albany, NY: State University of New York Press, 2004); *Access to God in Augustine's Confessions, Books X–XIII* (Albany, NY: State University of New York Press, 2005). See *Thomas O. Buford, The Idea of Creation in Plato, Augustine, and Emil Brunner* (Ph.D. diss., Boston University Graduate School, 1963): 112–229.

12. See Buford, *Trust*, 40–43.

13. Master Narrative as connective among premises and conclusion solves the problem of existential import, the sense of "is" present in Classical Aristotelian logic and contested by many modern logicians. See Joseph G. Brennan, *A Handbook of Logic*, 2nd edition (New York, NY: Harper and Brothers, 1957), 21–22. Unless logic is regulated to the realm of the mind in mind-body dualism, leaving problematic the existential status of universal propositions, and arguments employing universal propositions (whether in classical or mathematical language) little more than useful ways of organizing experienced "data," the argument from irony outlined above is no

more than an hypothesis. Arguments are finally rooted in the fullness of ordinary living. If so, how? We contend logic's roots lie in creative-finding. Kosik summarizes, "The primary and immediate attitude of man toward reality is not that of an abstract, cognizant subject, a pondering brain with a speculative approach to reality, but that of a perspicuously and practically active being, historical individual, who performs his practical activity in connection with nature and man, the realization of his motives and interests, in a given context of social relations. Reality, therefore, does not appear in the human being primarily in the form of an object for contemplation, examination and theorizing, of which the opposite, complementary pole would be the abstract subject of cognizance, but as a sphere of sensuous-practical activity, on the basis of which the direct, practical view of reality develops." K. Kosik, *Die Dialektik des Kondreten* (Frankfort / M., 1967). 7. Quoted by Ernesto Grassi. *Rhetoric as Philosophy, The Humanist Tradition* (University Park, PA: The Pennsylvania State University Press, 1980), 66.

14. Recall the discussion of creative-finding in chapter 3, particularly its roots in the sensuous, in practical living.

15. Speak the truth, as in *aletheia*, *a* as alpha privative and *lethe*, forgetting, not forgetting but recollecting

16. H. Richard Niebuhr's argument, though not without its difficulties, makes the essential point: "The certainty of faith may be stated in somewhat Cartesian fashion: I believe (i.e., trust-distrust, swear allegiance and betray) therefore I know that I am, but also I trust you and therefore I am certain that you are, and I trust and distrust the Ultimate Environment, the Absolute Source of my being, therefore I acknowledge that He is. There are three realities of which I am certain, self, companions, and the Transcendent. I assume the reality of these three even when I communicate my doubts to another. . . ." H. Richard Niebuhr, *Faith on Earth* (New Haven, CT: Yale University Press, 1989), 61.

17. Grassi, *Rhetoric as Philosophy,* 20.

18. This is reminiscent of Plato's Third Man argument.

19. The problem of existential import is a secondary problem; import finally rests in something being before the mind through *memoria, fantasia,* and *ingegno*. It rests in the natural sensuously grasped as the activity potentially of sensing is called forth.

20. This is the outcome of triadic trust. However, seen from the vantage point of logic, it is a hypothesis. If it is to be believed it must be a more reasonable hypothesis than any other one. However, the connections among premises and between premises and conclusion, that make the argument logically plausible, rest in metaphor, Persons-in-triadic-trusting-relations, Authority legitimizing the connections and thus the cogency of the argument.

21. The Cappadocian Father, Gregory of Nazianus, interpreted by Zizioulos, understands *ex nihilo* as ontological freedom. If creation is not *ex nihilo*, the Creator would chose from Being and thus be limited and controlled by it. See John D. Zizioulas, *Being as Communion, Studies in Personhood and the Church*, Foreword by John Meyendorff (Crestwood, NY: St. Vladimir's Seminary Press, 1985), chapters 1 and 2.

22. Niebuhr, *Faith on Earth*, 41.

23. Borden Parker Bowne, *Principles of Ethics* (New York, NY: American Book Company, 1892), 139.

24. In this both Kant and Levinas agree, though from different perspectives. See Emmanuel Levinas, "Is Ontology Fundamental?" chapter 1 in *Entre Nous, Thinking-of-the-Other*, trans. Michael B. Smith and Barbara Harshav (New York, NY: Columbia University Press, 1998), 1–11.

25. This scheme is repeated in Augustine. See his *On Free Choice of the Will*. Translated with Introduction and Notes, Thomas Williams (Indianapolis, IN: Hackett Publishing Company, 1993), Book Three.

26. Consider those relationships and their significance for *gnothi seauton* in chapter 7, "Dancing."

Chapter 7

Dancing

Our quest for self-knowledge nears its end. As whole persons, we are situated in temporal environments from triads, the natural, society and culture, to that which is there, the Personal, the Ultimate Environment. In those rich environments, we begin to understand who we are to be and what we ought to do. As temporal, both require connections between their background and foreground. To explore these relationships, we shall use the metaphor, dancing. Consider first, dancing as a metaphorical extension of The Personal; second, dancing and the environments; third, dancing the Dance, solving the problem of suspicion; fourth, dancing to self-knowledge in The Personal world. Before proceeding, focus again on the obstacle to self-knowledge, suspicion.

We yearn for *gnothi seauton*, yet we despair. The master images of cultural dyadic objectivism and those of cultural monadic subjectivism, led not to self-knowledge but to suspicion, to the antinomy of suspicion. Recall that both cultural dyadic objectivism and cultural monadic subjectivism have sufficient evidence supporting the truth of each one. It appears both are true. Yet, they are contradictories. The antinomy formally stated is p & –p. Formally, if contradictories, p is true, –p is false; p and –p cannot both be true or both be false. Thus, the antinomy. Beneath its logical form lies an experiential basis. Both sides of the antinomy lie at the core of our cultural Background contributing to our identity, the society we are, the culture we have, the Book of Knowledge we live by. We cannot help but live by them, yet they are contradictory! Suspicion saturates our social/cultural identity, our second nature, our self-knowledge. Turning from master cultural images permeating our tacit assumptions, Philosophy promises to pry us from the clutches of problematic cultural conundrums and set us on the path to *gnothi seauton*.

Philosophy offers two compelling grounds of master narratives, Being and Rationalism. First, interpretations of being fall along a "vertical axis" from Naturalism, the metaphysics of the infrastructure, to Idealism, the metaphysics of the superstructure. Second, Rationalism, the scaffold of our reflective reason directed to Being, guides to an understanding of and critical support for each terminus and those along the axis. Being and Rationalism cannot properly ground *gnothi seauton*. It appears nothing can do so. Without reliable connections between background and foreground, solidarity and stability erode and remain only as cultural, social habituation. Background and Foreground disconnected, unaided by reliable reason, we live on impulse, desire; barbarism governs individual, isolated living. For individuals without a trustworthy and reliable society and culture, death looms. We cannot know ourselves. Or, so it seems. Reconsider. The Master Narrative, Persons-in-triadic-trusting-relations, and the Personal provide help. Before discussing how, sharpen the issue.

Suspicion arises as the connections between Background and Foreground of our culture and second nature move out of sync precipitating suspicion, a logical conundrum and deep anxiety. Cast asunder are fundamental elements of any society and culture whose connection is required for achieving self-knowledge. Those elements include an Ultimate Environment, Authority that legitimates goals, stabilizers, solidars of whole persons in triads of mutual trust. How can they be reconnected in a way that lays the basis for self-knowledge? We have shown that The Personal grasped through the Master Narrative of persons-in-triadic-trusting-relations provides the best *topos* for *gnothi seauton*, it identifies the environments to be related, the connections among them, and how those connections bring into sync Background and Foreground. The Personal as Trustworthy, Authority legitimates solidarity among people living through time, stability for their second nature and culture, and causes or purposes of individuals, society, and culture. Doing that solves the problem of suspicion. Within that topos directing us to interpersonal relations with the Personal, we can discern what we are to be and what we are to do. How best grasp those connections? Do so through the metaphor of dancing. There we gain an understanding of life lived with self-knowledge. Turn first to dancing the Dance as a *topos*, one that extends the metaphor central to creative-finding, persons-in-triadic-trusting-relations.

DANCING

First, why dancing? It is an act of creative finding, an art form; it is not frenzied or mechanical motion without any design or point.[1] Earlier discussions moved from the fullness of practical living and its triadic structure bound and stabilized by trust, to knowing through creative-finding, to the *topos* of Master Narrative, Persons-in-triadic-trusting-relations, to environments of triadic-trusting, to the Personal. Using dancing as a metaphor continues developing the central role metaphor plays in the fullness of practical living, specifically creative-finding from triadic-trusting through various environments to The Personal and their integrating relationships. "Dancing the Dance" helps us explore the relation of the Personal to the fullness of practical living, notably to what we are to be and do.

The relationships among persons, their environments, and The Personal are best grasped via the metaphor of dancing. Dancing is always triadically performed within the structures given by the choreographer. That is, I-Thou-It (cause and the natural) and The Personal in mutual trustworthiness creatively find a good performance within the social structures (institutions and causes) created and structured by the choreographer, The Personal. Dancing though beautiful is fundamentally moral.

DANCING THE ENVIRONMENTS

Second, dancing always takes place in environment. Whether solo or in groups, dancing is triadic-trusting social action. The triadic structure of dancing persons has at least four dimensions. First, it is natural in the sense of bodily movement in a habitat in the natural expanse whose orderliness, malleability, and continuity are trustworthy. Second, it is temporal, social, cultural, institutional. It is relations through time among whole persons in society/culture involving other, contingent freedom, and creative finding. Third, it is moral. Bound by trust, dancing involves fidelity, promise making and keeping, obligation, and *kenosis*. Finally, the choreographer, exploring within the potentials of the medium of action of whole persons, creatively finds a plan for dancing, a choreography. This is a plan prepared for dancers who creatively find its aesthetic possibilities and dance them. That is, Swan Lake has one original choreography. Subsequent directors interpreted the plan as they explored the aesthetic possibilities of the medium for artistic creation.

Similarly, the Personal creates *ex nihilo* persons who live full practical lives, their environments, and their interrelationships for the purpose of mutual well-being, specifically trust, mercy, and justice. Further, The Personal creates *ex nihilo* the needs, potentials, and implicit causes of those environments. Their fulfillment requires triadic-trusting and the development of the structures rooted in it, its moral framework and purposes. Social, cultural structures created *ex nihilo* by the Personal, the Choreographer, are primary; those creatively-found by the director and dancers are secondary.

DANCING THE DANCE

Third, the Dance solves the problem of suspicion; dancing the Dance is morally living the connections. As the choreographer stands to dancing, The Personal stands to the created order as the Creator. Through the choreography, the choreographer sustains the orderly change of the dancers as they creatively find the aesthetic possibilities of the mediums of their bodies, the dance space, and accompanying music. The Personal is continuant through the orderly change of whole persons in triads of mutual thrust who creatively find the possibilities of primary institutions for forming secondary institutions for mutual care and well-being of whole persons. As with the artists, so it is with the Personal and the created order. Their relations are permeated by triadic trust, persons in freedom making and keeping (or breaking) promises, as well as ought, transcendence, and *kenosis*. Dancing with The Personal is a triadic relation within the created order that is, at its core, ethical. How parry suspicion's thrust and disarm it? Background and Foreground must be connected. The connections, legitimized by the Personal, not only solve the problem of suspicion, but also provide the social, cultural base and environment for discerning and living what we are to be and what we are to do.

Reconnecting Background and Foreground

What does reconnecting Background and Foreground mean? It does not mean creating a new society and culture. It is not an exercise in utopian thinking as Plato's *Republic*, Samuel Butler's *Erehwon*, or Skinner's *Walden Two*. Each advances a vision to show what society could be. To fit the ideal, utopian writers remove the ragged edges of the fullness of patterned practical living. Neither does it mean appealing to memory lodged deep in cultural Background and recollecting a cherished ideal. Chesterton in *Orthodoxy* appeals to Aristotle and Aquinas to solve cultural problems of his day, ignoring that the Master Narrative Order contributes to suspicion. More recently, Robert Heinlein in *The Moon is a Harsh Mistress* portrays an individualistic and libertarian utopia, ignoring the contribution of The Emerging Self to suspicion. Skinner in *Walden Two* presents a scientific understanding of humans and their life in society and culture, ignoring the contribution of scientific naturalism to suspicion.

Turn to what reconnecting does mean. First, it elevates triadic-trust from a vague assumption to clear prominence. It reconnects Background and Foreground through persons-in-triadic-trusting-relations. Recall that assumed in the fullness of patterned practical living and by previous Master Narratives, Ultimate Authorities, triadic-trusting remained submerged and undetected. Each Master Narrative identified an aspect of living and elevated it to dominance. Under conflicting and imploded Master Narratives undergirded by exhausted and violent Being and Rationalism, suspicion arises. Shorn of excess and finding its proper place within the Master Narrative, each environment plays its appropriate role. How can triadic-trusting subdue suspicion and reconnect Background and Foreground?

Triadic-trusting pervades the fullness of practical living, from eating a peach through patterns common to human existence. Once recognized, the pervasiveness of triadic-trusting in human existence and contexts becomes the *topos*, the most complete perspective available to us, the Master Narrative. We and our friends trust each other to fulfill an agreed on goal, for example. Being faithful to promises made, we do not break them, though we are aware that we have the freedom to break promises. Trust is expressed among friends and associates, as in Sue trusts Bill to keep his promise to pick her up after work. Continuing, trust occurs in the triadic structure of any human social/cultural living. Persons grow and develop within triads in which they trust the person teaching them a skill, a body of knowledge, an attitude. Everything they learn, know, and feel, mediated through persons they trust, recedes into the Background providing guidance to successfully negotiate the Foreground, present and future. The authorities in a person's life trust her to be faithful. Persons-in-triadic-trusting-relations permeates all human living, making possible society and culture. How can the Master Narrative and The Personal help us solve the antinomy of suspicion?

Suspicion occurs when trust is broken. The siren song of power, wealth, culture of personality, prestige, and narcissism call us away from keeping promises, caring for the well-being of others, and *kenosis*, to deserting the well-being of others, to the treason of the lie. Historically it occurs as the pervasiveness of trust is "forgotten," hidden in our social, cultural background. Under the cultural dominance of reason as Rationalism and Science (scientific materialism), we learn to trust only when rational to do so. Previous master narratives recognized only that sense of trust. Order and the Emerging Self, though exhausted, continue to be advocated as the best way to face the seismic shifts along the social/cultural fault lines disconnecting personal, social, and cultural Background and Foreground. However, previously unnoticed, past Master Narratives and their support systems, being and

Rationalism, rest on trust. Ironically, the antinomy of suspicion carries power only within everyday trusting. Master Narrative raised to *topos* contributes to allaying suspicion.

How? It does so in two ways. First, Persons-in-triadic-trusting-relations, though questioned, resists implosion by being assumed in forming and maintaining any society and culture, that we know of. The Personal as moral Authority legitimizes all connections uniting and stabilizing Background and Foreground. Second, the Master Narrative points to potentials in two areas of our lives. Each I, Thou, and It as numerically distinct individuals bring needs, potentials, and causes to a triad; each nexus of triadic-trust present potentials for meeting needs guided by causes. Connections are creatively-found by persons in triadic relations of trust who explore the needs, potentials, and causes numerically distinct individuals bring to triads as well as the potential connections of each nexus of triadic-trusting. Potentials, needs, structural possibilities, and causes contribute to connections binding and stabilizing triads and institutions.

Connecting, the Dance and Dancing

The Dance

The choreographer creates the Dance of whole persons. The Personal as Trustworthy Agent creates *ex nihilo* the pattern potentials both of each member of a triad and of the *nexus* of interacting triads. Consider first the members of the triadic relation. They are intrinsically situational: habitat, a culture, bodily I and Thou, and purposes.[2] Each individual I and Thou, as a whole person, is numerically distinct and triadically related both to other individuals possessing will agency and to the It. Though we can numerically distinguish each individual person within triads, they cannot be isolated from them. Anything that can be said about each person, anything that each person becomes, occurs within and is deeply influenced by the other members of the triad.[3] Whatever is said about individuals occurs within a triad.[4]

Next, some patterns are created by the Personal, and others are created by persons. Consider that some relations within the triad are stable, enduring, and maintained and others are not stable, enduring, or maintained. Two examples are an Oxford college and a momentary association such as giving directions to a stranger. Why are some relations within the triad stable, enduring, and maintained and others are not? Recall not only the possibilities I, Thou, and It bring to the triad but also the needs, purposes, and agencies of I and Thou as well as the exigencies of the It. In so far as the I-Thou-It are natural beings they are trustworthy; science tells us they operate according to the laws of physics and biology. There is a kind of permanency, a high degree of stability in these relations [gravity, for example]. Permeated by the natural context, each element within the triad both undergoes and acts on the other members of the triad. Limited by that environment as well as freed by its value possibilities, I and Thou intend to achieve common purposes, satisfy common needs, and collectively live according to norms built into purposive action. Institutional structures arise, stabilize, and remain rooted in the I-Thou-It triad within the orderliness of shared environments, society and culture, nature and intending shared needs, purposes, and norms. If there were no interaction within the triad there would be no shared norms, a solidar, or social structures, stable or otherwise. Where there is norm governed interaction within the triad to satisfy bodily, personal, and social needs or purposes there are stable, enduring structures, institutions.

The institutions that develop in any society rest both on shared needs, the activity potentials of each member of the triad, and causes, that with regard to which persons act. Each I and the Thou of the triad, brings to the triad various needs including food, shelter, clothing; social control; regulation for competing needs; organized religious practice; sexual expression and child bearing and rearing; passing on the ways of society's culture; and communication.[5] In the triad, I, the Thou, and the It interact to fulfill those needs guided by shared norms, or causes. As they do so, seven stable social patterns emerge appearing within the triad and nowhere else: economic, political, religious, productive, education, regulative, and communicative. Wherever a society with a culture appears these are present.

Each I and Thou of the triad brings to the nexus "bents," or "talents." Those talents are limited. No one member of the triad can care for all her needs. Here we find the basis of social difference and interdependence. For example, no one can be her own educator, can provide for all her economic needs, be her own priest, be her own media, set up her own regulations, be her own government. No one is isolated from all others and is talented enough to do everything. The only way one's needs are met is to depend on others. The I and Thou bring their inherent interdependence to the nexus of the triad. Here we find in the nexus the basis for social differentiation, both horizontal and vertical. In our discussion of solidarity we found the basis of social unity. On the basis of and within the pattern potentials of a nexus, a particular society with its habitat, history, Book of Knowledge creatively finds specific, concrete institutions. Examples in America include capitalism; representative form of democratic government; Baptist church; nuclear family; universal formal education K–12, technological schools, colleges, and universities; a constitution; and mass media. Each institution develops on the basis of trust and differentiated by the talents, giftedness of the members of the triad. Institutions stabilize social action.

Now we face a problem. Institutions form, decay, and die as new ones take their place. For example, in the West the extended family of the ancient world has been replaced in the modern world by the nuclear family. Though individual institutions last for awhile and die out, they are replaced by others of the same type. The extended family rarely exists in America; the nuclear has taken its place. Both are types of family, of reproductive institutional structure. Now how account for the continuity of the type, such as the reproductive institutional structure, as well as the changeableness of the token, the individual instances of family structure? Which institutions are created by The Personal, and which are created by persons in triadic-trusting relations?

Primary Institutions as Pattern Potentials of the Nexus of the Triad

Primary institutions are stable, enduring, norm governed social pattern potentials of natural triadic trust. I, Thou, and It interact on the basis of the natural possibilities (including their own bodies, needs, and talents), value possibilities (purposes and goals), and the potentialities each brings to the triad.[6] As the interaction occurs, it has a focus. The focus is present only in the interacting connection and is not reducible to the individual participants in the interaction. We shall call this focus of interaction a nexus. As the triadic interaction occurs, pattern potentials appear that are located neither in the individual participants of the triad nor external to them. They appear only in the nexus. These patterns are the potential ways of meeting the needs of the members of the triad and are required for the interaction to continue. For example, the possibility of communication occurs only within the triad and is required for the interaction to continue. Without the possibility of communication between I and Thou regarding an It, their social interaction would be severely limited. For I and Thou to relate to each other with regard to an It, they must be able to communicate with each other, to share information, knowledge, methods, procedures, and criteria. It is conceivable that an interaction could occur without communication; however, that would be only within the ecosystem (if at all). As one considers the living triad, particularly as it continues beyond its present members, it must be possible to teach members the ways of living generated within the triad, that is, their culture.

Further, the potentiality of communication would make possible education, whether informal or formal. In this sense the potential of education is intrinsic to and maintained within the structure of the triad. Here we find a pattern potential of the triadic relation that is not reducible to the individual members of the triad.

Finally, in general each I and Thou possess the same needs that range in intensity, extent. But each brings to the nexus different "bents," or "talents."

Furthermore, no one member of the triad can care for all her needs. For example, no one can be her own educator (even an autodidact can do so only on the basis of previous learning that was not self-taught), can provide for all her economic needs, or can be her own priest. The members of the triad are interdependent. Here we find in the pattern potentials the basis of social differentiation, for social hierarchy. In our discussion of solidarity, we found the basis for social unity, for our horizontal relationships. Here we find the basis for social difference, our vertical relationships.[7]

At least seven pattern potentials appear in every society: economic, educational, political, reproductive, religious, regulative, media and communicative.[8] The specific institutions a society forms varies with the possibilities of the habitat and the potentials of the members of the social group to transform the habitat to meet their needs. They could choose a barter system, capitalism, or some other specific economic system. Pattern potentials that arise only in the nexus of the interacting triad are primary institutions, or institutional types. They are created by the Personal.

Secondary institutions

The specific concrete institutions a society develops on the basis of and guided by the pattern potentials of the triad, we call secondary institutions, or institutional tokens. These are specific, historically concrete, relatively permanent pattern of social relations, (vertical and horizontal) sanctioned by norms that satisfy specific social desires, needs, and/or purposes. A particular school, say Furman University, is a secondary institution. What is the relation between a primary and a secondary institution? Secondary institutions are the numerically distinct, specific constructions made as we creatively find and explore the possibilities of primary institutions.[9] Though secondary institutions go out of existence, primary ones does not. They continue as pattern potentials required to meets needs, potentials, and purposes of members of triads. Persons live in triads, bringing with them needs for food, shelter, clothing; education; reproductive control; social control; regulation of competing needs; religious expression and development; and communication. The nexus of triads are pattern potentials for the satisfaction, development, and achievement of needs, potentials, and purposes of members of triads.

Institutions and Trust

Both primary and secondary institutions stabilize the socially common, including our second nature. Also, trust permeates institutions; if so, institutions are ethical. But is that true?

To locate the place of trust in relation to institutions, keep in mind the distinction between the activity potentials of individuals and the pattern potentials of the nexus found only in the triad. Consider belief as an activity potential. Without that potential individual humans could not trust. Trees do not seem to have it; many animals do. However, without the triadic interrelationship it would make no sense to mention trust, the recognition of an object or cause, and acknowledgement of a person in which confidence is placed or not placed. This means that trust can appear only within the potentials of the interrelationship among the members of the triad. It is here that primary institutions appear structurally possible (the range of these structures is limited by the individual potentials and relational potentials), and the possibility of trust can be made a reality. That is, if an individual remained alone, no trust could be formed. In the potentials of the nexus and the constructions made within and the basis of those potentials, we find trust as the unifier of concrete institutions.

Insofar as trust undergirds, permeates, and unites institutions, ethics does as well. Mutuality of trust, as we have seen, implies an obligation to keep promises, the promises to be trustworthy. Our mutual promising to be faithful requires limiting my own self-interests for the sake of fidelity, trust. Implied in trust is *kenosis* (renunciation of self-centeredness) for the well-being of others, for the care of others.[10] From this we recognize that institutions rest on trust, obligation, transcendence, and *kenosis,* all characteristics of ethical relations. Social stability, in so far as institutions provide it, is an ethical relation. Ethics does not rest on social stability.

Finally, the Dance forms a basis for international, cultural cooperation. All organized societies, societies with cultures, are secondary, are the creative-finding of persons exploring their pattern potentials. All societies' cultures structures and norms lie in triads, bound and stabilized by trust and exist in environments; social action, social, cultural, natural habitat, The Master Narrative, and The Personal. All resting in trusting triads, they ought to live up to their deepest values, persons, trust promising, obligation, freedom, and *kenosis*.

The basis for international and cultural understanding and cooperation lies in the morality of trust at the basis of primary institutions. Trust is deserted when secondary institutions are created for the self-interest of the few. That has significant implications for international relations. For example, international cooperation between two nations becomes difficult when one acknowledges persons and core trust, and the other does not. Further, different languages and religions, formative for cultural identity, hinder understanding and cooperation by forming an inside and an outside. Finding common ground in The Personal underlying any cultural identity is difficult but central for international and cultural cooperation. Turn to dancing the Dance responsibly.

Responsible Connecting

As we dance the Dance, we exercise responsible oversight on the interrelationships among secondary institutions, the structures of social action in a particular society's culture. Cherishes values lie at the base of triads and *nexuses*. These values compose the norms governing the cause, caring for the well being of persons.

Recall that societies have at least five institutions: religious, economic, political, reproductive, educational, and possibly two more, the communicative and the regulative. These institutions are primary. Built into the nexus of triadic-trusting they are required for the well being of citizens. They are that out of which persons creatively-find secondary institutions that enable them to meet their needs, develop their potentials, and care for themselves and each other.

Secondary institutions focus on a wide variety of needs, potentials with a view of fulfilling the cause of society, the well being of all its citizens. However, each has its own internal goals and momentum. The economic goal includes food, goods and services, wealth. It is organized around efficient creating and distributing. It depends on a hierarchy, not equality, to meet its goals. The political produces power and depends on authority, loyalty. The religious guides to salvation and is premised upon a fundamental inequality between God and humans, and between the shepherds of the flock and those they guide and instruct. The family is organized around passion and unconditional love, care for children, *kenosis*. It depends on authority and deference. Through education, a society transmits the best of its knowledge. It requires authority and deference. It is hierarchical and fundamentally unequal and unquestioning; the student critically questions in the manner taught by a teacher.

Consider their interrelations. Though distinct, institutions interpenetrate, affecting positively and sometimes negatively the legitimate work of each other. Occasionally one or more gains control over others to their detriment. President Eisenhower warned Americans of the tendency of the military industrial complex to gain control over their government, of the economic controlling the political, the economic controlling the media. And recently we have seen the impact of religion on government, not only in the Arab world but also in other countries.

Boundary line disputes are important. When each institution does its job and works with the others guided by causes of triads and nexus' and governed by morality of trust for the well-being of whole persons and triads lives are enhanced. But when one institution ignores causes that should guide actions deserts ethical trust and seeks to control another institution, lives are harmed. Each institution can desert or commit treason requiring oversight to ensure moral purposes to care for persons are met.

That leads us to recognize these institutions and their relations to each other ought to answer to causes and norms for guidance and correction. Under the moral vision of The Personal Trustworthy they ought to serve society and the persons living in it. Social Personalism espouses the moral character of institutions.

The Social Personalist, living within trust binding I-Thou-It triads, examines the possibilities of primary institutions for stable social relations, and creatively-finds secondary institutions that through time develop the potentials, meet the needs, and achieve the ends of persons bound by trust. Rooted in moral patterns implicit to trusting, primary institutions are potentially trusting and moral. Through creative-finding within triadic-trusting, particular institutions are formed to care for the well being of persons, including their legitimate needs, developing their proper potentials, and achieving purposes of love and justice.

SELF-KNOWLEDGE

Finally, for us dancers, what constitutes self-knowledge? What satisfies the command, *gnothi seauton*, Know Thyself? To know, we must give an eloquent answer to who I am, what I am to be, and what I am to do. First, what do we do?

A description of our full practical lives comes easily. If someone asks you who you are, you can tell them. Earlier we said, "I'm a husband, a father, a Baptist, a Texan who lives in South Carolina, a college professor, a Democrat, a capitalist, a regular reader of the local newspaper and the *Economist* magazine, a cellist, a flight instructor, an Eagle Scout, a weight lifter, and a walker." And, if speaking to a close friend, one might add, "I believe in civility, in hard work, fair play, equal rights, commitment to ideals beyond and greater than myself, equanimity, among others. That's the American Way." Straightforward, we are whole persons living a full practical life.

That means working a job to purchase food, shelter, clothing, education for oneself and family, voting, following the laws of society, practicing one's faith, communicating with family and friends, and participating in family living. These change over time, and we adapt, adopt, challenge, and reject.

Yet, we continue the basic patterns of our upbringing; we continue the way of Americans.

When an individual's book of knowledge connecting Background and Foreground is no longer reliable, as in a crisis, she appeals to her social/cultural Book of Knowledge. When it and the orientation it expresses, including the Master Narrative within which it is situated, implodes, losing authority and legitimacy, she continues her habituation. But, she no longer believes it without question. Suspicion grips her.

Pushed by suspicion to reflection, we recognize we are never isolated or alone; whole persons live in triadic-trusting structures in social/cultural, natural environments in relation to each other and to the Personal. Living, whole persons are natural, at least embodied narratives in habitats and physical expanse, distinguished by creative-finding agents, by action as self-initiated, planned, and purposive. In triads of trust, persons find solidarity and stability. A complex structure characterizes living persons in relation to their environments. Persons live bodily in triads governed by regnant ideals, purposes, morality of reciprocal trust. Each triad is formed, united, and stabilized by trust. Persons bring to triads common needs, potentials, and purposes. They also bring their own "bents," "tendencies." "Common" includes food, shelter, clothing, distribution of goods and services; religious expression; social control; social regulations; communication; learning; sexual expression and child-rearing. "Potentials" include at least sensing, feeling, desiring, oughting, acting, thinking. "Purposes" include surviving, knowing, associating in triadic-trust. "Bents" and "tendencies lean individual persons toward specific activities such as caring for others as a therapist, doctor, nurse; building as an engineer, architect, artisan; music; and politics. Persons cannot provide for all their individual needs, developing their individual leanings. Persons are interdependent in triadic-trust. Further, persons are temporal with a Background and a Foreground connected by a Book of Knowledge informing their habituation and guiding them culturally and individually.

Recognizing that we live as whole persons, continue the patterns and causes of our culture, and do so in environments of triadic-trusting including body, habitat, and natural expanse; social action; society and culture; what defeats suspicion, if anything? Suspicion arises as institutional structures lose their stabilizing and unifying power with no way to regain either one. No past Master Narrative, Order and Emerging Self once imploded, can allay suspicion. The straightforward answer is that trust defeats suspicion. Let me recount how.

Careful examination of triadic-trusting reveals a *nexus* the potentialities of which cannot be reduced to any one triad or member of a triad. Potentials of the nexus have multiple patterns, each one of which is oriented to satisfy the needs, potentialities, and purposes of members of a triad. These are primary institutions: economic, political, religious, reproduction and child-rearing, education, media, and regulative. Members of triads organize their society to meet needs, develop potentialities, and achieve purposes of their triadic-members. They creatively find secondary institutions. These are the actual institutions of a society, such as a constitutional, democratic political structure. Secondary institutions change; here lies suspicion. Yet, if one recognizes that primary institutions are potentials of nexus rooted in triads that in turn are the structure of any human association, that as secondary institutions change creating suspicion, primary institutions continue. They continue through social change, including suspicion, providing the basis for creatively-finding secondary ones. Since trust binds and stabilizes triads and their nexus, trust binds and stabilizes primary institutions.

The issue of self-knowledge drives to personal identity, that continuing through time, through personal, social, cultural, religious change. The answer is not found within the metaphysics of Being and Rationalism; searching there for essence is fruitless. Neither is it found within the empirical, as understood within modernity, Locke, for example. The answer is found within triadic trust and creative-finding the Personal and the personal world. To bring self-knowledge into bold relief, retrace our steps.

Persons in the fullness of ordinary living come to know through creative-finding, particularly recollective imagination. The triadic structure, I-Thou-It, permeates ordinary living; bound and stabilized by mutual trusting. It is inherently moral. Searching for a *topos*, a perspective, a new Master Narrative, we find it in the metaphor persons-in-triadic-trusting-relations. It is the *topos*, the perspective; it is also eloquent, the most complete speech we can tell about self-knowledge. This new Master Narrative brings into clarity what lay submerged under Order and Emerging Self: triads bound and stabilized by the moral relation of mutuality of trust central to which are promising, ought, freedom, other, transcendence, and *kenosis*. Rather than impersonal frameworks, such as Being and Rationalism, we live in the interpersonal moral framework of triadic-trust with The Personal.

Further, consider the body, cultural habitat, and the natural expanse. The Master Narrative points out that persons, mediated through I-Thou-It triads, in ordinary living, are whole; we live holistically. Reflection brings analysis, distinctions within the whole. Distinctions, made through reflection, introduce disciplines such as philosophy, theology, sociology, psychology, the natural sciences. Though insightful and contribute to understanding, they are parasitic on ordinary holistic living. We are whole persons; we live bodily-interpersonally-purposively-trustingly. Dualism of mind and body is an artificial construction developed within the metaphysics of Being and Rationalism that ignores the *topos*, the Master Narrative within which it is developed. Depending on holistic living understood within the Master Narrative of Persons-in-triadic-trusting-relations, mind-body dualism is not an eloquent speech.

Bodily living of mutuality of trust occurs in an environment, a habitat, and the natural expanse. These are integral to holistic living; they are dimensions of triadic-trusting. All living is caring for each other, holistically. We are morally responsible for the whole, each other, our social and natural environments. Being interrelated, we contribute our developed potentials to the sustainability of all environments viewed from the *topos*, the Master Narrative, including the Personal.

Further, persons find themselves in triads of mutual trusting; though bodily bearing the distinctive potentials of persons, they form personalities in triadic relations of mediation. Potentials are what persons can do as the opportunity arises mediated by culture resting on triadic-trusting. As persons form personalities mediated through triads of trust, they act in society bound by trust. They also form cultures, social organizations through time that by connecting Background and Foreground allow persons on the basis of the individual and cultural book of knowledge to move confidently into the foreground. Connections are specific institutions that meet the needs of individuals and society. Though specific institutions, secondary ones, becoming unsteady, unreliable and lack charisma, the connections remain steady through primary institutions present in potentials of nexus' common to triads that continue and remain rooted in fundamentally moral trust that binds and stabilizes triads.

Finally, what is the relation among persons and the Personal? Persons are created *ex nihilo* by The Personal. Persons can trust or break trust; they are free. This has important consequences. We are free; nothing compels actions of choice, though the exercise of free will has constraints. Distinguish between will power and will agency. Will agency means that an agent can choose among genuine options. Will power means that an agent can choose among genuine options and can carry out the choice. The Personal possesses will agency and will power. Nothing, so far as we know, constrains The Personal. This means that persons have dependent freedom; the freedom of the Personal is not dependent. The relation between the non-dependent and the dependent is interpersonal and *ex nihilo*. Persons creatively-find through exploring within a medium; The Personal creates the medium that which is formed through the medium. The Personal is trustworthy, ultimate authority, creator related to the creation through triadic-trust.

Thus, who am I, what am I to be, what am I to do? Whole persons in the fullness of practical living are called to triadic trust by the Personal are morally obligated to seek the good of ourselves and others, to feed the poor, to care for the fatherless, the care for the homeless, to care for every dimension of triads under the trustworthy, creator, moral authority of the Personal.

CONCLUSION

The Personal implied by the Master Narrative allows achieving two tasks, allaying suspicion and gaining self-knowledge. Background and Foreground connect through triadic-trusting and the primary institutions found in the *nexus* of triads. Essentially ethical, those connections receive their legitimacy from the Authority, The Personal. Within the pattern potentials of primary institutions, I and Thou seek to meet their own and others' needs, develop potentials, and achieve purposes. They do so by creatively finding secondary institutions. Though secondary institutions come into existence, stay for awhile, and die out, primary ones do not. Primary institutions connect Background and Foreground wherever persons live socially. Suspicion focuses on secondary institutions; primary institutions remain. Suspicion is allayed.

Self-knowledge is best grasped through the metaphor, dancing the Dance. Dancing as an art form, involves dancers together performing a Dance choreographed by a choreographer. Exploring the aesthetic, artistic possibilities of the choreography, dancers, whole persons, in triadic relation united and stabilized by mutual trust, creatively-find particular dances to achieve their needs, potentials, and purposes. They creatively find the potentials of the choreography. The "Swan Lake" they dance is their creative-finding as they explore the choreography of the choreographer's Swan Lake. Through their creative-finding, they come to know themselves.

As they creatively-find in triadic-trusting-relations, their social actions are moral. The relations of trusting, promising, oughting, *kenosis* are social actions. Acting kinetically, each dancer must curb and channel her interests to keep her mutual promises with other members of the triad, other dancers dancing the Dance, and to aid each other to fulfill their potentials, meet their needs, and achieve their purposes.

But, trust is violated. Secondary institutions fail. Person's hunger, lack clothing and shelter; their needs are not met; their potentials remain a dream, their hopes dashed. Dancing breaks asunder. Turn to Broken Dances.

Notes

1. See Sparshott's excellent study of the history of dance theory and analysis of dance as an art form. Cf. Francis Sparshott, *Off the Ground, First Steps to a*

Philosophical Consideration of the Dance (Princeton, N.J: Princeton University Press, 1988). Used here, the Dance is a metaphor for the interrelations among the elements identified by the *topos*, Master Narrative.

2. Cf. Theodore R. Schatzki, *The Site of the Social* (University Park, PA: The Pennsylvania State University Press, 2002).

3. Each person brings to the triad activity potentials, at least, that allow her to develop. However, the particular personality she becomes occurs in the triadic context. It is crucial to distinguish self, personality, and person: the activity potentials, the way the activity potentials develop and take form in the context of Thou and It, and the one whose these are. See Peter A. Bertocci's, "The Person, His Personality, and Environment," *Review of Metaphysics* 4 no.32 (1979): 605–621. See also Niebuhr, *Faith on Earth*, and Josiah Royce, *Outlines of Psychology: An Elemental Treatise with Some Practical Applications* (New York, NY: The Macmillan Co.), 1911.

4. The triadic relation can be conceived graphically as a triangle, with I, Thou, and It appearing as the three points.

5. That humans have needs is well established by Gordon Allport in *Pattern and Growth in Personality* (New York, NY: Holt, Rinehart and Winston, 1961); by Paul Ricoeur, *Nature and Freedom: The Voluntary and the Involuntary*, part I, trans. Erazim V. Kohak (Evanston, IL: Northwestern University Press (1950) 1966); and by Peter A. Bertocci, *Introduction to the Philosophy of Religion* (New York, NY: Prentice-Hall, 1951), 191–222. Bertocci's discussion of needs distinguishes between primary drives (physiological) and native mental motives, as well as their interconnectedness. Their place in institutions is noted by James K. Feibleman, *The Institutions of Society* (New York, NY: Humanities Press, [1956] 1968).

6. "Potential" is what can be done when the occasion calls for it.

7. See James Alexander, *The Civil Sphere* (New York, NY: Oxford University Press, 2006), 206. He says that "In social systems . . . every actor occupies a dual position. He or she is a subordinate or superordinate actor in a whole series of vertical hierarchies and, at the same time, a member of the horizontal community of civil life."

8. This list is from Alexander, *Civil Sphere*, 203–204. They are derived from empirical studies of societies, not logically deduced from axioms.

9. This discussion of institutions appearing in triadic relations gains strength through building on the insights of dyadic cultural objectivism and monadic cultural subjectivism. The former recognizes that humans find themselves enmeshed in a society; humans are inherently social beings. They need stable horizontal and vertical structures in which to live. The latter recognizes that humans through their imaginations, power of rational reflection, and free will can and sometimes must challenge and change established vertical and horizontal institutional relations that fail to meets their needs. Humans need the freedom to modify or revolutionize those social patterns that are not responsible and that are unfair. However, the weakness of the former is its resting social structures in a rationalistic, hierarchical metaphysics that limits freedom, social alternatives, and human growth and development. The weakness of the latter is its tendency to reject all social structures that do not meet one's specific interests and needs. Such a view taken to extreme can result in disorder. The view outlined here provides for social order in the patterned potentialities of the triad and

for human freedom, imagination, and reflective thought in individual potentials and capacities the I and Thou bring to the triad. Further, this view is a type of "natural law" theory, if one interprets the word "natural" to mean what is inherent to the triad relation, the pattern potentials. Pattern potentials are not the universal, eternal possibles of reality, Plato's eternal forms or the eternal forms of the mind of God, that receive existence as the demiurge or God in its goodness persuades the Receptacle to take unto itself their likeness, creating the best of all possible worlds. They exist, however in the pattern potentials of the nexus of the I-Thou-It triad.

10. Cf. Virginia Held, *The Ethics of Care, Personal, Political, and Global* (Oxford, UK: Oxford University Press, 2006). Held recognizes that care is a value as well as a practice and finds trust to be essential to practice. Her analysis, however, assumes ethical individualism. Though she sees it as developing within social relations, she does not account for those relations. We do so by appealing to the triadic structure of experience and the centrality of trust to that relation. That is, Held lacks a social ontology adequate to account for the ethics of care.

Chapter 8

Broken Dances

Finding self-knowledge through dancing the Dance created by the Choreographer solves the problem of suspicion. But does it? In the created order it does. Through triadic trust, the Master Narrative, we learn that institutions connecting Background and Foreground are legitimated by Authority, the Personal. The problem of suspicion solved, self-knowledge becomes possible. The optimistic cast of that solution ignores a dark backdrop common to all persons dancing the dance of life. Persons and nations trust; they distrust. Trustworthy, they are untrustworthy. The sinews of trust, making and keeping promises, bridling self interest for the well being of others, remaining loyal to worthwhile causes continue to bind and stabilize triads, institutions, society, and culture. Lying, cheating, stealing, abandoning causes without consent or legal justification, and overthrowing that to which loyalty is sworn, break trust. In breaking trust, we reject *kenosis*, self-renunciation for the sake of creative-finding around one's own self-center. Why do we seek to create a world around ourselves? Distrust persists in the world illuminated by the *topos*, the Master Narrative.

A more profound and menacing suspicion than rejecting *kenosis* while dancing the Dance, threatens the achievement of self-knowledge through the master narrative and the Personal. What we shall call profound suspicion focuses on the Choreographer of the Dance, the Creator, and the Personal. Self-knowledge requires finding ones place and work in that which is and without which a person would not be, the Personal. Could it be that the Creator Authority Personal is both Trustworthy and not Trustworthy? If so, the created person's self-knowledge may be trusted, and it may not be trusted. The Personal is enigmatic and so are we.

We discussed how we can respond to suspicion. In the created order suspicion is overcome through the fullness of practical living rooted in triadic trusting, in society/culture, the natural (body, habitat, and natural expanse) and the Ultimate Environment, that which is and without which a person would not be, The Trustworthy Personal. But, what if The Trustworthy Personal is also untrustworthy? If so, Authority is self-contradictory, and cannot be trusted to legitimate connections between background and foreground. How respond to profound suspicion? Can the most complete story help us? To explore, examine the problem, consider possible solutions, return to the fullness of practical living, and appeal to trust.

PROBLEM

While searching for self-knowledge, a deeply felt unease becomes increasingly clear, uneasiness more profound than the brokenness of culture and society. It is "the great suspicion that we are being deceived."[1] Seeking the contours of that which is and without which a person would not be, we find the Ultimate Environment, The Personal to be Trustworthy. The most complete story, it is eloquent, we claim; but if it is, it fails to address an anomaly. It may be the most complete story, but we are suspicious it is an inadequate story. Profound suspicion remains. Persons cannot penetrate deeply enough that which is and without which a person would not be to dispel profound suspicion. Not dispelled by trusting the trustworthy Personal, profound suspicion remains. The trustworthiness of the Creator crumbles under the challenge of profound suspicion; self-knowledge follows close behind. What is that challenge?

In the foreground we face natural and social disasters. Natural disasters include the vast devastation of the Lisbon earthquake and Hurricane Katrina.[2] Social disasters include Auschwitz and the bombings of Dresden and Hiroshima.[3] Common to both are destruction and death. Facing that Foreground, we appeal to our Background, including cultural Book of Knowledge and developed potentials. They cannot help us to understand and guide us in the face death and destruction. Background and Foreground separate, standing awkwardly apart, disconnected. In the disconnection, we stand speechless, appealing only to negatives such as nothing or lack of being.[4] Though we resume the pattern and solidarity of life, the profound suspicion that life is meaningless lingers. Trust is challenged.

Consider the focus of the challenge. Does the Personal, the Ultimate Environment that is and without which we would not be, deceive us? If so, The Personal is both Trustworthy and Untrustworthy, making the Master Narrative, The Personal, self-contradictory and unintelligible. Can any sense be made of the events prompting profound suspicion?

Note the deep cut profound suspicion makes in the fabric of the *topos*, threatening meaning of the fullness of practical living and the possibility of self-knowledge. Trust gone, we neither understand ourselves and our place in what is nor what we are to be and do. What about the story we have told? Profound suspicion renders it incoherent: what is there, without which we would not be, is both trustworthy and untrustworthy! Profound suspicion says the Personal cannot be trusted to legitimate connections between Background and Foreground, between Background and Lisbon and Auschwitz. Nothing can connect Background to such events; any connection supplied may be untrustworthy! How penetrate death and tell the most complete story about it? No resources in the Background can do so. Note how profoundly suspicion affects the speech we are developing.

Profound suspicion infects the *topos*, from the fullness of practical living and triads of reciprocal trust and commitment to common causes, to the natural, social triadic action in societies and cultures, the Master Narrative, and the trustworthy Personal. Succinctly, Background and Foreground connect through trust and disconnect through distrust. The most complete story is completely enigmatic. Mutual trust binds and stabilizes triads; triads loosen and wobble through distrust. Trust in the natural from bodies, to habitat, to the natural expanse allows continuity of triads, social action, society, culture, the *topos*, the Master Narrative; continuity of the natural wavers, and breaks under distrust. Communal trust permeates the *topos*, the Master Narrative, unifying it; the *topos*, the Master Narrative separates through distrust. Trustworthiness of The Personal Authority legitimizes solidarity and stability through all environments and triads of trust; but solidarity and stability through all environments and triads of trust become unreliable through the untrustworthiness of The Personal.

Significantly, under distrust, Master Narrative implodes. Master Narratives are susceptible to internal destruction. Two exhausted Master Narratives, Order and Emerging Self, imploded as science and skepticism that developed under them, focused their critical powers on the Master Narrative that were accepted without reflection or criticism. It can be argued that once internal criticism begins no Master Narrative can be accepted without thought or criticism. Thought and criticism resting on trust are no threat to the Master Narrative, Persons-in-triads- of mutual trusting-relations. However, the Master Narrative implodes under profound suspicion. In the face of sheer destruction, of the threat of non-existence, of Death, the Master Narrative, internally incoherent, lacks power to speak eloquently.

The mystery we seek to corner is profound; reaching to the core of what is there, the Ultimate Environment and our standing in relation to it. Self-knowledge dissolves into a mystery. Facing the mystery, what can be said? The mystery cannot be dispelled, but it can be cornered.

SOLUTIONS

Responding to the challenge of profound suspicion, at least four attempts to dispel the mystery have been made; they roughly correspond to the metaphysics of being, society and culture, the emerging self or individualism, and science. They are religious, social/cultural, individual, and scientific. Two seek to allay the mystery by resting responsibility on God and two on society and the individual. According to them, understanding who bears responsibility for catastrophes provides a basis for connecting Background and Foreground. If so, we do not stand speechless in the face of evil.

The appeal to religion, at least Abramic religion under the spell of Being and Rationalism, attributes to God the responsibility for connections between background and foreground. Consider two lines of reasoning. First, God allowed but did not create events in the Foreground, whether earthquakes or the devastations of war. Drawing on the metaphysics of being and rationalism, the backdrop of traditional theism, God is good and all powerful, greater than any force causing natural and social/cultural devastation. Eventually, God achieves God's purposes. If we could see all events from God's perspective, it would be clear that they are good. That argument is susceptible to the traditional dilemma attributed to Epicurus and Lactantius.[5] If God is willing and unable, then God is impotent. If God is able and not willing, then God is not good. Either God is willing and unable or God able and not willing. Therefore, God is impotent or God is not good. That problem arises from holding three propositions: God is good, God is all powerful, and evil exists. Caught in the dilemma, one could argue that God bridles God's power and allows evil to exist for the moral and religious development of persons. The emphasis on *kenosis* in relation to evil raises serious questions about God's benevolence. God allows events in creation to miss the mark, *hamartia,* and cause suffering both physical and moral for the betterment of persons. If so, how can the earthquake in Lisbon and the death chambers of Auschwitz enhance the lives of persons who died there? They cannot; the argument fails. The dilemma remains.

According to a second line of reasoning, the dilemma can be challenged by rejecting one of the propositions on which the dilemma rests. It is not the case that God is all powerful. It is claimed that some evil is meaningful. For example, God allows (*kenosis*) disciplinary evil for the moral development of persons. But some evil is not meaningful; it is non-disciplinary. God does not allow non-disciplinary evil. That evil derives from God's non-rational given, that in God's nature which God in God's goodness seeks to control, to bring it under the rational given.[6] However, a modern form of manicheistic dualism, this solution raises the dispute between monism and Dualism, and renders the unity of God problematic. Furthermore, though Personalistic, this argument is framed by Being and Rationalism.

Influenced by Renaissance and modern understanding of society and culture, the responsibility for natural disasters rests on social actions of societies and cultures. Regarding natural disasters such as Lisbon, we build cities in places susceptible to natural events potentially damaging to them. Lisbon, built on a fault line, was susceptible to seismic activity, to earthquakes. Earthquake is a natural event; destruction refers to the city, its people, its culture. Builders of Lisbon had a choice to build the city on a fault line or someplace else. Responsibility for consequences does not lie with God; it lies with the people who choose the place and built Lisbon. Persons who build homes and cities on coasts susceptible to hurricanes bear the responsibility for destruction of their homes and businesses in event of a hurricane. Responsibility for catastrophic destruction rests on social actions of societies and cultures.

However, societies may be held responsible for their actions; catastrophic destruction of hurricanes and level-5 tornadoes is beyond social control. Destructive tendencies are pervasive in the natural expanse; there is no safe place to stand, no safe place to build a city or a society. Responsibility for social catastrophes such as Auschwitz also rest on social action of societies and cultures. Specifically, some develop narratives that guide us to destroy persons, such as Hitler's racial purity doctrine that led to Auschwitz and the holocaust.

Third, responsibility rests on the individual person; I did it. That view rests in the Emerging Self of the Renaissance. In what sense can a particular person acting alone cause or be the occasion for Lisbon or Auschwitz? Consider another sense of "I did it." Each one of us denies *kenosis* and through creative-finding orients all around our self-center; we create the world around our individual self-interests. Yet, what about persons leads them to deny *kenosis* and to lie and kill other persons? Why do individual persons freely choose to break trust, to destroy? That solution raised the problem of why persons break trust. To say, "I just did it," is all we can say, but that provides no basis for legitimized connections between background and foreground.

Fourth, appealing to theories, methods, and procedures, scientists provide explanations of events in our bodies, habitats, and the natural expanse. They bring Lisbon and Auschwitz under the umbrella of scientific explanation, whether physics, chemistry, biology, sociology, psychology, or psychotherapy. In those disciplines, we find explanations that are rational, objective, value free. That argument dodges the central issue of accounting for destruction of life, societies, and cultures. Evil is at least not good, and as such it is a moral category. Evil is only an appearance.

Each appeal flounders under internal problems stemming from its roots in Order, the Emerging Self, modern science, and the metaphysics of being. Articulating the problem of evil from those perspectives implies that the formation of the problem bears the weakness of each perspective. Succinctly, each perspective, though helpful, is a limited narrative. A more complete narrative is persons-in-triadic-trusting-relations. If so, how best formulate the problem from that *topos*? The central problem lies in connecting the Foreground of natural and social catastrophes to Background capabilities and competencies for speaking. Before Lisbon, Auschwitz, and Dresden we stand speechless. We cannot trust connections among triads of mutual trust, nature, society and culture, or The Personal. The *topos*, the Master Narrative implodes in the face of Lisbon, Auschwitz, Dresden, and Hiroshima. Distrust penetrates to the core of the most complete story. Profound suspicion is the profound mystery. Mystery has not been cornered. Can it be?

TRUST

What resources can Social Personalism call on to ally profound suspicion? Recall the argument. Beginning with fullness of practical living, seeking to understand the social and cultural uneasiness we feel, and articulating it as suspicion, a disconnection of our Background and Foreground, we attempted to allay suspicion. Two former narratives, Order and Emerging Self, imploded and exhausted, lost their master status. They could not be revived by Idealism Naturalism, or Rationalism. However, insight into the fullness of practical living revealed triads, I-Thou-It, unified and stabilized by trust that eventually led the Master Narrative, persons in-triadic-trusting-relations. Persons form personalities mediated through triads of trust. Our understanding of that which is and without which we would not be is mediated through relations of triadic-trusting. That *topos* helps us recognize three environments of triadic-trusting: habitats and the natural expanse, society/culture, and The Personal. The Personal is Authority that legitimizes connections between Background and Foreground, allaying suspicion. As the most complete story, it is eloquent. But we tell the story amid distrust, deception beyond that of our companions; we see dimly.

On the one hand, we overcome suspicion through triadic trust, but only to a point. Suspicion as social/cultural can be defeated through triadic-trust. Persons build the fullness of practical living on mutual trust, not on the assumption of deception, on treason, on desertion. The Ultimate Environment that we grasp as The Personal, "that which is and without which I am not," is Trustworthy, Authority.[7] On the other hand, the *topos* of the Master Narrative does not defeat "the great suspicion that we are being deceived."[8] The Great Mystery remains: all religions and philosophies (ancient Greek) face it; Greek Philosophers faced it, and ran into the argument from evil; religious traditions of Abram, including Jesus the Christ, face it.

Nevertheless, Social Personalism claims the following insight: profound suspicion cannot be articulated without trust. Each attempt to penetrate the mystery of possible deception is formed within triads of mutual trust and filtered through mediation. Recognizing the limits of an eloquent Master Narrative, triadic-trusting is our relation to the trustworthy Personal. In that relation, we find what we are, what we are to be, and what we are to do. Though hobbled by broken trust, we continue dancing the Dance.

Notes

1. H. Richard. Niebuhr, *Faith on Earth, an Inquiry into the Structure of Human Faith*, ed. by Richard R. Niebuhr (New Haven, CT: Yale University Press, 1989), 82.

2. The Lisbon earthquake happened on Saturday, November 1, 1755, at around 9:40 in the morning and lasted about 10 minutes.

3. The bombing of Dresden began February 13, 1945 and lasted 14 hours. 250,000—possibly as many as a half a million persons died within a 14-hour period; estimates of those who died at Hiroshima range from 90,000 to 140,000.

4. See Augustine, *On Free Choice of the Will*, trans. Thomas Williams (Indianapolis, IN: Hackett Publishing Company, 1993), 69.

5. Cited by Susan Neiman, *Evil in Modern Thought, An Alternative History of Philosophy* (Princeton, NJ: Princeton University Press, 2002), 118.

6. Edgar Sheffield Brightman, *A Philosophy of Religion* (New York: Prentice-Hall, Inc., 1940), 336–341. "Disciplinary" and "non-disciplinary" is used by Bertocci in *Introduction to the Philosophy of Religion* (New York, NY: Prentice-Hall, Inc., 1951), 395–399.

7. Niebuhr, *Faith on Earth*, 67.

8. Niebuhr, *Faith on Earth*, 82.

Selected Bibliography

ARTICLES AND CHAPTERS IN BOOKS

Peter A. Bertocci, "The Essence of a Person." *The Monist* 61, 1 (1978): 28–41.

_____. "The Person, His Personality, and Environment."*Review of Metaphysics* 4 no. 32 (June 1979), 605–21.

Bandura, Albert. "Exploration of Fortuitous Determinants of Life Paths." *Psychological Inquiry* 9 no. 2 (1998): 95–115.

Bowne, Borden Parker. "The Failure of Impersonalism." 217–267 in *Personalism*, edited by Borden Parker Bowen. New York, NY: Houghton Mifflin, 1908.

_____. "The Significance of the Body of Mental Action." 16–23 in *Representative Essays of Borden Parker Bowne*, edited by Warren E. Steinkraus. Utica, NY: Meridian Publishing Company, n.d.

Buford, Thomas O. "Institutions and the Making of Persons." 290–304 in *A William Ernest Hocking Reader with Commentary*, edited by John Lacks and D. Micah Hester. Nashville, TN: Vanderbilt University Press, 2004.

Churchland, Paul. "Eliminative Materialism and the Propositional Attitudes." *Journal of Philosophy* 78, no. 2 (1981): 67–90.

Davidson, Donald. "What Metaphors Mean." *Critical Inquiry* 5, 1 Special Issue on Metaphor (Autumn, 1978): 31–47.

Hadot, Pierre. "Philosophy as a Way of Life." 264–275 in *Philosophy as a Way of Life: Spiritual Exercises from Socrates to Foucault*, edited with an introduction by Arnold I. Davidson, translated by Michael Chase. Oxford, UK: Blackwell Publishing Ltd., 1995.

Hall, Edward T. "The Dance of Life." 153–176 in *The Dance of Life, The Other Dimension of Time*. New York, NY: Anchor Books, 1989.

James, William. "The Thing and its Relations." 214–226 in *The Writings of William James, A Comprehensive Edition*, edited with an introduction and a new preface by John J. McDermott. Chicago, IL: University of Chicago Press, 1977.

_____. "A World of Pure Experience." 194–214 in *The Writings of William James, A Comprehensive Edition*, edited with an introduction and a new preface by John J. McDermott. Chicago, IL: University of Chicago Press, 1977.

Kalberg, Stephen. "Max Weber's Types of Rationality: Cornerstones for the Analysis of Rationalization Processes in History." *American Journal of Sociology* 85, no.5 (1980): 1145–1179.

Kohak, Erazim. "I, Thou, and It: A Contribution to the Phenomenology of Being-in-the-World." *The Philosophical Forum* 1 (Fall 1968): 36–72.

Levinas, Emmanuel. "Is Ontology Fundamental?" Pp. 1–11 in *Entre Nous, Thinking-of-the-Other*. Translated by Michael B. Smith and Barbara Harshav. New York, NY: Columbia University Press, 1998.

Livingston, Donald W. "David Hume and the Conservative Tradition." *The Intercollegiate Review* 44, 2 (Fall, 2009): 30–41.

Marty, Martin E. "Christians' Cultural Taint." *The Cresset*. Michaelmas. 73, 1 (September 2009): 63–65.

Parsons, Talcott. "Prolegomena to a Theory of Social Institutions." *American Sociological Review* 55, no.3 (June 1990): 313–345.

Ritzer, George. "The 'McDonaldization' of Society." *Journal of American Culture* 1, no. 6 (Spring 1983): 100–107.

Russell, Bertrand. "Logic as the Essence of Philosophy." 82–84 in *Readings on Logic*, edited by Irving M. Copi and James A. Gould. New York, NY: The Macmillan Company, 1964.

Schneider, Herbert W. "Introductory Essay: Bowne's Radical Epiricism." xi–xv in *Representative Essays of Borden Parker Bowne*, edited by Warren E. Steinkraus. Utica, NY: Meridian Publishing Company, n.d.

Singer, Marcus G. "Institutional Ethics." 223–253 in *Ethics*, edited by A. Phillips Griffiths, Royal Institute of Philosophy Supplement no. 35. Cambridge, UK: Cambridge University Press, 1993.

White, Lynn Townsend Jr. "The Historical Roots of Our Ecologic Crisis." *Science*, 155, 3767 (March 10, 1967): 1203–1207.

BOOKS

Aguiar, Peter A. Pagan and Teresa Auer, O. P., eds. *The Human Person and a Culture of Freedom*. Washington, DC: American Maritain Association, Washington, DC 2009; distributed by The Catholic University of America Press.

Alexander, James. *The Civil Sphere*. New York, NY: Oxford University Press, 2006.

Allen, Sarah. *The Philosophical Sense of Transcendence, Levinas and Plato on Loving Beyond Being*. Pittsburgh, PA: Duquesne University Press, 2009.

Allport, Gordon. *Pattern and Growth in Personality*. New York, NY: Holt, Rinehart and Winston, 1961.

Aristotle. *Poetics*. Trans with an introduction and notes by Gerald F. Else. Ann Arbor, MI: The University of Michigan Press, (1967) 1970.

Augustine, *On Free Choice of the Will*. Translated with introduction and notes, Thomas Williams. Indianapolis, IN: Hackett Publishing Company, 1993.

Bruce Aune, Bruce. *Metaphysics, the Elements*. Minneapolis, MN: University of Minnesota Press, 1985.

Bandura, Albert. *Social Foundations of Thought and Action, a Social Cognitive Theory*. Englewood Cliffs, NJ: Prentice-Hall, Inc., 1986.

Barfield, Owen. *Poetic Diction, a Study in Meaning*. Oxford, UK: Barfield Press, (1928) 2010.

Bengtsson, Jan Olof. *The Worldview of Personalism, Origins and Early Development* (Oxford, UK: Oxford UP, 2006).

Peter L. Berger, *The Social Construction of Reality; a Treatise in the Sociology of Knowledge*. Garden City, NY: Doubleday, 1966.

Bertocci, Peter A. *Introduction to the Philosophy of Religion*. New York, NY: Prentice-Hall, 1951.

Biesanz, John and Mavis Biesanz. *Modern Society, an Introduction to Social Science*. Inglewood Cliffs, NJ: Prentice-Hall, Inc., 1959.

Bloom, Harold. *The Anxiety of Influence*. 2nd ed. Oxford, UK: Oxford UP, 1997.

Borgata, Edgar F. and Henry J. Meyer, eds. *Sociological Theory, Present-Day Sociology from the Past*. New York, NY: Alfred A. Knopf, 1956.

Bottomore, T. B. *Sociology, a Guide to Problems and Literature*. New York, NY: Pantheon Books, 1971.

Bowne, Borden Parker. *Kant and Spencer, a Critical Exposition*. New York, NY: Houghton and Mifflin Company, 1912.

———. *Personalism*. New York, NY: Houghton Mifflin, 1908.

———. *Principles of Ethics*. New York, NY: American Book Company, 1892.

Brand, Myles, ed. *The Nature of Human Action*. Glenview, IL: Scott, Foresman and Company, 1970.

Brennan, Joseph G. *A Handbook of Logic*. 2nd ed. New York, NY: Harper and Brothers, 1957.

Brightman, Edgar Sheffield. *An Introduction to Philosophy*. New York, NY: Henry Holt, 1951.

———. *Person and Reality, An Introduction to Metaphysics*. Ed. by Peter A. Bertocci, Jannette E. Newhall, and Robert S. Brightman. New York, NY: The Ronald Press, 1958.

———. Edgar. *A Philosophy of Religion*. New York, NY; Prentice-Hall, Inc., 1940.

Bubner, Rudiger. *Modern German Philosophy*. Translated by Eric Matthews. Cambridge, UK: Cambridge University Press, 1981.

Buford, Thomas O., ed. *Essays on Other Minds*. Urbana, IL: University of Illinois Press, 1970.

———. *The Idea of Creation in Plato, Augustine, and Emil Brunner* (Ph.D. diss., Boston University Graduate School, 1963).

———. *In Search of a Calling*. Macon, GA: Mercer University Press, 1995.

———. *Trust, Our Second Nature; Crisis, Reconciliation, and the Personal*. Lanham, MD: Lexington Books, 2008.

Burtt, E. A. *Metaphysical Foundations of Modern Science.* Revised Edition. Garden City, NY: Doubleday and Company, Inc., (1924) 1932.

Byrant, Joseph M. *Moral Codes and Social Structure in Ancient Greece, Sociology of Greek Ethics from Homer to the Epicureans and Stoics.* Albany, NY: State University of New York Press, 1996.

Cassirer, Ernst. *An Essay on Man, an Introduction to a Philosophy of Human Culture.* New York, Garden City, NY: Doubleday and Company, Inc., 1944.

Chesterton, G. K. *Orthodoxy, a Companion to Heretics.* Vancouver, BC: Eremitical Press, 2009.

Churchland, Paul. *A Neurocomputational Perspective: The Nature of Mind and the Structure of Science.* Cambridge, MA: Massachusetts Institute of Technology Press, 1989.

Caputo, J. D. *Deconstruction in a Nutshell: A Conversation with Jacques Derrida .* New York, NY: Fordham University Press, 1977.

Cochrane, Charles Norris. *Christianity and Classical Culture, a Study of Thought and Action from Augustus to Augustine.* New York, NY: Oxford University Press, 1957.

Cooley, Charles Horton. *Social Organization.* New York, NY: Scribner's Sons, 1909.

Copi, Irving M. and James A. Gould. *Readings on Logic.* New York, NY: The Macmillan Company, 1964.

Cornford, F. M. *From Religion to Philosophy, a Study in the Origins of Western Speculation.* New York, NY: Harper and Row, Publishers, 1957.

_____. *Principium Sapientiae, a Study of the Origins of Greek Philosophical Thought.* New York: Harper and Row, Publishers, (1952) 1965.

Coulanges, Fustel de. *The Ancient City, a Study on the Religion, Laws, and Institutions of Greece and Rome.* New York, NY: Doubleday Anchor Books, 1956.

Cousins, Ewert. *Christ of the 21st Century.* Rockport, NY: Continuum, 1994.

Grassi, Ernesto. *Rhetoric as Philosophy, The Humanist Tradition.* University Park, PA: The Pennsylvania State University Press, 1980.

Crosby, Donald A. *A Religion of Nature.* Albany, NY: State University of New York Press, 2002.

Dalai Lama. *The Universe in a Single Atom.* New York, NY: Broadway Books, 2005.

Dampier, William C. A *History of Science and Its Relations with Philosophy and Religion.* Cambridge, UK: Cambridge University Press, 1961.

Deloria, Barbara, Kristen Foehner, and Sam Scinta, eds. *Spirit and Reason, The Vine Deloria, Jr., Reader.* Foreword by Wilma P. Mankiller. Golden, CO: Fulcrum Publishing, 1999.

Deloria, Vine, Jr. *The Metaphysics of Modern Existence.* New York, NY: Harper and Row, Publishers, 1979.

_____, and Daniel R. Wildcat. *Power and Place, Indian Education in America.* Golden, CO: American Indian Graduate Center and Fulcrum Resources, 2001.

Derrida, Jacques. *The Postcard from Socrates to Freud and Beyond,* translated by Alan Bass. Chicago, IL: University of Chicago Press, 1987.

Descartes, Rene. *Discourse on Method and Meditations*. Trans with an introduction by Laurence J. Lafleur. New York, NY: The Library of Liberal Arts Press, Inc., 1960.

Descombes, Vincent. *Modern French Philosophy*. Trans by L. Scott-Fox and J. M. Harding. Cambridge, UK: Cambridge University Press, 1980.

Dewey, John. *Experience and Nature*. Chicago: Open Court Publishing Company, 1926. (Reprinted New York, NY: W. W. Norton, Inc., n.d.)

———. Reconstruction in Philosophy. Boston, MA: Beacon Press, (1920) 1957.

Douglas, Mary. *How Institutions Think*. Syracuse, NY: Syracuse UP, 1986. New York, NY: Psychology Press, 2000.

Erikson, Erik. *Childhood and Society*. New York, NY: W. W. Norton and Company, (1950) 1963.

Farrer, Austin. *The Freedom of the Will*. London, UK: Adam and Charles Black, 1957.

Feibleman, James K. *The Institutions of Society*. New York, NY: Humanities Press, (1956) 1968.

Freud, Sigmund. *Civilization and Its Discontents*, intro by Louis Menand, trans and ed by James Strachey, biographical afterword by Peter Gay. New York, NY: W. W. Norton Company, (1961) 2005.

Garrett, Brian. *What Is This Thing Called Metaphysics?* London, UK: Routledge, 2006.

Gehlen, Arnold. *Man, His Nature and Place in the World*. New York, NY: Columbia University Press, (1974) 1988.

———. *Man in the Age of Technology*. Trans Patricia Lipscomb. Foreword by Peter L. Berger. New York, NY: Columbia University Press, 1980.

Gergen, Kenneth J. *The Saturated Self, Dilemmas of Identity in Contemporary Life*. New York, NY: Basic Books, 1991.

Gilmore, David, ed. *Honor and Shame and the Unity of the Mediterranean*. Special publication, number 22. Washington, DC: American Anthropological Association, 1987.

Glymour, Clark. *The Mind's Arrows, Bayes Nets and Graphical Causal Models in Psychology*. Cambridge, MA: The Massachusetts Institute of Technology Press, 2001.

Goodenough, Ursula. *The Sacred Depths of Nature*. Oxford, UK: Oxford UP, 1998.

Goosen, Gideon. *Spacetime and Theology in Dialogue*. Milwaukee, WI: Marquette University Press, 2008.

Gorman, Peter *Pythagoras, a Life*. London, UK: Routledge and Kegan Paul, 1979.

Grassi, Ernesto. *Rhetoric as Philosophy, the Humanist Tradition*. University Park, PA: The Pennsylvania State University Press, 1980.

Griffiths, A. Phillips, ed. *Ethics*. Royal Institute of Philosophy Supplement, 35, Cambridge, UK: Cambridge University Press, 1993.

Govier, Trudy. *Social Trust and Human Communities*. Montreal, ON: McGill-Queen's University Press, 1997.

Hadot, Ilsetraut. "The Spiritual Guide" in *Classical Mediterranean Spirituality. Egpytian, Greek, Roman* (n.d.), 436–459.
Habermas, Jergen. *The Legitimation Crisis.* Trans by Thomas McCarthy. Boston, MA: Beacon Press, 1973.
Hadot, Pierre. *The Inner Citadel, The Meditations of Marcus Aurelius.* Trans by Michael Chase. Cambridge, UK: Harvard University Press, (1998) 2001.
_____. *Philosophy as a Way of Life. Spiritual Exercises from Socrates to Foucault.* Edited with an introduction by Arnold I. Davidson. Trans by Michael Chase. Oxford, UK: Blackwell Publishing Ltd. 1995.
_____. *Plotinus or the Simplicity of Vision.* Trans by Michael Chase with an introduction by Arnold I. Davidson. Chicago, IL: University of Chicago Press, (1989) 1998.
_____. *The Veil of Isis. an Essay on the History of the Idea of Nature.* Trans by Michael Chase. Cambridge, MA: Harvard University Press, 2006.
_____. *What Is Ancient Philosophy?* Trans by Michael Chase. Cambridge, MA: Harvard University Press, 2002.
Hall, Edward T. *The Dance of Life, the Other Dimension of Time.* New York, NY: Anchor Books, (1983) 1989.
Hallowell, John H. *Main Currents in Modern Political Thought.* New York, NY: Holt, Rinehart and Winston, 1965.
Hasker, William. *The Emergent Self.* Ithaca, NY: Cornell University Press, 1999.
Heclo, Hugh. *On Thinking Institutionally.* Boulder, Co: Paradigm Publishers, 2008.
Heidegger, Martin. *Being and Truth.* Trans by Gregory Fried and Richard Polt. Bloomington, IN: Indiana University Press, 2010.
_____. *Introduction to Metaphysics.* New Haven: Yale University Press, 2000.
Held, Virginia. *The Ethics of Care, Personal, Political, and Global.* Oxford: Oxford University Press, 2006.
Herskovits, Melville J. *Cultural Anthropology.* Abridged revision of *Man and His Works.* New York, NY: Alfred A. Knopf, (1947) 1960.
Hocking, William Ernest. *Human Nature and Its Remaking.* New Haven, CT: Yale University Press, 1918.
_____. *Man and the State.* New Haven, CT: Yale University Press, 1926.
_____. *Types of Philosophy.* With Richard B. O. Hocking. 3rd ed. New York, NY: Charles Scribner's Sons, (1929) 1959.
Hollis, Martin. *Trust within Reason.* Cambridge, UK: Cambridge University Press, 1998.
Holmes, Stephen Taylor. "The Barbarism of Reflection." Pp. 213–222 in *Vico: Past and Present,* ed. Giorgio Tagliacozzo. Atlantic Highlands, NJ: Humanities Press, 1981.
Honderich, Ted. *How Free Are You? The Determinism Problem.* 2nd edition. Oxford, UK: Oxford University Press, 2002.
van Inwagen, Peter and Dean W. Zimmerman. *Metaphysics: The Big Questions.* Oxford, UK: Blackwell, 1998.

James, William. Letter to Bowne, August 17, 1908. Pp. 190 in *Representative Essays of Borden Parker Bowne*, ed. Warren E. Steinkraus (Utica, NY: Meridian Publishing Company, n.d.).

Jaspers, Karl. *The Origin and Goal of History*. Westport, CT: Greenwood Press Reprint, 1977.

Kant, Immanuel. *Anthropology from a Pragmatic Point of View*. Trans by Victor Lyle Dowdell. Introduction by Frederick P. Van De Pitte. Carbondale, IL: Southern Illinois University Press, (1978)1996.

Keller, Timothy. *The Reason for God*. New York, NY: Dutton, 2008.

Kemeny, John G. *A Philosopher Looks at Science*. Princeton, NJ: D. Van Nostrand Company, Inc., 1959.

Kestenbaum, Victor. *The Grace and the Severity of the Ideal, John Dewey and the Transcendent*. Chicago, IL: University of Chicago Press, 2002.

Kirk, G. S., and J. E. Raven. *The Presocratic Philosophers*. Cambridge, UK: Cambridge University Press, (1957) 1966.

Kohak, Erazim. *The Embers and the Stars, a Philosophical Inquiry into the Moral Sense of Nature*. Chicago, IL: University of Chicago Press, (1984) 1987.

Kosik, K. *Die Dialektik des Kondreten*. Frankfort / M., 1967.

Lachs, John and D. Micah Hester (Editors). *A William Ernest Hocking Reader with Commentary*. Nashville, TN: Vanderbilt University Press, 2004.

Lakoff, George and Mark Johnson. *Philosophy in the Flesh, the Embodied Mind and Its Challenge to Western Thought*. New York, NY: Basic Books, 1999.

Lemmon, E. J. *Beginning Logic*. Indianapolis, IN: Hackett Publishing Company, Inc. (1965) 1978.

Levinas, Emmanuel. *Entre Nous, Thinking-of-the-Other*. Trans Michael B. Smith and Barbara Harshav. New York, NY: Columbia University Press, 1998.

_____. *Otherwise than Being*. Trans Alphonso Lingis. Duquesne, PA: Duquesne UP, 2004.

_____. *Totality and Infinity*. Trans Alphonso Lingis. Duquesne, PA: Duquesne University Press, 1969.

Loux, Michael J. *Metaphysics, a Contemporary Introduction*. London, UK: Routledge, 1998.

Lubling, Yoram. *The Person Vanishes: John Dewey's Philosophy of Experience and the Self*. American University Studies V: Philosophy. New York, NY: Peter Lang Publishing, 2011.

Lyotard, J. F. *The Postmodern Condition: a Report on Knowledge*. Trans Geoff Bennington and Brian Massumi. Foreword by Frederic Jameson. Manchester, UK: Manchester University Press, (1979) 1984.

Macmurray, John. *The Boundaries of Science*. London: Faber and Faber, 1939.

_____. *The Clue to History*. London, UK: Student Christian Movement Press, 1938.

_____. *Persons in Relation*. London, UK: Faber and Faber Limited, 1961.

_____. *Reason and Emotion*. New York, NY: Humanity Books, 1992 (originally 2nd ed. New York, NY: Barnes and Noble, 1962).

———. *The Self as Agent*. London, UK: Faber and Faber Limited, 1957.
———. *The Structure of Religious Experience*. London, UK: Faber and Faber Limited, 1936.
MacIntyre, Alaisdair, *After Virtue*. South Bend, IN: Notre Dame University Press, 1981.
Malina, Bruce J. *The New Testament World, Insights from Cultural Anthropology*, 2nd ed. Louisville, KY: Westminster/John Knox Press, 1993.
McGrath, Alister E. *The Open Secret, A New Vision for Natural Theology*. Oxford, UK: Blackwell Publishing, 2008.
McGuckin, John Anthony. *The Westminster Handbook to Patristic Theology*. The Westminster Handbooks to Christian Theology. Louisville, KY: Westminster John Knox Press, 2004.
———. *The Order of Things, Explorations in Scientific Theology*. Oxford, UK: Blackwell Publishing, 2006.
Miller, Seumas. *Social Action, a Teleological Account*. Cambridge, UK: Cambridge University Press, 2001.
Moran, Richard. *Authority and Estrangement, an Essay on Self-Knowledge*. Princeton, NJ: Princeton UP, 2001.
Moreland, J. P., and William Lane Craig, *Philosophical Foundations for a Christian World View*. Downer's Grove: IL: Inter Varsity Press, 2003.
Murphy, Nancey and George F. R. Ellis. *On the Moral Nature of the Universe; Theology, Cosmology, and Ethics*. Minneapolis, MN: Augsburg Fortress, 1996.
———. *Theology in the Age of Scientific Reasoning*. Ithaca, NY: Cornell University Press, 1990.
Neiman, Susan. *Evil in Modern Thought, an Alternative History of Philosophy*. Princeton, NJ: Princeton University Press, 2002.
Neville, Robert C. *God the Creator, on the Transcendence and Presence of God*. Chicago, IL: University of Chicago Press, 1968.
Niebuhr, H. Richard. *Faith on Earth, an Inquiry into the Structure of Human Faith*. Ed. by Richard R. Niebuhr. New Haven, CT: Yale University Press, 1989.
Niebuhr, Reinhold. *Moral Man and Immoral Society, a Study in Ethics and Politics*. New York, NY: Charles Scribner's Sons, 1936.
Nikkel, David H. *Radical Embodiment*. Eugene, OR: Pickwick Publications, 2010.
Norton, David. *Personal Destinies, aPhilosophy of Ethical Individualism*. Princeton, NJ: Princeton University Press, 1976.
Oliver, Harold. *Metaphysics, Theology, and Self*. Macon, GA: Mercer University Press, 2006.
Ong, Walter J. *Orality and Literacy, the Technologizing of the Word*. London, UK: Routledge, 1982.
Pepper, Stephen C. *World Hypotheses, a Study in Evidence*. Berkeley, CA: University of California Press, 1942.
Plantinga, Cornelius. *Engaging God's World*. Grand Rapids, MI: Eerdmans, 2002.
Plato, *Meno*. Trans G. M. A. Grube. Indianapolis, IN: Hackett Publishing Company, Inc., 1976.

_____. *Philebus* 23 c-d. Trans R. Hackforth. Hamilton, Edith and Huntington Cairns, eds. *The Collected Dialogues of Plato including the Letters.* With introduction and prefatory notes. Princeton, NJ: Princeton University Press, (1961) 1994.

_____. *The Republic of Plato.* Trans with notes and an interpretive essay by Allan Bloom. New York, NY: Basic Books, Inc., 1968.

Pagano, Joseph. *The Origins and Development of the Triadic Structure of Faith in H. Richard Niebuhr.* Lanham, MD: University Press of America, Inc, 2005.

Pelikan, Jaroslav. *Christianity and Classical Culture, the Metamorphosis of Natural Theology in the Christian Encounter with Hellenism.* New Haven, CT: Yale University Press, 1993.

Polanyi, Michael. *Science, Faith, and Society.* Chicago, IL: University of Chicago Press, (1946) 1964.

Price, H. H. *Thinking and Experience.* Cambridge, MA: Harvard University Press, 1953.

Proust, Marcel. *Remembrance of Things Past.* New York, NY: Random House, 1981.

Ricoeur, Paul. *Freedom and Nature: The Voluntary and the Involuntary.* Trans with an introduction by Erazim V. Kohak. Evanston, IL: Northwestern University Press, 1966.

_____. *Interpretation Theory, Discourse and the Surplus of Meaning.* Fort Worth, TX: Texas Christian University Press, 1976.

Rogozinski, Jacob. *The Ego and the Flesh: An Introduction to Egoanalysis.* Trans Robert Vallier. Palo Alto, CA: Stanford University Press, 2010.

Rorty, Richard. *Contingency, Irony, and Solidarity.* Cambridge, UK: Cambridge University Press, 1989.

Rousseau, Jean-Jacques and Johann Gottfried Herder. *On the Origin of Language.* Trans with afterword by John H. Moral and Alexander Gode. Introduction by Alexander Gode. Chicago, IL: University of Chicago Press, 1966.

Royce, Josiah. *Outlines of Psychology: An Elemental Treatise with Some Practical Applications.* New York, NY: The Macmillan Co. 1911.

_____. *The Philosophy of Loyalty.* Nashville, TN: Vanderbilt University Press, [1908] 1995.

Rorty, Richard. *Contingency, Irony, and Solidarity.* Cambridge, UK: Cambridge University Press, 1989.

Russell, Bertrand. "Logic as the Essence of Philosophy." Pp. 78–91 in *Readings on Logic*, ed. by Irving M. Capi and James A. Gould. New York: The Macmillan Company, 1964.

Ryle, Gilbert. *The Concept of Mind.* Chicago, IL: University of Chicago Press, 1949.

Schatzki, Theodore R. *The Site of the Social.* University Park, PA: The Pennsylvania State University Press, 2002.

Scheler, *Man's Place in Nature.* Trans with introduction by Hans Meyerhoff. New York, NY: Beacon Press, 1961.

Scholz, Sally J. *Political Solidarity.* University Park, PA: The Pennsylvania State University, 2008.

Schrag, Calvin O. *God as Otherwise than Being*. Evanston, IL: Northwestern University Press, 2002.

———. *The Self after Postmodernity*. New Haven, CT: Yale University Press, 1997.

Schutz, Alfred. *The Phenomenology of the Social World*. Evanston, IL: Northwestern University Press, (1932) 1972.

Shay, Jonathan. *Achilles in Vietman, Combat Trauma and the Undoing of Character.* New York, NY: Touchstone, 1995.

Simon, Herbert A. *The Sciences of the Artificial*. 2nd ed. Cambridge, MA: Massachusetts Institute of Technology Press, 1992.

Smith, Christian. *What is a Person? Rethinking Humanity, Social Life, and the Moral Good from the Person Up*. Chicago, IL: The University of Chicago Press, 2010.

Southgate, Christopher. *The Groaning of Creation; God, Evolution, and the Problem of Evil*. Louisville, KY: John Knox Westminster Press, 2008.

Sparshott, Francis. *Off the Ground, First Steps to a Philosophical Consideration of the Dance*. Princeton, NJ: Princeton University Press, 1988.

Springsted, Eric O. *The Act of Faith, Christian Faith and the Moral Self.* Grand Rapids, MI: William B. Eerdmans Publishing Company, 2002.

Shrinivasan, Gummaraju. *Personalism, an Evaluation of Hindu and Western Types*. Delhi, IN: Research Publications in Social Sciences, 1972.

Spengler, Oswald. *Decline of the West*. 2 volumes. New York, NY: Alfred A. Knopf, 1961.

Stein, Howard F. *Beneath the Crust of Culture. Psychoanalytic Anthropology and the Cultural Unconscious in American Life*. Amsterdam, NL: Rodopi, 2004.

Steinkraus, Warren E., ed. *Representative Essays of Borden Parker Bowne*. Utica, NY: Meridian Publishing Company, n.d.

Stowell, Robin, ed. *The Cambridge Companion to the Cello*. Cambridge, UK: Cambridge University Press, 1999.

Stumpf, Samuel. *Socrates to Sartre*. New York, NY: McGraw-Hill, Inc., 1993.

Swidler, Leonard. *Death or Dialogue: From the Age of Monologue to the Age of Dialogue*. Trinity, 1990.

Tagliacozzo, Giorgio, ed. *Vico: Past and Present*. New York, NY: Humanities Press, Inc. 1981.

Talliaferro, Charles and Chad Meister, eds. *The Cambridge Companion to Christian Philosophical Theology*. Cambridge, UK: Cambridge University Press, 2010.

Tarnas, Richard. *The Passion of the Western Mind*. New York, NY: Ballantine Books, 1991.

Taylor, Charles. A Secular Age. Cambridge, MA: Harvard University Press, 2007.

Taylor, Mark C. *After God*. Chicago, IL: University of Chicago Press, 2007.

———. *The Moment of Complexity, Emerging Network Culture*. Chicago, IL: University of Chicago Press, 2001.

Temple, William. *Nature, Man and God*. London: Macmillan and Co., Limited, 1934.

Tetsuro, Watsuji. *Rinrigaku*. Trans Yamamoto Seisaku and Robert E. Carter. Albany, New York, NY: State University of New York Press, [1937] 1996.

Thilley, Frank and Ledger Wood. *A History of Philosophy*. 3rd ed. New York, NY: Holt, Rinehart, and Winston, (1914) (1951) 1963.

Tillich, Paul. *The Courage to Be*. New Haven, CT: Yale University Press, 1952.

Toulmin, Stephen, Richard Rieke, and Allan Janik. *An Introduction to Reasoning*. New York, NY: Macmillan Publishing Co., Inc., 1979.

Turnstall, Dwayne E. *Yes, But Not Quite, Encountering Josiah Royce's Ethico-Religious Insight*. New York, NY: Fordham University Press, 2009.

Vaught, Carl G. *The Journey toward God in Augustine's Confessions, Books I–VI*. Albany, NY: State University of New York Press, 2003.

———. *Encounters with God in Augustine's Confessions, Books VII–IX*. Albany, NY: State University of New York Press, 2004.

———. *Access to God's Confessions, Books X–XIII*. Albany, NY: State University of New York Press, 2005.

Verene, Donald Phillip. *Philosophy and the Return to Self-Knowledge*. New Haven, CT, Connecticut: Yale University Press, 1997.

———. *Speculative Philosophy*. Lanham, MD: Lexington Books, 2009.

———. *Vico's Science of Imagination*. Ithaca, NY: Cornell University Press, 1981.

Vernant, Jean-Pierre. *The Origins of Greek Thought*. Ithaca, NY: Cornell University Press, (1962) 1982.

———. *The Universe, the Gods, and Men*. Trans Linda Asher. New York, NY: HarperCollins, 2001; (1999).

Vico, Giambattista. *The New Science of Giambattista Vico, Unabridged Translation of the Third Edition (1744) with the Addition of "Practic of the New Science."* Trans Thomas Goddard Bergin and Max Harold Fish. Ithaca, NY: Cornell University Press, 1948.

Merriam-Webster's Collegiate Dictionary. 11th ed. Springfield, MA: Merriam-Webster, Incorporated, 2003.

Weintraub, Karl J. *Visions of Culture, Voltaire, Guizot, Burckhardt, Lamprecht, Huizinga, Ortega Y Gasset*. Chicago, IL: University of Chicago Press, 1966.

White, Morton. *A Philosophy of Culture, the Scope of Holistic Pragmatism*. Princeton, NJ: Princeton University Press, 2002.

Whitehead, Alfred North. *Religion in the Making*. Cleveland, OH: The World Publishing Company, 1963.

Will, Frederick. *Induction and Justification: An Investigation of Cartesian Procedure in the Philosophy of Knowledge*. Ithaca, NY: Cornell University Press, 1974.

Willard H, ed. *The Philosophy of Nietzsche*. New York, NY: The Modern Library, 1954.

Windelband, Wihelm. *A History of Philosophy*. Trans James H. Tufts. 2nd ed. revised and enlarged. Cresskill, NJ: The Paper Tiger, Inc. 2001; The Macmillan Company, 1901.

Wojtyla, Karol. *The Acting Person*. Trans Andrzej Potocki. Dordrecht, NL: D. Reidel Publishing Company, 1979.

Wolgast, Elizabeth. *Ethics of an Artificial Person, Lost Responsibility in Professions and Organizations*. Stanford, CA: Stanford University Press, 1992.

Yoder, John Howard. *The Politics of Jesus. Vicit Agnus Noster.* 2nd ed. Grand Rapids, MI: William B. Eerdmans Publishing Company, 1972.

Zimmerman, Carle C. *Family and Civilization.* Wilmington, DE: Intercollegiate Studies Institute, (1947) 2008.

Zizioulas, John D. *Being as Communion, Studies in Personhood and the Church.* Foreword by John Meyendorff. Crestwood, NY: St. Vladimir's Seminary Press, 1985.

_____. *Communion and Otherness, Further Studies in Personhood and the Church.* Ed. Paul McPartlan. New York, NY: T&T Clark, 2006.

Index

action, 131–33; definition of, 131; will agency and will power, 133; warrants and backings, 154–55; whole persons, 132
agency, 79
Alexander, James, 187nn7–8
Apology (Socrates), 14–16; honor and shame in, 14–16
Aquinas, Thomas, 51, 79, 112–113
argument, 76, 80; deconstruction of, 76; ironic, 158–60. *See also* backing; warrant
atamvidya, 30n1
Augustine, 24, 33n31, 33n34, 33n43, 48, 59, 112–13, 124n2
authority, xiii, 43, 75–76; and profound suspicion, 191

background, xiii, 4–7, 73–74, 77–78, 92–93, 117, 142
backing, 68, 76, 80; master narrative, 158–59; and trust, 159
being, xii, xiv–xv; metaphysics of, 36, 73, 111, 115–116
Bertocci, Peter A., x, 148n19, 148n22; non-disciplinary and disciplinary evil, 195n6
body, 107

Bowne, Borden Parker, ix, xii, 31n6, 43, 125n10
Brand, Myles, 147n8
Brightman, Edgar Sheffield, x, xii, 69n7

causality, 12–13; Aristotelian, 3; mechanistic, 21; teleological, 21, 37, 39
Christendom, 25, 76
Christianity, 16
Churchland, Paul, 69n9
Cooley, Charles Horton, 147n12
Cornford, F. M., 125n8
creatio ex nihilo, xvii, 37, 50–51, 53, 59, 78, 113; 163, 173
creative finding, 78, 83, 124, 172–73; institutions, 142; medium, 78
creator, freedom of, 166
cultural dyadic objectivism, definition of, xii, 9–10
cultural monadic subjectivism, xiv; definition of, xiv, 19
culture, 89; definition of, 136; triads, rest in, 121

the Dance, xvii, 172–73, 176–78; basis for international cooperation, 180

dancing, xvii, 172–76; dimensions of, 17; environments, 173; moral, 172–73; natural, 173
Democritus, xii, 16
Descartes, 22–23, 38–39, 51, 82, 114
Douglas, Mary, 147n10
dualism, xv–xvi; appeal of, 108; Cartesian, 7; cul-de-sacs, 115–16; mind-body, xv, 22–23, 51; Plato, 110–11; types of, 108–15

eloquence, definition of, xi
emerging self, ix, xiii, ix, 19–24, 35
environment: definition of, 89, 136; and the Personal, 163–66
evil, xviii. *See also* profound suspicion
experience, 79; social character of, 104n51

Flewelling, Ralph Tyler, ix, xviiinl
foreground, xiii, 4–7, 73–74 77–78, 92–93, 117, 142
foundationalism, 129–30; certainty, 130
freedom, 19, 43, 112
Freud, Sigmund, 69n9

God, 112
gnothi seauton, 24, 27–28, 7; definition of, vii–ix, 3
Grassi, Ernesto, 162
great chain of being, 16, 17, 18, 37–38, 48, 50
Greek Enlightenment, 14

Habermas, Jurgen, 30n1
Habitat, 117, 136; definition of, 89
habituation, 84
hamartia, 112
Hegel, xii
Held, Virginia, 149n28, 188n10
Heraclitus, 110
Hesoid, 14
Hobbes, Thomas, 22
Hocking, William Ernest, x, 147n11
Homer, 14

honor, 11–12, 19

I-Thou-It, xii, 85
idealism, xi–xii, 43; allaying suspicion, 49–52; modern, 51; and nature, 54–55; Platonic, 46–47; senses of, 45; types, 50–52;
imagination, 81–82; recollective, 81. *See also* memory
impersonalism, xi–xii, 155–58; failure of, xii; formal, xii; substantive, xi
individuation, 65–66
infrastructure, xii
institution, 131; created by the Personal, 176; created by persons, 176; definition of, 135–36; found and made, 143–44; primary, 140–41, 181; secondary, 142, 179, 181; trust, 142–43, 180
irony, 76

Jacobi, Friedrich Heinrich, x
James, William, ix
Jaspers, Karl, 31n4

Kemeny, John G., 68n3, 68n5
kenosis, xvi, 96, 105n59, 130, 161, 173, 174; definition of, xv
knowledge, 79, 83; direct, 86; indirect, 86; society, 86, 128–131; triads, 85–90
Kosik, K., 167–68n13

law: Aquinas, 21; social, 21–22
lebenswelt, xi
Levinas, Immanuel, 94–95, 97–98
Locke, John, 83
Lyotard, Jean-Francois, xixn4, 77, 101n2, 101n5, 105n64

Macmurray, John, x
mathematics, 39
mediation, 83, 86
memory, 81–82. *See also* imagination
metanarrative, 101n2

metaphor, 102n18; knowing through, 160–62
metaphysics, xii
Milesians, 37, 56–57
motion, Aristotelian view of, 37
Mounier, Emmanuel, x

narrative, master, xiv, xv, 73, 98–100, 124, 153–54; authority of, xv, 41; definition of, x
naturalism, xi–xii; allaying suspicion, 40–41; appeal of, 36; correcting illusions, 40; *gnothi seauton,* 44; modern, 38
nature, xvi; ancient view of, 37; characteristics of, 118–22; law and uniformity of, 122–23; modern view of, 38–40
Nazianus, Gregory, 32n31, 33n34, 48; 169–70n21
Net Work, 25
nexus, xvi, 139, 161; institutions, primary, 139–40, 177, 178; pattern potentials, 140–42, 177
Niebuhr, H. Richard, 168
Nietzsche, Frederick, 34n49
norms, cultural, 136

Oakley, Francis, 71n27
order, xii, 35
other, xvii, 94–95; as mysterious, xvii, 164; domestication of, 165; transcending, 95–98, 164
other minds, 128–31, 160; antinomy, 129; certainty, 130; skeptic's argument, 128

Parmenides, 46, 51, 57, 110
Parsons, Talcott, 136
Pepper, Stephen, xixn5
person, 13, 17, 32n31; activity potentials of, 120; other of, 166; triads, 138; whole, xvi, 117–122, 127
the Personal, xv, xvii, 151; argument for, 154–58; characteristics of, 158, 162–63; dancing, 174; environments of, 163–66; relation to the created, 164–165
Personalism: definition of, ix; Social, ix–xi, 182
perspective, ix, 74, 100n1
philosophy, 36
phusis, 37, 45–46, 70n16, 110, 113, 115
the Plague, 38, 114
Plato, xii, 16, 58, 99, 112
Polanyi, Michael, 104n47
potential, activity, 103n31; types of, 120
profound suspicion, 189–91; and mystery, 195; and the Personal, 190; solutions, 192–94; and trust, 194–95
proposition, 80

rationalism, xi–xii, xv, 35, 111, 115; ancient and medieval, 57–60; formation of, 56–57; modern, 60–62; and suspicion, 62–64; and violence of persons and society, 66, 96–98
rationality, technical, 25
realism, moderate, 79
recollection, 43
reflection, 87, 89
relations, triadic, xv
Renaissance, xiv, 19–20
res cogitans, 23
res extensa, 23
Ricoeur, Paul, xix, 30n4
Rorty, Richard, xixn4
Royce, Josiah, x

Schutz, Alfred, 129
science, xvi, 20–21; modern, 38–40, 114; and triads, 122–23; as *Wissenschaft,* 38
Searle, John, 77
second nature, 4–6, 41
self-knowledge, viii–ix, 182–86
sensus communis, 74, 98–99
shame, 12, 18
Singer, Marcus, 135–36
skepticism, 90

Social Personalism, ix–xi
Socrates. See *Apology* (Socrates)
solidarity, xvi, 41–42, 52; definition of, 133–34; root of, 134; triads, 134–35
Sparshott, Francis, 186n1
Spengler, Oswald, 31–32n4
stability, xvi, 41, 42–43, 52; institutions, 138–40; meaning of, 137; root of, 137
suprastructure, xii
suspicion, xii, xiii, xiv, 26, 30n4, 76, 171–72; antinomy of, xiv, 29; background and foreground relations, 26–29; the Dance, 174; elements, 26–28; profound, xvii–xviii, 189–91

Taylor, Mark C., 34n48
Tetsuro, Watsuji, 104n47
topos, ix–x, xii, xv, 74, 98, 100n1, 172; and profound suspicion, 191
transcendent, 164
triads, 77, 84; and body, 118–121; knowledge, 85; natural dimension of, 117–121; place of members in, 121; potentials of, 84–85; role of members in, 121; stability of, 138–39; structure of, 88
trust, xii, 76, 90–98; belief, 91–92; dancing, 174–76; institutions, 140–43; ought, 93–98; *Rinrigaku*, 104n47
truth, 75, 79

Vaught, Karl, 167n11
Vedic texts, 30n1
vera narratio, 98
Verene, Donald Philip, xixn4 and 5, 101n4
Vico, Giambattista, xixn5, 82

warrant, 76, 80, 82; being and rationalism, 160–61
Will, Frederick, xixn8, 146n6
Wittgenstein, Ludwig, 76, 77
Wojtyla, Karol, x

CPSIA information can be obtained at www.ICGtesting.com
Printed in the USA
BVOW021432131111

275978BV00001B/4/P